New York University Studies in Near Eastern Civilization
Number 12

General Editor
Bayly Winder

ALSO IN THIS SERIES

Number I: F. E. Peters, *Aristotle and the Arabs*

Number II: Jacob M. Landau, *Jews in Nineteenth-Century Egypt*

Number III: Lois Anita Giffen, *Theory of Profane Love Among the Arabs: The Development of the Genre*

Number IV: Lewis V. Thomas, *A Study of Naima*, Norman Itkowitz, editor

Number V: Carl Max Kortepeter, *Ottoman Imperialism During the Reformation: Europe and The Caucasus*

Number VI: Linda Fish Compton, *Andalusian Lyrical Poetry and Old Spanish Love Songs: The Muwashshah and Its Kharja*

Number VII: Peter J. Chelkowski, *Ta'ziyeh: Ritual and Drama in Iran*

Number VIII: Arthur N. Young, *Saudi Arabia: The Making of a Financial Giant*

Number IX: Donald Quataert, *Social Disintegration and Popular Resistance in the Ottoman Empire, 1881–1908: Reactions to European Economic Penetration.*

Number X: Tawfiq Al-Hakim, *The Return of Consciousness*, Bayly Winder, translator

Number XI: F. E. Peters, *Jerusalem and Mecca: The Typology of the Holy City in the Near East*

New York University Studies in Near Eastern Civilization

The participation of the New York University Press in the University's commitment to Near Eastern Studies provides Americans and others with new opportunities for understanding the Near East. Concerned with those various peoples of the Near East who, throughout the centuries, have dramatically shaped many of mankind's most fundamental concepts and who have always had high importance in practical affairs, this series, New York University Studies in Near Eastern Civilization, seeks to publish important works in this vital area. The purview will be broad, open to varied approaches and historical periods, including the range of social scientific approaches. It will, however, be particularly receptive to work in two areas that reflect the University and that may have received insufficient attention elsewhere. These are literature and art. Furthermore, taking a stand that may be more utilitarian than that of some other publications, the series will welcome translations of important Near Eastern literature. In this way, an audience, unacquainted with the languages of the Near East, will be able to deepen its knowledge of the cultural achievements of Near Eastern peoples.

Bayly Winder
General Editor

The Origins of Western Economic Dominance in the Middle East

Mercantilism and the Islamic Economy in Aleppo, 1600–1750

BRUCE MASTERS

NEW YORK UNIVERSITY PRESS
New York and London

Manufactured in the United States of America

Library of Congress Cataloging-in-Publication Data

Masters, Bruce Alan, 1950–
The origins of western economic dominance in the Middle East.

(New York University studies in Near Eastern civilization ; no. 11)
Bibliography: p.
Includes index.
1. Aleppo (Syria)—Commerce—History—17th century. 2. Middle East—Commerce—Europe—History—17th century. 3. Europe—Commerce—Middle East—History—17th century. 4. Middle East—History—1517–
I. Title. II. Series.
HF3758.Z9A435 1987 382'.0956913 87–24886
ISBN 0-8147-5435-X

Clothbound editions of New York University Press books are Smyth-sewn and printed on permanent and durable acid-free paper.

Book design by Ken Venezio

To Abdul-Karim Rafeq

Contents

	Figures	ix
	Acknowledgments	xi
	Abbreviations	xiii
	Note on Transliteration	xv
	Note on Weight and Currency Terms	xvii
	Introduction	1
I	Aleppo and the Caravan Trade	8
	THE RISE OF ALEPPO, 1516–1600	
	THE TIME OF TROUBLES, 1600–1630	
	THE RETURN OF THE SILK TRADE, 1630–1730	
	THE DECLINE OF THE CARAVAN TRADE	
II	Population, Society, and Merchants in Ottoman Aleppo	37
	POPULATION AND ETHNICITY	
	THE QUESTION OF "CLASS"	
	ALEPPO'S MERCHANTS	
	MERCHANTS AS FREE AGENTS	
	THE PRACTICE OF COMMERCE IN ALEPPO	
III	Merchant Diasporas and Trading "Nations"	72
	THE EUROPEAN TRADING COMMUNITIES	
	TRADING DIASPORAS FROM WITHIN THE *UMMA*	
	THE SYRIAN CHRISTIANS: A NEW TRADING DIASPORA	

IV The Commercial Institutions of a Caravan City 110

THE CARAVANS
KHANS, *SŪQS*, AND COFFEEHOUSES
GOVERNMENTAL INSTITUTIONS OF TRADE

V Money, Credit, and Investment 146

MONEY, TRADE, AND CREDIT
LOANS AND CREDIT
CAPITAL INVESTMENT
WOMEN AS INVESTORS

VI An "Islamic Economy" in an Age of Mercantilism 186

FOUNDATIONS OF THE ISLAMIC ECONOMY
THE OTTOMAN RESPONSE TO SHIFTS IN INTERNATIONAL TRADING PATTERNS
THE GOVERNMENT AND THE GUILDS

Conclusion 216

Glossary 223

Selected Bibliography 227

Index 237

Figures

1	*Jizya* Payers	40
2	*Shāhbandar*s of Aleppo, 1610–1726	58
3	Abstract of Commercial Cases	62
4	Sample Rental Costs for Pack Animals from Aleppo	114
5	*Emin-i Gümrük*s of Aleppo	140
6–8	Summaries of Court Cases Involving Loans	154
9–11	Composition of Wealth Held By Aleppo's Economic and Political Elite	166

Acknowledgments

This monograph began, as so many do, as a doctoral dissertation. But in the years since the dissertation's writing, I have had the opportunity to research and think further about Aleppo's role in the history of the modern Middle East. I have not strayed measurably from any of the conclusions I reached in the dissertation, but I am thankful for the time to have thought in more detail about the questions raised there. Additionally, Chapter 3 first appeared in a slightly different form in *The International History Review* 9/3, while parts of Chapter 2 appeared in an article in *The International Journal of Turkish Studies* 4/1.

I owe a debt of thanks to a number of people who have helped me through the various stages of my research on Aleppo. I am appreciative of the grants provided by the U.S. Office of Education, in the form of a Fulbright-Hays Doctoral Dissertation Research Abroad Fellowship, and by the Social Science Research Council, which enabled me to conduct research in the archives of Syria and Turkey for the dissertation; and by Wesleyan University, which provided support for postdoctoral research visits to Istanbul and London.

I would like to thank the government of the Syrian Arab Republic for permission to conduct research in their National Archives; Dr. ʿAfīf Bahnassī, Director of the Department of Antiquities; and Mme Daʿd al-Ḥakīm, Director of the National Archives, and her staff, for the numerous cups of coffee and good humor with which they plied me while dealing with my inquiries in Damascus. My gratitude is also owed to the Prime Minister's Office of the Republic of Turkey for permission to conduct research in the Başbakanlık Arşivi in Istanbul; to the former director of that archive, Dr. Atilla Çetin, and his staff, for their help; and likewise to the staff of the Public Records Office in London, for allowing me to consult the records of the Levant Company.

The genesis of the interest that carried me through the researching and writing of the dissertation came from the lectures given by Halil Inalcik at the University of Chicago, on various aspects of Ottoman social and economic history. To Professor Inalcik I owe a special debt of gratitude for his guidance and insights over the years. I am also fortunate to have enjoyed the friendship and assistance of Abdul-Karim Rafeq, who has helped me to understand the complexities and richness inherent in the study of the history of Ottoman Syria. I dedicate this book to him in partial repayment of all that he has given me so freely.

I would also like to thank Richard Chambers and Bruce Craig at the University of Chicago and Tony Greenwood and Gülen Aktaş in Istanbul for their friendship and help all these years. In preparing this manuscript, I was thankful for the advice I have received from Palmyra Brummett, William Ochsenwald, Richard Elphick, and Abdul-Karim Rafeq. I am further indebted to my colleagues at Wesleyan, for their interest, hospitality, friendship, and moral support. I would especially like to mention Russ Murphy and Philip Pomper, both good friends and scholarly colleagues. Lastly, I would like to thank my parents for their love, support, and understanding.

Abbreviations

Aleppo Aleppo Sharīᶜa Court Registers, Syrian National Archives, Damascus

AS Awāmir al-Sulṭānīya (Imperial Orders), Syrian National Archives, Damascus

b. *ibn* ("son of"), applied to Muslim males

bnt. *bint* ("daughter of"), used with females' names, regardless of religion

BSOAS *Bulletin of the School of Oriental and African Studies*, University of London

*EI*² *Encyclopedia of Islam*, 2nd edition

FO Foreign Office Papers, Public Record Office (PRO), London

IJMES *International Journal of Middle Eastern Studies*

JESHO *Journal of the Economic and Social History of the Orient*

MD Mühimme Defterleri, Başbakanlık Arşivi (BBA), Istanbul

MM Maliyeden Müdevver, BBA, Istanbul

SP State Papers, PRO, London

Venice Calendar of State Papers, Venice, PRO, London

w. *walad* ("son of"), used for non-Muslims in the Aleppo sources

Note on Transliteration

It was not easy to decide on a system of transliteration for the names and terms encountered in this book. Aleppo is and was a cosmopolitan center. Its inhabitants belong to several different ethnic groups and are often multilingual. In addition to the predominant Arabic-speaking population, there are significant numbers of Armenians, Kurds, and Turks living in the city now, as there were in the Ottoman period.

The local records on which the city's history in the Ottoman period can be based were kept in both Arabic and Ottoman Turkish. Generally, the entries in the court records were kept in Arabic, while all official communications to and from the central government in Istanbul were in Turkish. There was some overlap, however, as in the registration in Ottoman Turkish of court cases that involved persons who had come to the city from Anatolia.

To reflect this official and unofficial diglossia of Ottoman Aleppo, I have chosen to transliterate the local names occurring in the court records as if they were Arabic, following the system recommended by the *International Journal of Middle East Studies*. Likewise, various terms used in the context of local institutions are treated as being Arabic in origin. The names of individuals who are identified in the sources as being either Ottoman or Anatolian, including Armenians and Kurds, and terms that are either of Turkish origin or that took on a specific meaning in the Ottoman period, even if originally from Arabic, are transliterated according to the rules of Modern Turkish. In some cases, both Arabic and Ottoman Turkish forms of a word have been given. To reduce confusion, a glossary of the more important terms has been provided at the end.

Note on Weight and Currency Terms

Throughout the Ottoman period, the standard measure of solid goods in Aleppo was the Aleppo *qinṭar (qinṭar Ḥalabī)*, which was in turn divided into 100 *raṭls*. According to various European sources, the *raṭl* was the equivalent of 1.984 to 2.040 kilograms. Although there seems to be some confusion over what the Western equivalent of the *qinṭar* actually was, we do know that the *qinṭar* was considered to be the equivalent of a standard camel load. In addition, the Ottoman measurements of *okka* (approximately 1.2 kg.) and *kile* which apparently equaled 64 *okka* in Syria were used in some customs regulations. (For a discussion of the often confusing system of weights and measures in the Ottoman Empire, see Halil Inalcik, "Introduction to Ottoman Metrology," *Turcica* 15:311–48.)

Currency values could be equally ambiguous. The official Ottoman currency in most of the period covered by this study was the *akçe*, referred to locally in Aleppo as the *ʿuthmānī*. This was the unit of money most frequently employed in state documents, but it was seldom used in the court cases in the city. The preferred currency was European, either the *ghurūsh asadī* (the Netherlands *leuventhaler*), or the *ghurūsh riyālī* (the Spanish *réal*). After the first quarter of the eighteenth century, the Ottomans introduced a new silver coin, called the *zolota* in Turkish, *zalāṭa* or sometimes simply *ghurūsh jadīd* in Arabic. The value of the two coins of European origin varied over the course of the Ottoman period, with respect both to each other and to the *akçe*, which was constantly being devalued. The two European coins were often used indiscriminately in the Aleppo sources, but it would seem that in general, the *ghurūsh asadī* was worth slightly more.

Introduction

Her husband's to Aleppo gone, master o' the Tiger.—*Macbeth* I, iii, 7.

The Aleppine is a gentleman; the Damascene is ill-fortuned; the Cairene, a thief.
(Ḥalabī shalabī, Shāmī Shūʾmī, Miṣrī Ḥarāmī)—Syrian proverb

The quotations above present two differing images of one city in the same period. Linking it to the Tigris rather than the Euphrates River, Shakespeare evokes an exotic Aleppo through an effective, if geographically inaccurate, pun. Nonetheless, as he placed its name on the tongue of a Scots witch, we can assume it was a city already recognized by his audience as being the sort of place to which an Englishman might set off to seek his fortune. The Levant, as the eastern Mediterranean coast was known in Shakespeare's day, was, after all, one of the first regions outside of Europe to be visited by errant Englishmen, and a chartered Levant Company existed in London (1581) before there was an East India Company or a Virginia expedition. Aleppo had already won a place in the geographical imagination of Elizabethan Englishmen, even if it is largely unknown to Americans today.

In sharp contrast to the wandering Elizabethan Englishman are the qualities extolled in the Syrian proverb. It presents Aleppo as the home of staid, unobtrusive, dignified gentlemen who displayed those virtues that over the centuries the Sunni Muslim burghers of Syria's cities had come to cherish. Although trade is not mentioned explicitly in the Syrian proverb, the honorific title *çelebi* was often applied to the city's merchant elite. Taken as metaphors of the time in which they were voiced, the quotations represent the two peoples who with their different styles and economic ideologies came into contact in the markets of Aleppo.

Between 1600 and 1750, Aleppo was one of the premier cities of the vast Ottoman Empire and one of those rare locations in human history where two cultures competed for a prolonged period without resorting to violence. Like Beirut in the nineteenth and early twentieth centuries, it was a commercial entrepôt where East mingled with West, with the underlying motor being the quest for profit on each side of the cultural divide. In the case of Aleppo, however, unlike the latter-day Beirut, the two were on a roughly equal footing, politically and technologically. Yet despite the absence of the physical coercion that so often marks the encounters between different civilizations, the city was an economic battlefield where two distinct commercial traditions struggled to control the trade of the Levant.

The ideology that motivated the English merchants consisted of the newly emerging theories of mercantilism. This vision of a world economy sought, in brief, to increase exports, limit imports through protective tariffs, and use government power wherever possible to promote the foreign trade of the nation in an attempt to accumulate specie, which, in turn, would guarantee the health and vigor of the state and its people.[1] Arrayed against it was an Islamic philosophy of the economy that was based on the centuries-old traditions and institutions of trade as they had evolved in the Middle East. Included in this set of inherited truths, which the Ottomans held governed their economy, was an understanding that the caravan trade was the lifeblood of empires, to be preserved at all costs, and that the survival of the state's revenues was dependent on justice in the marketplace. While this philosophy was not nearly as consciously articulated as that of mercantilism, it permeated the ways in which Middle Easterners conducted business and the trade policies implemented by the Ottoman state as fully as did mercantilism those of England.

Yet by 1750, it was the western European version of a world economy that had emerged triumphant. While there were Middle Easterners who adapted to these new conditions and profited from the Western victory, they were increasingly required to play the game of international commerce by Western rules. Entry into a Western-dominated economic relationship was not a fate unique to the Middle East, however. From the seventeenth century through the nineteenth, most of the world was becoming economically, and often politically, dependent on one or another of the western European powers.[2]

Although the end was much the same, the historical developments that created this new relationship were not identical in all parts of the globe. What makes the economic fate of the Ottoman Empire different was that its incorporation into the modern system dominated by Europe and capitalism, to use Wallerstein's terminology, resulted from conscious policies implemented by a non-Western power—in this case, the Ottoman government. While Ottoman officialdom generally believed that its policies would benefit the state's revenue base, they most often had the opposite results.

Ironically, the incorporation of the region into a European economic world system represented a reversal of the relationship that had endured for centuries between the Muslim world and western Europe, when world trade had largely been a Muslim monopoly. It had been, after all, their desire to break out of dependency on Muslim caravans to bring them the goods of the fabled East that set the Europeans off on their voyages of discovery, which would remake the world. In what has become the classic study of this struggle between two competing worldviews and economies, Niels Steensgaard argued that at the start of the seventeenth century, the English and the Dutch succeeded in breaking the Muslim caravans' hold over the trade of Asia.[3] Although his dating of the demise seems premature, there is no question that the West's technology and commercial policies eventually succeeded in effecting an Asian trade revolution.

Obviously, the question of why the Muslim Middle East was surpassed by western Europe, first economically and then politically, is complex. It involves not only differing political institutions but harder-to-pinpoint attitudes toward technology, trade, profits, and even the legal position of corporations in two different societies. Nonetheless, the demise of the Ottoman Empire and its legacy of lingering political and economic dissonance in the region confirm the failure of the Islamic economy to compete in a changing world.

But without an understanding of the internal dynamics of the Ottoman economy, we are left with the explanation that the failure was inevitable, an unfortunate side effect of the historical necessity of the rise of capitalism. This explanation is only slightly more satisfying than saying it was all due to kismet, or fate. This deemphasis of the internal dynamics of non-Western economies seems to be the major drawback of research in the dependency-theory mode, by historians such as Wallerstein.[4] In the Middle East, at least, domestic conditions in the Ottoman Empire often seem to have propelled the region into the world economy much more rapidly than did the external forces of European greed or ambition.

For an understanding of why this occurred, Aleppo, perhaps more than any other city in the Ottoman Empire, provides a model of the inherent strengths and weaknesses of an Islamic economy. Not only was it the most important commercial center in the Middle East, in terms of its volume of trade with the West in the period between 1600 and 1750, it was the only traditional caravan center to retain its pride of place in an age of increasing Western economic presence. Furthermore, as a result of a host of complex historical developments, Aleppo never engendered a strong local political elite that could promote the city's economic interests. Its fortunes as a trading city were consequently determined by the currents of international commerce and the policies implemented by Istanbul, its political capital. As such, the city's success or failure serves as a virtual litmus test for the effectiveness of those policies.

Aleppo's story tells us how the merchants of the Middle East adapted to the initial challenge of Western competition to the caravan trade and why they were eventually supplanted by the West. Their failure was Aleppo's, and Aleppo's decline in turn mirrored the fate of the Middle East. By the second half of the nineteenth century, the city had become an unimportant provincial Syrian center, handling a meager export of raw cotton for Europe's industries, while the Middle East had lost its economic independence.

Although the role Middle Easterners played in this transition is important, it is a subplot in world history that has not received much attention. This lacuna has to some extent been the product of the European sources that were used to tell the tale. The Europeans present in the Ottoman Empire clearly were not privy to the inner workings of either the Ottoman state administration or the subtleties of Islamic commercial life. Their reports, therefore, were often only partially correct, and recent scholarship relying on them has produced an incomplete account of the formation of the Middle East's dependent economic relationship with western Europe.

This shortcoming has not necessarily been a product of negligence. Any researcher into this subject who seeks the Muslim perspective is struck at first by the absence of corresponding documentation of the types utilized in the study of European mercantilism. The merchants of the Middle East were, on the whole, very private people. This was partly a result of the social mores of Islam and partly derived from their history. The vagaries of their sometimes despotic political leadership had taught the peoples of the region the follies of conspicuous consumption, and the merchants were circumspect in making themselves known. The extant Muslim court records inform us that many merchants kept private records, but none of these are known to have survived. A further loss to historians seems to have been the Ottoman customs records from the various Levantine cities, which would have provided some balance to those in the European archives. What do remain are the orders from the central government in Istanbul regulating trade, and the court records of Aleppo and of various other commercial centers of the Ottoman Empire. While not as complete as the records from Europe, these, at least, give us some insight into the ideology of the state toward commerce and the actual Muslim practice of trade in the region.

Primarily based on these indigenous records of the Levant trade, this study deals with the native merchants of Aleppo, their institutions, their patterns of investment, their composition as a social group, and their relationship with the Europeans and the Ottoman central government. In order to treat the complexities of the transformation of Aleppo's economy, the book is divided into six chapters, each of which seeks to explain one reason for the failure of Aleppo to adapt to new conditions in the world economy. Chapter 1, "Aleppo and the Caravan Trade," deals with the historical development of Aleppo's role in Middle Eastern trade during the Ottoman period (1516–1918). It stresses that while Aleppo had always had the potential for being one of the great caravan cities of the region, it was the Ottoman conquest of Syria in 1516 that catapulated the city to preeminence. Aleppo's fortunes were primarily linked to those of the caravans bringing the silk of Iran to the Mediterranean. Once that trade halted in the middle of the eighteenth century, it became increasingly difficult for the local merchants to translate their former advantage into any lasting benefit.

Chapter 2, "Population, Society, and Merchants in Ottoman Aleppo," examines the composition and role of Aleppo's merchants in a larger context of the city's population. While trade was the most accessible means for a Muslim Aleppine to create wealth, there was not a true class of merchants. Rather, almost everyone who had any capital at all invested in trade. Once someone had acquired excess capital through trade, the usual pattern was to diversify his or her investments into other less risky endeavors. Given this diversity of opportunities, there was not an organized body of influential individuals who were solely dependent on trade for increasing their wealth. Hence there was no one to lobby for commercial interests in the capital, Istanbul, in the way English merchants could, and did, apply pressure in London.

If conditions for the creation of a strong merchant class were not present among the Muslim community of Aleppo, the same could not be said for the various ethnic and religious minority communities of the Levant. Chapter 3, "Merchant Diasporas and Trading 'Nation's.' " examines these, concentrating on the Armenians from Iran, the Sephardic Jews, and the Syrian Christians, to demonstrate how changing economic conditions in the region advanced these groups' economic positions relative to that of their Muslim neighbors.

Chapter 4, "The Commercial Institutions of a Caravan City," describes the ways in which the caravan trade was conducted in Aleppo during the Ottoman period, concentrating on its Islamic underpinnings and its inherent durability. The trade's institutional strengths enabled it to survive but at the same time, paradoxically, limited the Islamic economy's ability to expand.

Chapter 5, "Money, Credit, and Investment," looks at the ways in which Aleppo's citizens invested their wealth. Its conclusions are based on a sample of 1,196 individual loan cases chosen at random from the thousands of such cases registered in the seventeenth and eighteenth centuries and from a register of estate property of deceased Muslims. These samples demonstrate that while wealthy Muslims invested in a number of diverse activities, moneylending was the most widely and avidly pursued. The bulk of the loans went to peasants in the surrounding countryside, establishing a credit relationship that was transformed to virtual property ownership in the eighteenth century.

The last chapter, "An 'Islamic Economy' in an Age of Mercantilism," contrasts the commercial ideology of the Ottoman Empire with that of mercantilist England. It suggests that the Ottomans consciously implemented policies, such as low tariffs and the discouragement of local production, that hastened the region's incorporation into the modern world system. This chapter traces the origins of Ottoman economic policies to two often contradictory sources: an Islamic ideal of marketplace ethics and the secular traditions of a Middle Eastern political economy. In conclusion, it suggests that a reliance on those philosophies made the collapse of the Islamic economy and the incorporation of the region into the modern world system possible, as the traditional Islamic goals of justice and order ironically served to complement the mercantilist economic goals of the Europeans. Aleppo's incorporation into the modern world system as a peripheral region, again to borrow Wallerstein's categories, was not inevitable, given the hindsight of history. Rather, it was a result of several different internal factors, each of which, had it existed solely on its own, might have produced far different results. It is to those factors that we must now turn our attention.

NOTES

1. See for example, J. R. McCulloch, ed., *Early English Tracts on Commerce* (Cambridge, 1954), for an articulation of mercantilist ideology by Englishmen in this period. For a modern account of English mercantilism, see Jan de Vries, *The Economy of Europe in an Age of Crisis, 1600–1750* (Cambridge, 1976). Further discussion of English mercantilism in the context of Aleppo can be found in chapters 5 and 6.

2. The dynamics of this process, which created the modern world, has absorbed the interest of many contemporary scholars who see the seventeenth and eighteenth centuries as crucial to the understanding of the relations of dependency that exist between the First and Third Worlds in the twentieth. See, for example, Immanuel Wallerstein's work *The Modern World System,* vols. 1–2 (New York, 1974, 1980).

3. Niels Steensgaard, *The Asian Trade Revolution of the Seventeenth Century* (Chicago, 1974).

4. A sympathetic critique of Wallerstein is found in Charles Ragin and Daniel Chirot, "The World System of Immanuel Wallerstein: Sociology and Politics as History," in *Visions and Method in Historical Sociology,* ed. Theda Skocpol (London, 1984).

CHAPTER I

Aleppo and the Caravan Trade

How Aleppo came to be the premier commercial center of the eastern Mediterranean is neither geographically nor historically self-evident. The city did not possess the political or historical importance of Istanbul, Cairo, or Damascus. Nonetheless, in the sixteenth and seventeenth centuries, the mere mention of Aleppo's name could evoke for western Europeans images of the wealth of the fabulous East. Much of the city's luster was undoubtedly linked to its traditions and its citizens' business acumen, but as Aleppo's glory had faded by the end of the eighteenth century, we must assume that competing dynamics of the city's social and political order stymied any translation of its historically brief period of prominence into long-lasting economic or political benefits. Before we have a chance to examine those, however, we must look at the conditions that created Aleppo's renown in the first place.

Although Aleppo is some fifty miles distant from the Mediterranean, its geography supplied the potential for its becoming a great commercial center. Located on a fertile plain and watered by the small but adequate river Quwayq, the city has easy access to both the olive groves of northern Syria surrounding the towns of Idlib and Maʿarrat al-Miṣrīn and the silk-producing mulberry orchards located in the hills of the Mediterranean coast near the biblical city of Antioch (the present-day Turkish province of Hatay). In a wider geographical context, it lay astride the caravan trails connecting Anatolia to Syria and is almost equidistant from the sea and the Euphrates River, for millenia the favored trade route to Iraq and India beyond. Location made Aleppo's commercial success in the Ottoman period possible, but Aleppo, which has a history that extends back at least four thousand years, has rarely played as dominant a role in the economy of the eastern Mediterranean as it did from the sixteenth through the eighteenth centuries. Indeed, it has largely been overshadowed throughout most of its recorded history by one or another of Syria's other major cities.

All the great cities of Syria—Damascus, Homs, Hama, and Aleppo—lie near the edge of the Syrian desert but are graced with fairly large, cultivable regions in their immediate vicinities. They stand in marked contrast to Syria's seaports, which are cursed by a narrow coastal plain and have therefore been traditionally dependent on outside sources of grain to feed their populations. This disparity in easily obtainable grain supplies has given Syria's desert "port" cities, with their autonomous sources of foodstuffs, the upper hand strategically, and hence militarily and politically, over the towns that face the sea. The only exceptions have occurred when the coastal towns have been allied to, or dominated by, powers from across the sea.

Such was the case during the Crusading period (1095–1291), when the Syrian coast was physically detached from the interior by the invaders. In the era following the expulsion of the Europeans, the inland centers reasserted their political supremacy. With it came their cultural and economic dominance, as the seaport cities, with the exception of Tripoli, declined to little more than villages.[1] In the post-Crusading centuries, caravans entering Syria terminated in the inland towns, rather than winding their way over the coastal ranges to the sea. In part, this pattern was the result of purely political and strategic motives, as the Mamluk rulers of Syria (1260–1516) feared recurring Frankish—that is, western European—incursions and piracy and so discouraged the development of the coastal cities. But an economic motivation was in evidence as well, as long as what was being transported was largely consumed in the urban centers of the Middle East. Once established, the caravan routes exhibited a remarkable tenacity. Long after Europe became the final destination of much of what was being transshipped, these interior cities retained their monopoly as the dowagers of the caravan trade, to be replaced as Syria's major commercial centers by the coastal towns only with the advent of the steamship.

Given Syria's geography, any of the four inland cities could have emerged as the most important of the regional termini of the caravans in the Ottoman period. Palmyra and its neighbor Homs (the classical Emessa) had held the honor in Hellenistic and Roman eras, and throughout the Muslim centuries Damascus had predominated. The reasons for Damascus's central role in the earlier centuries are apparent. Damascus is nearer than Aleppo to not only Egypt and the Arabian Peninsula but the important Red Sea routes to the East that during the troubled fifteenth century provided a more secure passage to the Indies than did the Euphrates.

Additionally, Damascus held a decided advantage over Aleppo in that it served as the starting point for the yearly hajj (Muslim pilgrimage) caravan to the Hijaz. This is not to be underestimated, as the arrival of thousands of pilgrims annually generated political prestige and economic advantages for the city.[2] Furthermore, Damascus was traditionally the region's political capital, with the accompanying power that entailed. Even Aleppo's apparent advantage of being physically closer to the Euphrates route than Damascus did not preclude the latter's serving as the terminus of the Iraqi caravans on occasion. To understand, then, why Aleppo and not Damascus succeeded, we have to look to historical developments whose origins lay beyond Syria.

A major boost to Aleppo's possibilities came at the end of the fifteenth century, when Venice and the other Italian cities trading to the Middle East began seeking different goods in the bazaars of the region. Previously, they had bought the products of Middle Eastern workshops—primarily silk cloth, but also carpets, glass, and steel, in addition to the Eastern spices transported into the region by the caravans. With the increase in indigenous European craft output, however, their interest turned to primary products, principally cotton and silk, which could supply Europe's craftsmen. This evolution in consumption patterns created increased commercial opportunities for those centers that afforded relatively easy access for both the European merchants and the products being sought.[3] In this context Damascus suffered several liabilities.

Most important, Damascus had no primary products close at hand of interest to the Europeans. Aleppo, by contrast, was near to the raw-silk- and cotton-producing areas of northern Syria. To purchase this cotton, the first Venetian trading houses were established in Aleppo during the course of the fifteenth century.[4] Second, even though Damascus is only fifty miles from the Mediterranean as the crow flies, it is separated from the sea by the Lebanon and Anti-Lebanon ranges, which, in addition to being difficult to traverse, were inhabited by peoples often at odds with the political leadership in Damascus.

Geography and caution forced travel between Damascus and the coast to follow the more circuitous, albeit safer, route that went south of the city, through the Galilee and over to the coast at either Tyre, Sidon, or Acre. Another, equally cumbersome route led north, either through the Biqaʿ or along the western slopes of the Anti-Lebanon range to Homs and then west to the sea at Tripoli. Aleppo's easier access to the sea gave it a definite advantage over its rival, although this was diminished as long as Tripoli, some eight days distant from the city for pack animals,[5] remained its principal port.

Aleppo's ability to challenge Damascus was enhanced further by geopolitical changes in the region. The fall in 1375 of the Armenian kingdom of Cilicia, a major regional trading center, and political unrest in southeastern Anatolia in the fifteenth century encouraged the caravans bringing the raw silk of Iran to shift their route southward to one that went via Mosul and Aleppo. The change in the trade routes came at a time when both the demand for and the volume of Iranian raw silk was growing in Aleppo. The caravans bringing that silk advanced the city's viability as a trading center and established a symbiotic relationship between its economic fortunes and the silk trade that would be a hallmark of the city's economic life for the next few centuries. Furthermore, in the second half of fifteenth century, as the situation in Anatolia stabilized with the ascendancy of the Ottoman state, the strength and economic prosperity of the new regional superpower helped to direct trade north from Syria, with Aleppo serving as the conduit. But despite these indicators that the tide of history was ebbing for Damascus, it remained the major commercial center of Syria throughout the fifteenth century. It was there that the majority of Italian merchants active in the Syria trade resided, and it continued to control the bulk of the trade in eastern spices.[6] By 1600, however, that had all changed.

THE RISE OF ALEPPO, 1516–1600

The primary impetus to the amelioration of Aleppo's commercial position in the Levant in the sixteenth century was the Ottoman conquest of Syria in 1516, and the consequent changes in regional geopolitical alignments it engendered. The reason for the Ottoman move into Syria against the Mamluk Sultan Qānsūh al-Ghawrī—whether to forestall their archrival the Iranian Shah Ismaʾil Safavi, as the Ottoman conqueror of the city,

Sultan Selim I (1512–20), explained to the city's notables;[7] to pursue some long-range plan to unite the Muslim world under one political leadership; or, alternatively, to secure the trade routes—mattered little to the people of Aleppo caught between two opposing armies. They were clearly tired of the Mamluks, who had ruled the city despotically since the middle of the thirteenth century. Their apathy became apparent as the Ottoman army approached the city and the civilian leadership of the town chose wisely to do nothing, remaining neutral in the conflict.

After Qānsuh al-Ghawrī's ignoble defeat at Marj Dābiq on August 23, 1516, the city's gates were barred to the remnants of his army while the citizenry heaped abuse on the soldiers from the safety of the city's walls. In contrast, the Ottoman army headed by Sultan Selim was welcomed with gowns of honor (the Islamic equivalent to the keys of the city) and speeches of welcome, while the Sultan's name was mentioned as sovereign in the Friday prayers offered throughout the city.[8] It can not be known how much of this display was engendered by genuine feelings of relief to have the Mamluks gone or simply by an astute understanding of the direction the political winds were blowing. Nonetheless, whether the city's population understood it or not, a new era in the city's history had commenced.

Aleppo's loyalty to the new order was soon tested in 1520, when upon the accession to the Ottoman throne by Süleyman (1520–66), to be known as the "Magnificent" in the West, the governor of Damascus, the ex-Mamluk Jānbirdī al-Ghazālī, rose in revolt. Al-Ghazālī apparently dreamed that all the former Mamluk domains, including Egypt and Syria, would rally to his standard. When the leadership of Aleppo failed to follow his lead, he marched on the city. Aleppo's populace resisted and together with the city's garrison were able to withstand a siege until an Ottoman relief army arrived. They were thus spared the sacking by those same Ottoman troops that the inhabitants of Damascus were soon afterward forced to endure for having had an ambitious governor.[9]

The revolt of al-Ghazālī sealed the division of Syria into two provinces, to become three with the creation of a province centered in Tripoli around 1570. Until 1567, however, the finances of Syria were maintained under one directorate, the Treasury of Arabia *(Arabistan Defterdarı)*, located in Aleppo.[10] The lack of a clear-cut division of fiscal jurisdiction among Syria's provincial centers provided the military of Damascus with a continuing excuse to meddle in Aleppo's affairs. Throughout the sixteenth century, janissaries (the Ottoman professional infantry) from Damascus, obviously not willing to accept Damascus's reduced status, would show up in the province's villages to help collect the taxes, creating havoc for everyone involved. Despite this continuing interference, the political separation of Aleppo from Damascus ended the historic de facto domination of Syria's traditional capital over its rival and put both cities on an equal footing with regard to the new center of power in Istanbul. Aleppo had suffered throughout the Mamluk era in its role as a political backwater and a frontier city in an unsettled region. With the Ottoman conquest, however, it now stood to benefit from peace and suddenly widened markets.

Its geopolitical potential was aided further with the Ottoman conquest of Baghdad in 1534, and the subsequent incorporation of the port of Basra into the empire in 1549.[11] With this expansion, the Ottomans not only checked a threatened Iranian advance into the region but also announced a policy designed to prevent Portuguese incursions into the Arabian and Red seas. Indian products—spices, indigo, and cotton cloth—were once again free to travel up the Euphrates route, and Aleppo benefited at the expense of Damascus.

In addition to the security it gave the eastern trade routes, this *pax ottomanica* provided Aleppo's merchants with a much broader hinterland to exploit. This included an area bounded by a rough triangle, the legs of which rest in Diyarbakır to the north, Mosul to the east, and Aleppo to the west. By the end of the sixteenth century, Aleppo had become the leading center of commerce in this region, to the detriment of all other provincial towns. It was the domination of this large economic zone, coupled with political independence from Damascus, that enabled Aleppo to grow into a major metropolis—an assertion supported by evidence that regional products made up the bulk of the products sold in Aleppo's markets, despite the fame of the goods that came from further afield. Even after the transit trade began to dry up at the end of the eighteenth century, Aleppo retained its primary position as a commercial metropolis of a major geographical region, comparable to Beirut to the south. Acknowledging this regional role, a British observer, as late as 1851, could predict that without its markets in southern Anatolia and northern Iraq, Aleppo would wither and die.[12] This prediction would unfortunately come very close to realization in the years following World War I, when a new political border separated the city from its former hinterlands.

The formation of a greatly expanded economic zone for Aleppo helped to loosen the hold Damascus had exercised over the city in Mamluk times. It would, however, be an oversimplification of the city's emerging geopolitical realignment to accept Mustafa Akdağ's thesis that the city simply became an economic and cultural extension of Anatolia in the Ottoman period.[13] Rather, Aleppo and its hinterlands were linked to, but separate from, other similarly autonomous economic zones in southern Syria, Egypt, western Anatolia, and Iraq. In this context, the model of a world empire suggested by Braudel and Wallerstein for the Ottoman Empire—an overarching political structure encompassing smaller, largely self-contained economic units, each consisting of a metropolitan center and its hinterlands[14]—seems particularly useful in envisioning the interrelationship between the various regions of the empire. But even within such broadly defined geographical entities, we should be careful to distinguish between economic and cultural spheres of influence.

There can be little doubt that Ottoman, and therefore Turkish, influences became prominent in Aleppo's cultural life beginning with the sixteenth century. The architectural styles chosen by the city's elites mirrored those of the capital, as did their food and dress, while members of the prominent religious families sent their sons to study in the *madrasa*s (religious schools) of Anatolia. Turkish expressions crept into the vernacular Arabic spoken in the city, and the city's most famous figures in the world of Ottoman letters were Turks, the historian Naima and the poet Nâbî. Still, it would be a mistake to underplay the continuing pull Damascus exerted as a cultural center over all of Syria. Physically, Aleppo may have grown to resemble an Anatolian provincial center, but its literary and religious life continued to be conducted largely in Arabic, and in those cultural spheres that are harder to quantify the dominance of Damascus continued.[15]

But in the sphere of commerce Aleppo's position had become unchallenged, although it is difficult to know at what point Aleppo actually began to surpass Damascus as Syria's leading commercial entrepôt. Nonetheless, there are some indications that the process was under way soon after the Ottoman conquest. The most easily traceable is the two cities' changing relationship with their various European trading partners. In 1545, the Venetians transferred the residence of their consul for Syria from Damascus to Tripoli, and in 1548, from Tripoli to Aleppo, where it remained until 1675 when the Venetian Senate abolished the office altogether.[16] The Venetians' move from Damascus was accompanied by a general withdrawal of European merchant houses from that city to the coast or Aleppo, and it was not until the nineteenth century that they returned.[17]

In addition to the Venetians, other Europeans began to center the base of their Syrian commercial operations in Aleppo, in the half century following the Ottoman conquest. The French established consular representation in the city as early as 1557. Two decades later, in 1581, the Levant Company received its charter from Queen Elizabeth I. Although Damascus was listed as one of the cities in which factors (agents sent out from England to handle the company's trade) were entitled to operate, none in fact did so. Rather, the first company consul in Syria took up residence in Tripoli in 1583, and in the same year a vice-consul, William Barrett, arrived in Aleppo.[18] By 1586, Aleppo had replaced Tripoli as the consul's residence and chief company town in Syria, a position it held as long as the company was chartered.[19]

Tied to the growing interest of the Europeans in Aleppo was their increasing impatience with conditions at Tripoli, which had served as Syria's principal port up to that point. Not only was Tripoli at least eight days away from Aleppo by pack animal, a journey often made dangerous by the presence of bandits and rebellious tribal peoples in the coastal range,[20] but it lay in another province from Aleppo. This, in effect, doubled the number of government officials who expected gifts from the European merchants. Additionally, the region surrounding Tripoli was politically unstable, and its governors were less often under the direct control of the central administration than were those in Aleppo. Throughout the last decades of the sixteenth century and the first of the seventeenth, most of the province's governors were from the Sayfā family, who saw the European merchants as a source of revenue to finance their own political ambitions.[21]

Changes in the Levant trade also encouraged the Europeans to seek a port closer to Aleppo. From the mid–sixteenth century onward, pepper was replaced by raw silk as the major trade item in the city. As silk was bulkier and cheaper than pepper, the costs of transporting it by pack animal formed a greater percentage of its market value than was formerly the case with pepper. When these costs were added to the extortions that the Europeans were routinely encountering in Tripoli, that port became even less attractive, creating a pressing demand for an alternative.

This was found in the natural harbor at Iskenderun (Alexandretta), which could be reached from Aleppo in two to three days by pack animal and which fell under the jurisdiction of Aleppo's governor. Nonetheless, as a future international port city, the site had several distinct disadvantages. Not the least of these was its climate, which was perceived to contain—"unhealthy humors," no doubt produced by a malarial marsh that bordered the harbor. Moreover, there was neither a town nor any fortification already in place to protect the anchored shipping from pirates.[22] Despite these drawbacks, the Venetians, French, and English began to lobby in Istanbul to have Iskenderun made a customs station. In this, they were aided by local merchants and officials in Aleppo who perceived the potential of a nearby port for themselves.[23]

By 1590, Iskenderun was unofficially being used as a port, and in 1593, an imperial order was issued establishing a customs station there.[24] The Venetians were the first to take advantage of the port's official status, constructing warehouses and homes for their factors, but they were soon joined by the English and the French. By the middle of the seventeenth century, Iskenderun had grown into a small European town. The transition from Tripoli to Iskenderun did not pass unchallenged by the Sayfās, however, who correctly saw the new customs office in Iskenderun as a potential infringement on their revenues.

In an effort to get them back, the Sayfās offered counterbribes and petitions in the capital, winning a small victory in 1605 when the European ambassadors were informed that due to pirate raids, Iskenderun was being closed down.[25] This first order was evidently not obeyed, most probably because at that time the Ottomans had lost control of Aleppo, and a second order removing the European merchants to Tripoli was issued in 1609. This time mischief done by the European merchants in the port was cited as the reason for the port's closing. Additional orders were issued soon afterward, mandating the destruction of the European warehouses to encourage the implementation of the second closure decree.[26]

While it is not absolutely clear what the mischief perpetrated by the Europeans was, one historian has suggested that it included gunrunning to the rebel Ali Canpulatoğlu (see below).[27] Ironically, the removal of Iskenderun's port status corresponded to the fall from grace of the Sayfā family as governors of Tripoli. As such, Istanbul's reversal of its policy may have had its roots in the internal politics of the province as well as in a reaction to European interference.[28]

The Europeans, at first unsuccessfully, offered counterbribes to the grand vizier, the head of the Ottoman state council of ministers, to effect a rescission of the order. Apparently, however, they did not present a united front, and the English who were seeking at the same time to open up Trabzon as a conduit for the Persian silk trade were accused of being only lukewarm in their support by the continental merchants.[29] Nonetheless, the combined efforts of all the Europeans, English included, and the officials in Aleppo finally won the day, and in January of 1612, the European ambassadors at the Porte (as the Ottoman government in Istanbul was called in the European diplomatic dispatches) were informed that Iskenderun would again be open for business.[30]

The fate of Iskenderun provides an important watershed for Aleppo's changing fortunes, as it signals the city's transition from being primarily a caravan entrepôt of trade to one that was linked equally to the sea and the trade of the West. Iskenderun's growth into a city demonstrates the increased interest of the Europeans in the products available in Aleppo, as well as their power to affect the region's economic life. It was they who decided that Iskenderun would be the city's port and developed the facilities there to make it possible. Iskenderun had thus become the first of the "colonial" port cities—eventually to include Izmir, Beirut, and Alexandria—that grew up along the Levantine coast under Western tutelage and dominated the Middle East's commerce in the nineteenth and early twentieth centuries. Though the interior caravan cities would retain their control over the coast politically for several centuries more, in retrospect we can date the Syrian coast's entry into a world economy dominated by Europe with the establishment of the first customs station in Iskenderun.

The Western trading nations were not alone in showing an increased interest in Aleppo in the sixteenth century. The Ottomans, too, saw the city's potential, as the massive public building programs underwritten by various Ottoman officials during the century attest. These projects for the most part were financed by pious endowments, *waqf,* and consisted of mosques or other structures, such as schools, dedicated for religious purposes. Usually included in the *waqf* were various types of commercial buildings, which were endowed by the founder at the same time as the structures devoted to God and his community. The mundane revenues produced by the rental of the former were designed to maintain the higher goals of the latter, but, at least initially, they gave a boost to the city's economy as well.

The first of the many Ottoman-period *waqf*s was ordered by the governor Hüsrev Paşa and was completed in 1544. It included a large mosque bearing the governor's name and several acres of attached commercial properties. With this auspicious start, urban construction supported by *waqf* endowments continued unabated for four decades, reaching its apogee with the *waqf* of Bahram Paşa in 1583.

These various constructions more than doubled the city's core area, creating a vast interlocking network of miles of covered bazaar with shops, workshops, warehouses, and hostels for merchants all jostled together.[31] These pious endowments were undertaken to exploit Aleppo's rising economic fortunes, as the donors would not have invested their capital in projects to promote their eternal glory if they thought the projects were losing propositions. At the same time, however, this investment in the city's commercial infrastructure on such a vast scale gave impetus to the merchants traveling with the caravans to direct their movement toward Aleppo.

With the establishment of the port at Iskenderun and the growth of the city's commercial heart, the end of the sixteenth century saw Aleppo economically triumphant in its new role as the dominant commercial center in Syria. But just as developments coming from outside the city had engendered its good fortune, external developments at the beginning of the seventeenth century threatened to destroy it. The first challenge of the new century, however, came not from without, but from within Syria itself.

THE TIME OF TROUBLES, 1600–1630

The first decade of the seventeenth century was a time of crisis for the Ottoman Empire. Faced with wars on its borders with Iran and Hungary, governed by a weak and incompetent sultan, and in the midst of a fiscal crisis, the empire underwent a series of rebellions known collectively in Turkish historiography as the *Celali* (usually defined as "outlaw" or "rebel") Revolts,[32] which threatened its continued stability. One of the most serious of these revolts centered around Aleppo and was led by the Kurdish chieftain Ali Canpulatoğlu.

The Canpulatoğlu family had entered into the political limelight of northern Syria following the Ottoman conquest. Faced with an often turbulent political situation in its new province, the Ottomans relied on the cooptation of tribal leaders into the provincial government, both as a source of manpower to maintain order and as a means to pacify that leadership and make it amenable to Ottoman state interests. Such was the origin of the various local dynasties—including the Maᶜnīs, the Sayfās, and the Harfūshes, as well as the Canpulatoğlus themselves—that emerged in the more remote areas of the country. Such families were able to retain their positions by keeping order in the countryside and by walking a very delicate line, balanced between their own ambitions and what the central authorities would allow.

The Canpulatoğlus were the hereditary chieftains of the Kurds who inhabited the strategically important region surrounding the towns of Kilis and ᶜAzāz, present-day sister border towns of Turkey and Syria respectively. As leaders of an extended clan, they offered their kinsmen as levies in the service of the state and received in their stead official recognition as political bosses of the region. Although their base of power did not include Aleppo itself, the city was within their possible sphere of influence and contained numerous former subjects, Kurdish tribesmen who had migrated there.[33] The proximity of these tribal forces to the city made the clan an important power broker in the politics of the province in the early decades of Ottoman rule. Its leadership was especially important in the ongoing feud between the provincial governors of Damascus and Aleppo over the right to collect the tax revenues of northern Syria.

The conflict between provinces was engendered, as seen above, by the janissaries stationed in Damascus, who, despite the separation of the treasuries of the two provinces, still regarded the collection of taxes in Aleppo as one of their prerogatives. In 1603, as in 1599 and 1601, they took over the city, pillaging and looting, while the Ottoman governor looked on from the security of the city's citadel unable to restore order. In 1603, however, peace was restored by Hüseyin, the acting head of the Canpulatoğlu clan, whose tribesmen subdued the janissaries and sent them back to Damascus. In return for his service, Hüseyin was appointed governor of Aleppo. His appointment was, however, resisted by the acting governor of the city, Nasuh Paşa, a career Ottoman administrator who would later become grand vizier. He resented the Canpulatoğlus' upstart tribal status and was reported to have said that if the Porte had assigned a black slave to be governor of the city he would have acquiesced, but that he could not acquiesce in the appointment of the son of a Canpulat.[34]

In the face of Nasuh Paşa's adamant refusal to vacate the citadel, Hüseyin and his tribesmen laid siege to the city in 1604. The accounts of how long the siege lasted differ, but they concur that the end came when the city's chief judge effected a compromise that allowed Nasuh to leave Aleppo with his person and property unharmed, thereby giving the city over to Hüseyin. Hüseyin did not have long to consolidate his new position, however, before he was called up by the Ottoman army to aid in their war with the Iranians who were threatening to advance along the Empire's eastern front.

In November of 1605, the Ottomans suffered a resounding defeat at Urmia in Iran before Hüseyin and his forces could arrive. On his way to the front, Hüseyin met troops who had fled the battle and who informed him that the Ottoman army had fled the field. Rather than go on, he unwisely decided to direct his men to the Ottoman base camp in Van. There he encountered the wrath of the defeated Ottoman general, Çağalzade Sinan Paşa, who executed him on the ground that his men should have been at the battle, even if it had already been lost.

Shortly thereafter, Ali, Hüseyin's nephew, raised the clan's standard in revolt in revenge for his uncle's execution. In a short time, he was able to defeat the Sayfās and to emerge as the dominant military power in the province. Faced with a full-scale rebellion that it did not have the manpower to suppress, the Ottoman government attempted to mollify Ali by appointing him governor of Aleppo in 1606, while it prepared an army to punish his insubordination. The high stakes of his gamble were clear from the outset to Ali as well, and he set about trying to secure his political and military position in Syria. He is reported to have entered into direct negotiations with the duke of Tuscany, declaring himself in his correspondence with the West to be the "Prince and Protector of the Kingdom of Syria."[35] This grandiloquent title has a decidedly European ring about it and sounds designed for foreign consumption. His claim to Arabic speakers is not as clear, but a contemporary Kurdish source bespeaks hopes of his establishing a Kurdish principality.[36]

These possible visions of grandeur separate Ali from other *celali*-period rebels to whom he has been compared.[37] None of the others sought independence from the Ottoman state; rather, they hoped to use their rebellions to win concessions from Istanbul. Indeed, the apparent separatist coloration of the Canpulatoğlu revolt gave it a decidedly local Syrian character. For as we have seen, Jānbirdī al-Ghazālī entertained similar personal ambitions, and the Maʿnī dynasty in Mount Lebanon in the seventeenth century frequently acted to secure a position reminiscent of Ali's dreams.[38]

But the degree to which Ali actually wanted the independence of Syria remains an enigma. The accounts of his rebellion, while written largely by his contemporaries, were penned long after his death. Whether or not his ambitions included independence or merely personal aggrandizement, the Ottomans could not afford to let his insolence go unpunished. An army was formed in the summer of 1607 and arrived in Syria in September. Upon hearing that an army was on its way, Ali sought to gain support in Syria by saying that he was the loyal subject of the sultan and the rightly appointed governor of Aleppo, but this sudden show of fealty remained unconvincing.

The two armies met on October 24, 1607, and Ali's forces suffered a major defeat. Fleeing the field, he tried to rally various tribal forces and even went as far as to offer his services to the Iranian shah. He had little success, however, as the country sensed the tide had definitely turned against the Canpulatoğlu dynasty. Aleppo itself, which was garrisoned by forces still loyal to Ali, surrendered to the Ottomans on November 8, 1607, without a fight. Afterwards, having failed to win the acceptance of the shah or an alliance with other rebels in Anatolia, Ali Canpulatoğlu took advantage of the pardon that had been proffered to him by the sultan and went to Istanbul. There he received an imperial welcome and was given a government post in faroff Rumania. He never returned to Syria. In 1610, he was executed in Belgrade for treason,[39] bringing to an end the only episode in Aleppo's history as an Ottoman province in which a local figure dared to act upon such grand political ambitions.

The sole apparent legacy of Ali's revolt was an increased appreciation in Istanbul of Aleppo's strategic importance. Local personalities would never again be allowed to serve as the province's governor, and those Ottoman officials appointed there would be rotated frequently so as not to allow them to create local bases of power. Governors would rebel in

Aleppo after Ali, as in the case of Abaza Hasan Paşa in 1657,[40] but their ambitions would center on the capital and would not include hopes for a Syrian principality.

In the aftermath of the revolt, Aleppo was finally freed from the political intrigues of Damascus, but the cost was a much firmer control from Istanbul. Locally, Ali seems to have been forgotten, except among his Kurdish kinsmen, who for several years after his banishment continued to extort taxes in his name from caravans passing near Kilis.[41] Most of the family itself migrated to Mount Lebanon, dashing hopes for a rising. Without a leader such as the Canpulatoğlus provided, Kurdish unrest was confined to banditry, never to achieve the status of a rebellion again. Ali Canpulatoğlu remains a tragic hero in the ballads passed down in the Kurdish mountain villages around Kilis, but elsewhere his memory was reduced to that of another *celali.*

Despite the heroic potential of the legend of Syria's own Bonnie Prince Charlie in the personage of Ali, a threat of much greater consequence for Aleppo's commercial fortunes was occurring at roughly the same time, outside the empire's borders. In 1605, the city was reported to have conducted trade amounting to between one million and one-and-a-half million gold ducats with Venice, 800,000 with France, 300,000 with England, and 150,000 with the Netherlands. The exports consisted primarily of raw silk, indigo, cotton, gallnuts (used to set dyes), and some spices, while the imports were comprised of cloth (both silks and woolens) and coins.[42] Interestingly, this trade occurred between two major sieges of the city and may indicate how little effect Ali Canpulatoğlu's revolt actually had on Aleppo's transit trade. At that time, the key product being exported was Iranian silk, which more than anything else made Aleppo commercially important to the Europeans.

Silk formed the lifeblood of the long-distance caravan trade in the seventeenth century, just as pepper and spices from the East had done in the century before. But in the first quarter of the seventeenth century, an unusual coalition was taking shape to divert the silk trade away from the borders of the Ottoman Empire and the Mediterranean. Such threats were not new. The transit trade had long been hostage to political considerations. As recently as 1514, the Ottomans had sought to embargo Iranian products in an attempt to weaken their enemy.[43] By the seventeenth century, however, that trade was perceived as being too vital to the imperial interests for such an action to be contemplated. The Iranians, on the other hand, realizing the potential for damage to their rivals, began to consider the possibility of marketing their silk to the West by an alternative way that would avoid the Ottoman realm.

In this, they were aided in the first decades of the seventeenth century by the Englishman Robert Sherley and the combined efforts of the East India Company and the Netherlands Vereenigde Oost-Indische Compagnie (VOC), which drove the Portuguese from the Persian Gulf and diverted the silk trade away from the Mediterranean.[44] These efforts were abetted by Shah Abbas (1587–1629), who turned the silk production of Iran into a royal monopoly. The Ottoman grand vizier had naively protested to the Venetian ambassador that such a scheme was unfeasible, as it would take a year for ships to sail from Hormuz to Europe and besides the shah of Iran possessed no ships.[45] Yet by 1619, it had become apparent to many in the Mediterranean that the unthinkable had in fact happened. The camel caravan had apparently been bested at last by the sailing ship.

Such a radical shift in the trade routes was of obvious concern not only to the Ottomans, whose coffers were enriched by transit taxes, but also to the Venetians, the French, and the English Levant Company, all of whom had a stake in the continuance of the Levant trade. But there was not much any of them could do to correct the situation. The Ottomans were able to beat back an Iranian offensive and had secured their borders in Iraq by 1639,[46] but they lacked the military might to wrest the silk-producing region of Gilan away from the shah. For the French and the Venetians, the alternative lay in opening up trading relations directly with Iran, as the Venetians at least contemplated.[47] Such action was precluded, however, by the naval superiority of the English and the Dutch in the Persian Gulf. On their home front, the Levant Company lobbied Parliament to forbid the East India Company from engaging in the Persian Gulf trade, but in vain.[48]

Despite their collective inabilities to prevent the diversion of the Levant trade, the fears of the parties involved were cheered in 1629, with the death of Shah Abbas. His successor, Shah Safi, was unable to maintain the royal monopoly on silk, and the Armenian merchants who handled the trade moved back into the comfortable patterns of the old overland routes. As another Armenian merchant wrote almost a century later about similar circumstances, "that a marchant who has been long used to one sort of trade will not give that over to fall into another unless they can see some extraordinary profit in the new trade."[49]

Perhaps to counter the hemorrhage in his revenues that the resumption of the caravan trade entailed, Shah Safi greatly increased the taxes collected from the companies trading in Iran, thereby adding a nail to the coffin of the dream of a Persian Gulf trading empire. The Europeans in Iran were already finding it difficult to buy all of the country's silk, and with the new taxes, they dropped their dreams of a monopoly. By 1633, many of them had left Iran, causing the Venetians optimistically to predict a renewal of the Levant trade.[50]

THE RETURN OF THE SILK TRADE, 1630–1730

The failure of the shahs to maintain a state monopoly over their country's silk production and the subsequent return of Iranian silk to the markets of Aleppo were welcome events both for the city and for its European trading partners. For the Armenians, who must be credited for much of the effort in resurrecting the trade, the caravan option provided opportunities for both wider markets and greater profits. The caravans' freedom of movement also reduced the control the East India Company could potentially exercise over a trade the Armenians considered their own. At the time of Shah Abbas's death, Iran was estimated to be producing one thousand tons of silk annually, of which two-thirds was reaching Europe.[51] By the middle of the 1630s, this was almost all passing through Aleppo. The silk found a ready market in Europe, especially in England, where it was estimated that the number of people employed in the silk-cloth industry in London had risen from three hundred in 1600 to over ten thousand in 1640.[52]

The needs of a nascent silk industry in Europe heightened Aleppo's importance, at least temporarily, as Iranian silk formed the bulk of the cheap silk available on the world markets until the end of the seventeenth century, when Bengali silk became readily available.[53] The Iranians were unable to increase their production, however, and so the competition for those stocks available in Aleppo intensified. The Venetians, the veteran traders of the Levant, had held the undisputed lead in Aleppo's trade for well over a century, but their position was threatened by the French, English, and Dutch, as new products and organizations were introduced in the scramble for silk.

When the dust had settled, the English Levant Company emerged with the premier position in the Levant trade. Concomitantly, in England, raw silk became the dominant single commodity imported from outside of Europe during the seventeenth century.[54] The reason for England's success in dominating the Levant trade are as complex as the accompanying reasons for the failure of the Ventians and, to a lesser extent, the French to compete successfully.

Venice had its own source of raw silk in Italy, and its textile industry concentrated on luxury fabrics, which could not make use of the cheaper-quality Middle Eastern silk.[55] It did not, therefore, need to compete as fully for Iranian raw silk as did England, whose industry could find a use for it. Furthermore, Venice's industries did not keep pace with those of northern Europe, and its merchants had fewer items with which to barter on a grand scale in the Levant than did the English or the Dutch. The question of barter items was critical, as the Venetians refused steadfastly to pay for their purchases with coin, holding out for either barter or local sales to finance their purchases. This behavior was in marked contrast to their policy of a century before,[56] and lessened their ability to compete with those who had cash. The English, on the other hand, were more than willing initially to pay with coin, which the Iranian Armenians prefered to barter items, if it meant capturing the trade.[57] Once their control had been established, however, the English introduced a barter policy that was remarkably similar to the one employed by the Venetians earlier.

But, more decisive than the advantage the English gained by dealing with specie, the woolen broadcloths they introduced into the region proved to be the most popular European import to both the local Syrian consumers and the Armenians from Iran. This consumer acceptance lessened the dependency of the English merchants on cash and created an expanded market for English textiles.

In a short time, European broadcloth became a staple of the Levant trade for both Syrian and Iranian consumption. The English estimated that roughly half of the twelve thousand cloths they exported to Aleppo annually in the late 1680s, the high-water mark of their exports of broadcloth to the Middle East, eventually ended up in Iran.[58] Sober, darker colors were found to be preferred in Syria, while lighter cloth and brighter colors were destined for the Iranian market.[59] In Syria, the broadcloth was largely used for the outer street garments worn by both men and women and replaced the coarser cloth produced locally (called invariably *khām* in Arabic language sources, regardless of place of manufacture or composition). The developing trade in broadcloth fostered an alliance between the Levant Company and English textile producers. This community of interest contrasted to the often hostile relations between the textile industry and the East India Company, the Levant Company's rivals in the marketplace, and helps to explain some of the Levant Company's political influence in London.[60]

Perhaps the greatest advantage the English possessed, however, was the structure of their trading company. It allowed the English merchants to deal collectively with Ottoman officialdom, while permitting the individual factors to take the initiative in their quest for profits. The factors had to abide by the rules of their consul, if they were to remain members in good standing of the English "nation," but they were individually responsible only to the company member in London who had provided them with their operating capital. In fact, individual factors were often in direct competition with one another. It was this combination of strength and flexibility that the Venetians saw as giving the English the commercial edge in the Levant trade, and their consuls suggested the formation of a similar company to promote the republic's interests.[61]

The Venetians could not afford the luxury of revamping their mercantile traditions, however, as they faced severe external challenges from the Ottomans, who were seeking to expand in the Mediterranean at the expanse of the republic's trading stations. This competition culminated in the Ottoman-Venetian war over Crete in 1669, which ended with the island's annexation to the Ottoman Empire. After the war, Venice could no longer compete economically with the northwestern Europeans. Its industry was unable to keep up with that of its rivals,[62] and its middleman position between East and West became redundant with the opening of direct trade between producers and consumers.

The French faced many of the same disadvantages as the Venetians. Their traders, controlled by the Marseilles Chamber of Commerce, lacked the institutional freedom enjoyed by the factors of the Levant Company. What is more, their textile production lagged behind the innovations made by the English, while their products were seen, at least in the seventeenth century, as generally inferior to those offered by their competition in Aleppo's markets.[63] As a result, while at the beginning of the seventeenth century the Venetians had seen the French as their strongest competition, by its end both the Venetians and the French had been virtually eliminated from the field.

Having lost out in the competition for the trade of Aleppo, the French relocated their Syrian commercial interests to Tripoli, where they could obtain the silk of Mount Lebanon, more readily available but generally considered inferior to that of Iran, and to Sidon, where they concentrated in opening up the trade of southern Syria. This redeployment is reflected in the trade figures for Marseilles with various Levantine ports as reported at the end of the seventeenth century: Istanbul, 700,000 livres; Izmir, 800,000; Aleppo, 400,000; Sidon, 450,000; Tripoli, 200,000; and Egypt, 1,200,000. This was down from the trade levels reached in 1671, when it was reported that the trade of Marseilles with Aleppo had reached 1,650,000 livres.[64] By comparison, Aleppo had become very important to England. English exports to the Ottoman Empire, handled by the Levant Company amounted to £367,595 in 1663, while their imports were valued at £167,661. About half of the company's total trade was conducted at Aleppo. In the same year, England through the monopoly of the East India Company only exported to the rest of Asia goods worth £175,116, while importing £138,278 worth in 1664,[65] making the Middle East the primary arena of English trade outside of Europe.

Not only the Europeans were competing for Iranian silk, but so too were the cities of the Ottoman Empire. As in earlier centuries, the caravans' final destinations reflected political and economic as well as geographical realities. Formerly, Damascus had provided Aleppo with its major competition, but with the advent of silk as the major commodity traded between the Ottomans and Europe, Damascus's attractiveness diminished, as it was too distant from the sources to remain competitive. Rather, Izmir, which had previously been a minor seaport, became the major rival to Aleppo as the chief commercial emporium of the Levant, sometimes even to the exclusion of Aleppo. The Dutch, for example, concentrated almost all their efforts in the eastern Mediterranean there. Although the Netherlands had established a consulate in Aleppo in 1612, Dutch merchants were represented there by consul only intermittently throughout the period and were often under English consular representation.[66]

Although Izmir is on the sea with direct access to European shipping, a quick look at a map of the Middle East will reveal that Izmir is much further afield from Iran than is Aleppo, sixty days by caravan, as opposed to forty-five.[67] Geography alone again fails to explain why Izmir was able to attract the silk trade away from Aleppo, though the city had emerged in the seventeenth century as a commercial entrepôt in its own right, serving as a market for Anatolian raw materials: mohair from Ankara, silk from Tokat, and cotton. As such, it had attracted European merchants, who had established commercial facilities in the town. It also possessed the very real advantage of being much closer to the capital, Istanbul; it was therefore under the more direct control of the sultan and the influence of the European ambassadors, and the routes leading to it were relatively secure. By contrast, the route to Aleppo was remote and often troubled by bandits and by the Kurdish princes who dominated southeastern Anatolia.

But despite these very real detractions, it seems that the single most influential factor aiding the rise of Izmir was the higher rate of taxation merchants encountered in, and on their way to, Aleppo. In this, the development of Izmir offers an interesting parallel to the rise of the port at Iskenderun, which was promoted in response to the greed of the officials in control of Tripoli (see pp. 15–17 above). The French traveler Jean-Baptiste Tavernier reported in the first half of the seventeenth century that the tolls exacted along the route from Tabriz to Izmir totaled 36 or 37 *ghurūsh,* while those paid along the Tabriz-Aleppo route amounted to 67 *ghurūsh,* with additional exactions being demanded by the Kurdish chieftains in the region of Van.[68] Later in the century another Frenchman, the chevalier d'Arvieux, reported that the high customs tolls being exacted at Aleppo were forcing the Armenian merchants to shift their trade from Aleppo to Izmir,[69] a charge often repeated in the letters sent from Aleppo by the factors of the Levant Company.[70]

While it is clear from the volume of silk exported by the Levant Company from the rival cities that Izmir never completely replaced Aleppo as the leading destination of the silk caravans, it allowed the merchants the option to boycott Aleppo should the local officials there seek to exceed the limits set by law in collecting tolls. By the eighteenth century Izmir had indeed surpassed Aleppo in the volume of trade it handled with Europe. By then, however, the Iranian silk trade had all but ended, and it was the produce of its Anatolian hinterlands—wool, cotton, tobacco, and fruit—that made up most of Izmir's exports.

In addition to silk, the caravans continued to bring to Aleppo's markets much of the Indian goods sold there. The persistence of the trade with the East, via the Euphrates route, throughout the period is a formidable challenge to Steensgaard's theory that the seventeenth century saw an Asian trade revolution, whereby the caravans were bested by the European trading companies. Rather, it seems that a temporary equilibrium was reached throughout most of the century in which the caravans and the Europeans were in competition with each other for control of the Middle Eastern markets. Direct competition took place in a number of commodities. Those most often mentioned were indigo, spices, and Yemeni coffee. In the case of coffee and indigo, competition came from goods imported to the Middle East by the Europeans from their colonies in the New World; in the case of spices, it amounted to competitive modes of transport, the sailing ship versus the camel.

The English factors in Aleppo were keenly aware of the ramifications of the continued health of the caravan trade, and their letters to London are full of accounts of the costs of various products in the city with queries as to whether it would be profitable to compete by buying the goods elsewhere and shipping them to the Levant. Similarly, they wrote that local merchants looked with trepidation on reports of the direct India trade to England in the seventeenth century, because of what it could mean for their investments.[71] Much of what they reported was rumor, but rumor had a way of affecting the prices in the marketplace. For example, in 1701 accounts of a beduin attack on the hajj caravan sent coffee and indigo prices soaring in the city. As a consequence, the English found they could unload their Jamaican indigo at about the same price as that coming from the Indian subcontinent, either by way of Jeddah and the hajj route via Damascus or by Basra and the Euphrates route. But a year later, news of a large and well-stocked hajj caravan sent the prices plummeting.[72]

Yet despite the competition provided by English colonial goods, the trade with the East showed a remarkable resiliency. Even Southeast Asian spices, which were increasingly being imported to the region by the Europeans, continued, at least in part, to follow the old trade routes to the Middle East.[73] Although the prices paid for these in Aleppo were too high to make them profitably reexportable to Europe, as long as the caravan transportation costs remained low such goods could effectively compete locally with the same items transported either across the Atlantic or around the Cape of Good Hope. The willingness on the part of the Middle Eastern merchants to accept a lower profit margin on the trade than were the Europeans was the key to the caravans' continued existence, and such a potential for profit would remain as long as camel transport costs were lower than those of ships.

THE DECLINE OF THE CARAVAN TRADE

Despite the resiliency of the caravan trade, by 1750 there were clear signs of trouble. It was not only Aleppo that struggled to maintain its commercial position in the Levant against impossible odds, but also its old trading partner the Levant Company. Tied largely to one commodity, silk, the Levant Company never became a leviathan like its rival the East India Company, and by 1700 it faced several potentially lethal challenges to its continued survival. Ironically, its jealously guarded monopoly on the Levant trade proved a problem, as the Levant Company could only export as much broadcloth as could be absorbed by the Ottoman Empire and Iran, markets relatively small by world standards and becoming saturated by the beginning of the eighteenth century.

These shrinking exports were further threatened by the East India Company's plans to sell broadcloth directly to Iran in the 1690s and by a reorganized French textile industry whose products were lighter in weight and brighter in color than their English competition. To make matters worse, alternative sources of silk were becoming more plentiful outside the Levant, and the demand for Middle Eastern silk was declining.[74] Then war broke out in 1723 between the Ottomans and Iran, as Iran itself was convulsed in the political chaos that marked the end of the Safavid dynasty and the rise of Nadir Shah. Warfare between the Ottomans and Iran would continue off and on for some twenty years until Nadir Shah's death in 1747.

The troubled conditions in Iran led to an almost total halt in the caravan trade, as Iran's silk production dropped off dramatically, estimated by one observer to be only 160 tons in 1730. Furthermore, that greatly reduced crop was required almost exclusively in domestic production, so little was exported.[75] Deeply concerned, the English factors reported as early as 1725 that no Iranian silk was reaching Aleppo, and throughout the next two decades their letters were almost universally glum.[76] Although some Iranian silk occasionally did get through, the falloff in trade forced the Levant Company to switch its interests to locally produced

Syrian silk, from either Mount Lebanon or Antioch. The abrupt and almost total end to the Iran trade had disastrous consequences for the company's exports of broadcloth from Britain as well. This declining market engendered increased vigilance on the part of the Levant Company to maintain its monopoly position at home, both for the import of Levantine products to the British Isles and the export of goods eastward to the Ottoman Empire. An example of this was the company's prohibition of the independent import of Irish broadcloth directly from Dublin to the Levant, a stratagem that sought to avoid London's customs duties and provide a cheaper alternative to the higher-priced English broadcloth.[77]

By 1750, the Levant Company's position in Aleppo was in disarray. It was increasingly forced to pay for purchases of Syrian silk with cash rather than broadcloth. On July 30, 1765, the British consul in Aleppo reported that the average annual import of broadcloths to the city had dropped from one thousand bales in the period between 1748 and 1756, already down from the highs of the early decades of the century, to less than five hundred bales annually for the years 1756–74. He went on to say:

> The causes of this decrease are various but chiefly to be attributed to the depopulation of Persia from whence very considerable quantities of sherbasse, ardassette and other sorts of silks were brought to this market, for return for which the Persians took off the chiefest part of our cloth, but none of the Persian silk has been seen since the year 1750. Indeed some ten years ago about 300 bales of our cloth were by the channell of Baghdad annually run off in that city for Persia and countries adjacent. This poor residue of a very extensive trade is now however entirely lost to us by importations to Bassora of British cloth by the East India Company who for two or three years past by regular importations have supplied Baghdad and Persia with the little wanted. . . .[78]

The consul listed another reason for the decline in trade—the competition offered by French cloth. Citing its lower cost (due, he said, to lower labor and transportation costs), he also admitted the French had been more innovative in appealing to local tastes. The result had been to boost their annual export to Aleppo to fifteen hundred bales of cloth, trebling the British trade.

There were also signs that the Euphrates caravan route was in trouble. European imports of their colonial products were undercutting the prices charged by the merchants traveling with the caravans, and mention of caravans arriving with eastern trade goods became much less frequent. Furthermore, the collective rising star of the ʿAẓm family as governors of Damascus gave notice that the political leadership in that city was once again reasserting its position in Syria, reflected in a report that the ʿAẓms had used their influence to divert the Baghdad caravans to Damascus.[79]

Aleppo had never been able to develop an independent political leadership in the aftermath of Ali Canpulatoğlu's revolt. On the contrary, the eighteenth century witnessed an increasing fragmentation of the city's political elite into the factions of janissaries and *ashrāf* (to be discussed in the next chapter), which periodically errupted into open and bloody warfare. It could not, therefore, offer any effective political resistance to Damascus's resurgence. Caravans continued to come from Iraq to Aleppo for at least another century, but the city no longer had an effective monopoly on the trade.

While the transit trade was drying up at Aleppo, the city's trading relations with Europe were undergoing profound changes. Instead of being middlemen, the city's merchants were providing raw materials produced either within the immediate vicinity of the city or in its neighboring hinterlands. This trend had begun with the Levant Company's efforts to buy Syrian silk in the absence of imports from Iran, but it had been accelerated with French interest in Syrian cotton.

The Ottoman Empire had, in general, become the major supplier of raw cotton for the French textile industry by the end of the eighteenth century. While Izmir was by far the more important source, Aleppo also was becoming a major center in the trade. In the period between 1750 and 1754, the city's cotton trade with France averaged 15,000 livres annually, and by 1786–89 it had reached an annual average of 71,000 livres. This was far below the average of 6,920,00 livres for Izmir, but nonetheless important locally.[80] Furthermore, with the desire to be closer to the emerging sources of cotton in southern Syria and the silk of Mount Lebanon, the Europeans moved their major marketing efforts to the coast. Conditions outside of Syria had once again seemingly acted to change Aleppo's fate. Without a whimper to mark the transition, except from the Levant Company, the city had passed from being a caravan entrepôt to being a producer of "colonial" goods. While this transition was not necessarily bad for Aleppo's merchants, it forced them into a more dependent role vis-à-vis Western purchasers than they had known previously.

Fate had indeed been mercurial to Aleppo. Historical and geographical conditions had allowed it to benefit from the transit trade for two centuries. This happy situation provided Aleppo's merchants with a surplus garnered from the labor of others, the silk growers of Iran and the English broadcloth workers. The buying and selling of foreign goods enriched the city's economy, as a combination of a growing demand in Western Europe for the raw materials of Asia, in particular Iranian silk, and the security offered by the Ottoman Empire combined to make Aleppo a natural meeting place for buyers and sellers. In its role as commercial middleman, Aleppo and its merchants profited, as Muslim merchants had for centuries, from the trade of Asia to Europe that crossed their domain. Changes in the patterns of world trade in the seventeenth and eighteenth centuries, however, marked the end of that tradition. New technology allowed Western ships to supersede the caravans. With their decreasing viability as competitors in the transit trade, Aleppo's merchants found themselves in a strange new relationship with the West. No longer middlemen for goods from outside Syria, they had become sellers of locally produced agricultural products to the Europeans. Those who could not or would not change lost out to others who understood that a new age was upon them.

NOTES

1. Antoine Abdel-Nour, *Introduction à l'histoire urbaine de la Syrie Ottomane (XVIe–XVIIIe siècle)* (Beirut, 1982), pp. 76–77.

2. Abdul-Karim Rafeq, "Qāfilat al-ḥajj al-Shāmī wa-ahammiyatuha fī al-dawla al-ʿuthmānīya," *Dirāsāt Tāʾrīkhīya* 6:193–216.

3. Eliyahu Ashtor, "The Economic Decline of the Middle East during the Late Middle Ages: An Outline," *Asian and African Studies* 15:262–63.

4. Eliyahu Ashtor, *Levant Trade in the Late Middle Ages* (Princeton, 1983), p. 121.

5. Guglielmo Berchet, *Relazioni dei consoli veneti nella Siria* (Turin, 1866), p. 142.

6. Ashtor, *Levant Trade in the Late Middle Ages*, pp. 392, 461.

7. Ibn Ayās, Muḥammad Aḥmad, *Badāʾiʿ al-zuhūr fī waqāʾiʿ al-duhūr* (Istanbul, 1932), 5:58–61.

8. Ibid. See also al-Ṭabbākh, Muḥammad Rāghib, *Aʿlām al-nubalā bi-tāʾrīkh Ḥalab al-shahbā* (Aleppo, 1923–26), 3:166–72.

9. ibn Ṭulūn, Muḥammad, *Aʿlām al-warā bi-man wuliya nāʾiban min al-Atrāk bi-Dimashq al-Shām al-kubrā* (Damascus, 1964), pp. 259–67.

10. Muhammad Adnan Bakhit, *The Ottoman Province of Damascus in the Sixteenth Century* (Beirut, 1982), p. 145. Halil Inalcik, *The Ottoman Empire: The Classical Age, 1300–*

1600 (London, 1973), p. 106. This assessment is questioned, however, in Abdul-Karim Rafeq, *The Province of Damascus* (Beirut, 1966), p. 16.

11. The rulers of Basra had in 1636 pledged their fealty to Süleyman but reneged on their promises. Stephen Longrigg, *Four Centuries of Modern Iraq* (Oxford, 1925), pp. 31–32. See also Salih Özbaran, "Osmanlı İmparatorluğu ve Hindistan Yolu," *Tarih Dergisi* 31:66–146.

12. London, Public Records Office, Foreign Office Documents. (henceforth FO) 861/2:201, 30 Aug. 1851. Aleppo's regional commercial role is further documented by Eugen Wirth, "Aleppo in 19. Jahrhundert. Ein Beispiel für stabilität und Dynamik spätosmanischer Wirtschaft." Corrected reprint of article with the same title first published in *Osmanistische Studien Zur Wirtschafts-und Sozialgeschichte*, ed. Hans Georg Majer (Wiesbaden, 1986).

13. Mustafa Akdağ, *Türkiye'nin İktisadi ve İçtimai Tarihi* (Ankara, 1979).

14. Fernand Braudel, *The Perspective of the World*, vol. 2 of *Civilization and Capitalism, 15th–18th Century* (New York, 1984), and Wallerstein, *The Modern World System*.

15. This is apparent from the dominant position of seventeenth- and eighteenth-century Damascus chroniclers, poets, religious writers, and biographers in Syrian belles lettres and an accompanying dearth of similar intellectual output from Aleppo. See Usāmā ʿAnūtī, *al-Ḥaraka al-adābīya fī bilād al-Shām khilāl al-qarn al-thāmin ʿashar* (Beirut, 1970).

16. Berchet, p. 19. Venice did not retain a consul in Aleppo throughout this entire period, as is indicated by the account of the German merchant Wolffgang Aigen, resident in the city between 1656 and 1663. Aigen, as a protégé of a hostile power, Venice, had to maintain the fiction that he was a subject of France while in the city. Wolffgang Aigen, *Sieben Jahre in Aleppo*, ed. Andreas Tietze (Vienna, 1980), pp. 82–83.

17. Abdul-Karim Rafeq, "The Impact of Europe on a Traditional Economy: The Case of Damascus, 1840–1870," in *Économie et Sociétés dans l'Empire Ottoman*, ed. Jean-Louis Bacque-Grammont and Paul Dumont (Paris: 1983), p. 420.

18. Alexander Russell, *The Natural History of Aleppo* (London, 1794), 1:Appendix 5–6.

19. Alfred C. Wood, *The History of the Levant Company* (London, 1935).

20. Richard Pococke, *Description of the East and Some Other Countries*, in *Voyages and Travels in All Parts of the World*, coll. John Pinkerton (London, 1811), 10:545.

21. Damascus, Syrian National Archives, Aleppo Sharīʿa Court Records, (Dār al-Wathāʾiq al-Tāʾrīkhīya) (henceforth Aleppo) 22:458. In a depositon registered before the chief judge of Aleppo, the European merchants cited the oppression of the Sayfā family as the reason they sought to obtain port concessions at Iskenderun. They agreed to pay the same rate of taxation at Iskenderun as was levied in Tripoli.

22. Berchet, pp. 84–85.

23. Halil Sahillioğlu, "Taghayyur ṭurūq al-tijāra waʾl-tanaffus bayna mināʾay Ṭarablūs al-Shām waʾl-Iskandarūn fī al-qarn al-sābiʿ ʿashar," in *Muʾtammar al-duwwalī li-tāʾrīkh bilad al-Shām* (Damascus, 1980).

24. Ibid.

25. London, Public Records Office, Calendar of State Papers: Venice (henceforth Venice) 10:318.

26. Venice 11:267, 284.

27. William Griswold, *The Great Anatolian Rebellion 1000–1020/1591–1611* (Berlin, 1983), p. 78.

28. Abdul-Rahim Abu-Husayn, *Provincial Leaderships in Syria, 1575–1650* (Beirut, 1985), pp. 30–34.

29. Venice 11:407, 455, 497.

30. Venice 12:476.

31. André Raymond, "The Ottoman Conquest and the Development of the Great Arab Towns," *International Journal of Turkish Studiess* 1:84–101.

32. Griswold; Mustafa Akdağ, *Türk Halkının Dirlik ve Düzenlik Kavgası* (Ankara, 1979).

33. Bruce Masters, "Patterns of Migration to Ottoman Aleppo," *International Journal of Turkish Studies* 4(1) (forthcoming May 1987).

34. Muhammad Adnan Bakhit, "Aleppo and the Ottoman Military in the 16th Century," *al-Abḥāth* 27:27–38. For contemporary accounts of the Canpulatoğlu revolt, see Abū'l-Wafā b. al-ʿUrdī, *Maʿādin al-dhahab fī'l-aʿyān al-musharrafa bi-him Ḥalab*, MS, British Library, Or.3618, ff. 71–74; Muḥammad al-Amīn al-Muḥibbī, *Khulāṣāt al-athār fī aʿyān al-qarn al-ḥādī ʿashar* (Cairo, 1869), 2:84–87. For modern interpretations, see Griswold; Rafeq, "The Revolt of ʿAlī Pāshā Jānbulād (1605–1607) in the Contemporary Arabic Sources and Its Significance," *VIII. Türk Tarih Kongresi: Kongreye Sunulan Bildiriler* (Ankara, 1983), 3:1515–34.

35. Griswold, pp. 129–31.

36. Rafeq, "The Revolt of ʿAlī Pāsha Jānbulād," 3:1530–31.

37. Griswold; Akdağ, *Türkiye'nin İktisadi ve İçtimai Tarihi.*

38. For a discussion of other Syrian warlords, see Abu-Husayn.

39. Mustafa Naima, *Tarih-i Naima* (Istanbul: n.p.d.), 2:21–22.

40. Rafeq, "The Revolt of ʿAlī Pāsha Jānbulād," 3:1532.

41. Istanbul, Başbakanlık Arşivi, Mühimme Defterleri (henceforth MD) 79:156, Rebiyülevvel 1019/May–June 1610.

42. Pedro Teixeira, *The Travels of Pedro Teixeira,* Hakluyt Society, 2nd ser., no. 9 (London, 1902), pp. 118–21.

43. Halil Inalcik, "The Ottoman Economic Mind," in *Studies in the Economic History of the Middle East,* ed. M. A. Cook (London, 1970), pp. 212–13.

44. Steensgaard, *The Asian Trade Revolution.*

45. Venice 15:558–59.

46. Longrigg, p. 74.

47. Venice 16:11.

48. Steensgaard, pp. 367–74.

49. K. N. Chaudhuri, *The Trading World of Asia and the East India Company, 1660–1760* (Cambridge, 1978), pp. 49–50.

50. Venice 23:75.

51. *The Encylopedia of Islam,* 2nd ed. (henceforth EI^2), Niels Steensgaard, "Ḥarir."

52. Wood, p. 76.

53. Chaudhuri, *The Trading World of Asia,* pp. 343–53.

54. Ralph Davis, "English Imports from the Middle East, 1580–1780," in *Studies in the Economic History of the Middle East,* ed. M. A. Cook (London, 1970), p. 196.

55. Antoine Rabbath, *Documents inédits pour servir à l 'histoire du Christianisme en Orient* (Paris, 1905, 1911), 1:509.

56. Ashtor, "The Economic Decline of the Middle East during the Late Middle Ages."

57. London, Public Records Office, State Papers (henceforth SP) 110/20:1, 27 April 1696.

58. Wood, p. 116.

59. SP 110/21:188, 8 August 1700.

60. Chaudhuri, *The Trading World of Asia,* pp. 278–81.

61. Venice 36:139; 37:57–58.

62. Domenico Sella, "Crisis and Transformation in Venetian Trade," in *Crisis and Change*

in the Venetian Economy in the Sixteenth and Seventeenth Centuries, ed. Brian Pullan (London, 1968), pp. 88–105.

63. Davis, "English Imports from the Middle East."

64. Adel Ismail, *Documents diplomatiques et consulaires relatifs à l'histoire du Liban et des pays du Proche Orient du XVIIe siècle à nos jours* (Beirut: 1975–), 3:203; Rabbath 1:508. The French consul d'Arvieux estimated in 1680 that France imported one million livres of goods annually from Aleppo while England's exports to Aleppo and imports from the city both totalled six million livres. P. Masson, *Histoire du Commerce français dans le Levant au XVIIe siècle* (Paris, 1896), p. 374.

65. Wood, p. 102; Chaudhuri, *The Trading World of Asia*, pp. 507–08.

66. Russell 1: Appendix 8; G. R. Bosscha-Erdbrink, *At the Threshold of Felicity: Ottoman-Dutch Relations during the Embassy of Cornelius Calkoen at the Sublime Porte, 1726–1744* (Ankara, 1975), p. 153.

67. Jean-Baptiste Taverneir, *Les six voyages en Turquie* (Paris, 1679), 1:34.

68. Ibid.

69. Laurant Chevalier d'Arvieux, *Memoires du Chevalier d'Arvieux* (German trans.) (Leipzig, 1756), 6:361.

70. SP 110/16:57, 6 Dec. 1688; SP 110/14:144, 15 Dec. 1677.

71. SP 110/21:180, 2 Aug. 1700.

72. SP 110/22:111, 8 Sept. 1701; SP 110/22:337, 5 Aug. 1702.

73. SP 110/33:168, 15 March 1755.

74. Chaudhuri, *The Trading World of Asia*, pp. 343–58.

75. EI^2, "Ḥarir."

76. For example, SP 110/25:32, 18 Aug. 1725; SP 110/26:10, 1 Jan. 1734; SP 110/32:78, 1 Aug. 1754; SP 105/118:275, 2 April 1754.

77. SP 105/118:294, 19 Nov. 1754.

78. SP 110/29:211, 30 July 1765.

79. SP 110/29:214, 30 July 1765.

80. Bruce McGowan, *Economic Life in Ottoman Europe: Taxation, Trade, and the Struggle for Land, 1600–1800* (London, 1981), pp. 28–31.

CHAPTER II

Population, Society, and Merchants in Ottoman Aleppo

Key to our understanding of the reasons why Aleppines may or may not have been able to profit in the long term from the shifting patterns of trade in the Levant is the question of whether merchants in Ottoman Syria constituted a distinct social class, sharing a vision of economic and political interests. If they did, we would expect those Aleppines would have been able to effect policies that would have promoted, or at least maintained, their city's commercial position.

By comparison, merchants in western Europe in the same historical period were recognized, by insiders and outsiders alike, as constituting a subgroup with a distinct community of interests within a larger, newly emerging bourgeoisie. The European merchants were vocal and politically astute, promoting policies that would benefit their investments. As such, their ambitions often clashed with those of the traditional landed gentry over the direction their various countries' national economic policies should take. The outcome could be crucial, as the group that triumphed would determine its nation's economic fate for the next several centuries.

In those countries, such as England and the Netherlands, where merchants emerged as important economic and political pressure groups, mercantilism came close to being state doctrine. For their efforts, those early merchant capitalists are generally credited, or condemned, by historians for having pushed the economies of northwestern Europe down the road to capitalism. But before they could do this, they first had to be cognizant both of the fact that their individual success was subordinate to larger class interests and of their own political power to effect policies that would benefit individual and group economic interests.

In contrast to these early mercantilists, the merchants of Syria (or more properly the Muslim merchants of Syria, for, as we shall see in the next chapter, religious minority interests and commerce often went hand in hand) seem never to have evolved a sense of having shared economic and social interests as a distinct group. Rather, wealthy Muslim merchants were a part of the larger urban social and economic elite. As such, their desire or ability to influence policies to promote trade was marginal. Yet Syria has been from the dawn of its recorded history a country of merchants. That, at least, has been the national stereotype held not only by outsiders but to some extent by the Syrians themselves.

In the previous chapter, in which Aleppo's role in the great East-West trade of the sixteenth through the eighteenth centuries was outlined, it often seemed as if that city were little more than a *locus operandi* for actors from without. Which image is correct: a nation of traders, if not shopkeepers, or simply a grand bazaar, a Levantine equivalent of a shopping mall? The answer seems to lie in the social formations of Ottoman Aleppo, and with those who were involved in the city's trade.

POPULATION AND ETHNICITY

In the seventeenth and eighteenth centuries, European accounts of the Ottoman Empire commonly asserted that Aleppo had the third largest population in the realm, surpassed only by Istanbul and Cairo. While this assessment was obviously colored by the Europeans' consciousness of Aleppo's economic importance to them, their estimate was most probably correct. The only other cities that might have competed for third place were Damascus and Izmir, and they were in no position to challenge Aleppo's ranking, for different reasons, until the second half of the eighteenth century. But the question of exactly how many people lived in Aleppo in the Ottoman period remains far from clear.

The European observers' accounts were fairly consistent, if not totally accurate in their estimates of the city's population. In 1599, the Venetian consul, Giorgio Emo, stated that Aleppo had 200,000 residents.[1] This was a figure echoed by the mid-seventeenth-century visitor Wolffgang Aigen[2] and expanded to 250,000 by his contemporary Nicolas Poirresson.[3] The chevalier d'Arvieux, who served as France's consul in Aleppo, gave what is probably the highest guess of the city's population at 290,000 people in 1683, while Russell in 1753 gave an estimate of 230,000. These last figures are especially problematic, as they do not correspond realistically to the totals for the city's households given by the two observers: 13,660 and 10,742, respectively.[4]

Unfortunately, Ottoman sources are not particularly helpful in solving the population dilemma either. Ömer Lütfi Barkan pioneered the systematic study of the population of the sixteenth-century Ottoman Empire, using the ledgers of taxable households preserved in the Ottoman state archives.[5] For the most part his findings have remained unchallenged since their publication, although from the outset his results for Syria have been controversial. The primary objection, raised by Issawi, was the seeming undercount of Christians.[6] While this is troublesome, most historians have accepted his other, more important assertion that Aleppo and Damascus, in contrast to every other city in the empire, underwent a dramatic population loss during the course of the sixteenth century. His results for Aleppo indicate a drop in the city's population from an estimate of 67,344 people before 1520 to 46,365 in 1580,[7] a far cry from Emo's total.

In support of Barkan's thesis, it is possible that the city suffered a population loss in the sixteenth century. The chronicles and the Venetians report several major outbreaks of the plague during the century, and these could have served to reduce the urban population. On the other hand, it was clear that the city experienced a tremendous growth in its physical area during the latter half of the century, and it seems difficult to reconcile with Barkan's thesis of decline the picture of a city with a robust economy described in the letters of the Venetian consuls and other European visitors.

Recently André Raymond has put forward a revision of the theory of the city's declining population that seems to solve the problem. Accepting Barkan's findings as reflecting the reality of the demographic conditions in Aleppo in the sixteenth century, he suggests that the city experienced a substantial growth in the seventeenth century, contrary to general trends in the Ottoman urban population at large.[8] But this revision encounters problems of verification, as, with the exception of a few scattered records of the head tax levied on adult, non-Muslim males (in Arabic *jizya,* Turkish *cizye*), there are no Ottoman records to substantiate the assertion of population growth. Despite these drawbacks, Raymond's model of urban growth is strongly supported by numerous cases preserved in the city's court records involving what seems to have been an almost continual immigration of rural peoples from both northern Syria and southeastern Anatolia into Aleppo throughout the seventeenth and early eighteenth centuries. These individual cases taken together do not produce the aggregate numbers necessary to substantiate a theory of population growth in themselves, but they do seem to point to what was undoubtedly a larger trend when placed together with the undisputable growth in the non-Muslim population.

This evidence of Christian migration suggests a broad, tentative outline of Aleppo's demographic trends for the Ottoman period: The city's population declined in the sixteenth century. It then rapidly grew in the first half of the seventeenth century, reaching its peak about the time that d'Arvieux visited it. Then in the eighteenth century, Aleppo apparently entered into a population slump that paralleled the decline in the transit trade and lasted well into the nineteenth century. Without more complete population data, this model remains only hypothetical, but it does find support in topographical studies of the city.[9] It is further strengthened by evidence of the very real depopulation in Syria that occurred throughout the seventeenth and early eighteenth centuries, described by Constantine Volney at the end of the eighteenth century:

In consequence of such wretched government, the greater part of the pashalics in the empire are improverished and laid waste. This is the case in particular with that of Aleppo. In the ancient deftars, or registers of imposts, upwards of three thousand two hundred villages were reckoned; but, at present, the collector can scarcely find four hundred. Such of our merchants as have resided there twenty years, have themselves seen the greater part of the environs of Aleppo depopulated. The traveller meets

Figure 1. *Jizya* Payers

	Christians	*Jews*
1640	2,500	—
1672	—	380
1695	5,391	875
1740	8,120	—
1754	7,213	—

with nothing but houses in ruin, cisterns rendered useless, and fields abandoned. Those who cultivated them are fled into the towns where the population is absorbed, but where at least the individual conceals himself from the rapacious hand of despotism.[10]

While this description and others like it penned by European travelers are hauntingly evocative, the picture of desolation they provide may not be totally accurate. The European visitors to the Levant were struck by the glories of the area's antiquities, which they contrasted with the stark realities of its present. This nostalgia for worlds forever lost permeated and perceptibly colored their descriptions. As for the contemporary Middle East, their accounts had a clearly articulated bias against the Ottoman/Islamic culture, which could only be contrasted against their vision of a classical Hellenistic culture. In their minds, a golden tradition had been cruelly usurped by the infidel. As such, although their laments over the transience of human glory make for good literature, their historical accuracy, though often cited as primary evidence, may be dubious at best.[11] Exaggerated as these accounts might have been, it nevertheless seems undeniable that major demographic shifts were occurring in northern Syria at that time.

While the circumstantial evidence for Aleppo's growth seems strong, it is not irrefutable. Neither are the estimates for the total number of inhabitants the city had in the seventeenth century. Nonetheless, Raymond suggests, based on the number of households given by d'Arvieux as compared with the ratio of households to population from the end of the nineteenth century for which we have reasonably accurate data, that the population of the city in 1683 was 115,000.[12] This hunch seems as good as any other for establishing the city's population at its zenith, but the total most probably dropped to around 80,000 by the end of the eighteenth century, its nadir.

Whatever their numbers, Aleppo's people in the Ottoman period were ethnically diverse. In addition to the foreign merchants, who will be discussed in the next chapter, Aleppo then, as now, lay close to the linguistic border separating Arabic speakers from those who spoke Turkish. There is strong evidence to indicate there were still pockets of Arabic speakers at least as far north as Diyarbakır and that the cities of Mardin and Urfa, both currently in Turkey, may have had substantial Arabic-speaking populations.[13] But it is also evident from travelers' accounts that somewhere just to the north of the city, and definitely by Gaziantep, the local population was composed of Turkish speakers.[14] Turks were represented in the city not only by the Ottoman establishment but by merchants and migrants from Aleppo's northern hinterlands. Their presence in Aleppo is indicated by an occasional entry in the court records of a case that was conducted in Turkish for their benefit. In addition, Türkmen were a constant presence in the province, as both government-ordered deportees (to be discussed in chapter 4) and voluntary migrants. In particular, the region around Amık Gölü, in the present-day Turkish province of Hatay, was popular with the tribes as a winter grazing ground *(kışlak)* for their herds.

Kurds, from the nearby region of Kilis and further afield in eastern Anatolia, and beduin Arabs were also numerous in the city. We are able to track tribal migrants such as the Kurds, Türkmen, and beduin in Aleppo because the tribesmen were subject to special taxes in lieu of military service and were frequently brought to court by the tax collectors in attempts to gain back taxes. Furthermore, tribal identification was usually given as a part of an individual's name whenever tribespeople were involved in any way with the courts.

From such cases, it is apparent that the tribespeople migrating to Aleppo settled almost exclusively in the eastern suburbs of the city: Bānqūsā, Qārliq, Tātārlar, Maydānjik. It was there that the caravans were organized and the occupations supporting them were centered. The instability of those quarters, generated by the constant arrival and departure of the caravans, as well as the occasional lawlessness of tribal people separated from the social bonds of their tribes, is reflected in the court records, where residents of the eastern quarters appear often as perpetrators of theft and murder.[15]

Besides ethnic minorities, the city had large religious minorities: the Christians, who constituted approximately twenty percent of the total population in the seventeenth century, were divided among Greek Orthodox, Syrian Orthodox or Syriac-speaking Jacobite Christians (Suryani), Armenians, and Maronites; and the Jews, about five percent of the population, who were divided into Arabic-speaking and Spanish/Italian communities.[16] These religious communities will be discussed in more detail in the next chapter.

THE QUESTION OF "CLASS"

Ottoman society, as it existed in the sixteenth through the eighteenth centuries, presents barriers to historians who seek to understand how its component parts functioned in terms of social class. It has been argued that in economic systems such as existed in the Ottoman Empire, where the state appropriated the surplus and controlled the means of production (i.e., the Asian mode of production), there could be no true class formation. While such generalizations have been largely pushed aside, we are still faced with formidable problems in identifying class formation in the Ottoman case.[17] Not the least is the lack of any terminology recognizing what might be construed as economic classes in Ottoman literature or government archives (other than certain obvious ones—e.g., peasants) and the officially sanctioned organization of Ottoman society into clearly demarcated groups of people along religious, trade, tribal, or city-quarter lines. These units referred to invariably in the Ottoman sources as *taife* ("group") have been interpreted to demonstrate that Ottoman society was organized into units that were vertically rather than horizontally constituted, with an individual's identify arising from his or her membership in one or more of these groupings rather than from any sense of class identity formulated by economic roles.[18] In other words, commonality of economic interests was subordinated to loyalties arising out of alternative social identities.

These alternative identities have given rise to a historical interpretation that emphasizes ethnic and religious identification to reconstruct Ottoman society. This characterization has been criticized by Marxist historians as smacking of obscurantist Orientalism at its worst. Their critique holds that the establishment of what is termed the "mosaic" theory of Muslim society hides the true class-based dynamic of that society behind the walls of town quarters or the distinctive dress of the non-Muslim minorities. As Bryan Turner puts it:

> The mosaic theory of the Middle East social structure attempts to draw attention to supposed differences between the social organisation and history of European societies and the Islamic world. The central assumption is that while European societies from feudalism to capitalism can be adequately conceptualised in terms of a system of social stratification whose primary units are those of social class, the social structure of Islam can only be described in terms of semi-autonomous vertical units. Within

this mosaic of units, economic class is relatively unimportant when compared to ethnicity, religion, and tribe. Furthermore the Marxist version of the concept of "social class" is usually held to be too vulgar or too ideological to be of service in the analysis of Middle East societies. The modes of production—slavery, feudalism, capitalism—in the conventional Marxist scheme are regarded by most Orientalists as systems of "class-dominated" politics, and these schemes can only be applied to the Middle East when they have been radically redefined.[19]

There is obvious merit to this critique, as Western scholarship on Muslim societies has often been overawed by what was different from the Western experience and has emphasized this to the exclusion of what was similar. To voice a partial defense of a "mosaic" theory, however, it would seem that to understand how Ottoman society functioned in terms of its component parts, we have to begin with the building blocks that the Ottomans themselves employed, recognizing that these were, in fact, vertically constructed along other than economic lines. Sometimes, however, a recognizable economic class—that is, a group identifiable by its relationship to the means of production—and the Ottoman designation of a *taife* could coincide. We return again to the example of peasants. But even with such categories, there are pitfalls. It was not the peasants' role in rural production that distinguished them from others in the society, but simply that they lived in the country. Categories such as landholding or sharecropper did not enter into Ottoman rural surveys. Rather, peasants were distinguished by whether they were household heads.[20] This was a distinction important to the Ottomans in assessing equitable taxation, but arguably not a foundation of an economic class.

On the other hand, in support of the Marxist critique, it must be recognized that the *taife* did not produce, in most cases, an overpowering sense of solidarity among its membership in the way Marixists would argue class identities do. It was, after all, primarily a fiscal unit, either established by the Ottomans directly, or formed locally with their encouragement, to make the administration of their empire easier by facilitating, the all-important task of tax collection. The *taife* gave a collective identity to its membership only insofar as they had dealings with the government. In an application of the Middle Eastern axiom, "happy is the man whose name the government doesn't know," the *taife* allowed anonymity behind the facade of a spokesman: the *shaykh* of a craft corporation, the imam of a quarter, the bishop, and so on. Within each unit, however, there often existed internal conflict, and all too little solidarity.

The *taife* classifications did not exhaust the established Ottoman legal categories. Other, more important ones mandated by Muslim law clearly delineated heirarchies between various segments of the population: the difference in legal status between men and women, free persons and slaves, Muslims and non-Muslims, *ashrāf* (descendants of the Prophet Muhammad, singular *sharīf*) and other Muslims. The primary line of demarcation in the society, however, was between ruler and ruled, or, put another way, between those who were "Ottomans" (*askeri* in the sources, literally "military"; the term was applied to the soldiers and bureaucrats who were posted in Aleppo by Istanbul) and those who were not, whether they were Arabic, Turkish, or Kurdish speakers. But this distinction was not always scrupulously maintained. In the centuries following the Ottoman conquest, native members of the Muslim intelligentsia, the *ʿulamā*, ingratiated themselves into the legal system; indigenous tribal peoples became an increasingly important component of the provincial military establishment; and Ottomans posted in Aleppo married into local families, remaining there after their terms of office had ended.

In Aleppo, the distinction between military and nonmilitary was further blurred by the existence of a sizeable block of people claiming descent from the Prophet: the *ashrāf*. Such an exalted genealogy conferred considerable status in a society where identification was so closely linked to religion, but it also gave the descendants the distinct economic advantage of being exempted from certain taxes. It is not clear, however, why Aleppo of all the cities of the empire, with the obvious exceptions of the holy cities of Mecca and Madina, had such a high proportion of the Prophet's descendants (*sharīf*s, to use the English plural) among its population. The Ottomans themselves seemed puzzled by it.[21]

Nevertheless, the *ashrāf* constituted a formidable presence in the city. On the surface, they appeared to have been vertically constituted, with a membership ranging from the social and economic elite to humble tradesmen. But while it was true that one did not have to be rich to be a descendant of the Prophet, the rich eagerly sought that status. Once a nondescendant achieved wealth, the tendency was to become a member of the club, either through marriage or by buying a genealogy that would establish his descent from the noble line of the Banū Hāshim. In Aleppo, if not elsewhere in the Muslim world, *sharīf* status more often than not coincided with what might be labeled the political, economic, and cultural elite of the civilian population. But even here we have to be cautious in looking for clearly defined social interest groups. Although the *ashrāf* generally represented local, as opposed to *askeri,* interests, numerous members of the Ottoman governing elite also had *sharīf* status and there was frequent intermarriage between the top ranks of the *askeri* and daughters of the prominent *sharīf* families. Furthermore, there were *sharīfs* who worked at low-status jobs, such as porters.

The *ashrāf*'s chief rivals for political and economic power within the Muslim community in Aleppo were from the *askeri* group, or more precisely the janissaries, the Ottomans' feared professional infantry. The janissary corps in Aleppo had two distinct components: those who were sent from Istanbul and those who were recruited locally. The local recruits, who undoubtedly formed the overwhelming majority of the corps' membership in the seventeenth and eighteenth centuries, had little more than name in common with the classical Ottoman institution. Rather than being products of the child levy *(devşirme)* imposed on the Christian population of Anatolia and the Balkans, most of those identified as janissaries in Aleppo were born Muslim, as can be ascertained by their patronymics. Unlike the situation in Damascus, however, in Aleppo few tensions developed between locally recruited janissaries and those sent out from the capital.[22]

One of the most distinctive features of the Aleppo janissaries, a group with a well-defined sense of solidarity, was their frequent tribal origins. This can be determined not only by the occurrence of distinctly Turkish or Kurdish names among the corps's membership but also by the fact that the quarters most often mentioned as being their residential neighborhoods were the same as those inhabited by tribal peoples.[23] Military service was one of the prime attractions that drew tribesmen to the city in the first place, and once there, the corps provided the tribal migrants with a group identity in a new, alien environment, a substitution as it were for the tribal bonds they had left behind.

The inevitable tension between tribal newcomers and long-established urbanites was transformed into the often bloody faction fights between janissaries and the *ashrāf,* with the *ashrāf* serving as the staunch champions of the status quo. An indication of the social and economic roots of this urban conflict is found in the periodic disputes that erupted between the craft guilds and the janissaries. The court records contain many examples of petitions from guild members requesting that the janissaries who were attempting to enter into the trades without the guilds' permission be stopped. Significantly, members of the *ashrāf* figure prominently on the side of those defending the established practice, while it is possible on occasion to identify those individuals seeking to disturb the established practice as having had tribal origins, as well as being janissaries.[24]

Interestingly, a division can be made between trades that were janissary-dominated and those controlled by the *ashrāf*. The former had links to the tribes, such as butchers, renderers of sheep fat, workers in wool, and tentmakers, while the latter included the more established and respected trades, such as silk weavers and dyers. Similarly, merchants were often *ashrāf*, while brokers in the various markets were janissaries. This suggests that there were economic underpinnings to the groups' frequent hostilities, although the ethnic component of their respective identities was undoubtedly stronger.

In terms of social organization, the janissary corps offered the tribesmen an opportunity to create a collective identity to promote their interests. This allowed them to circumvent the closed nature of the guilds and the urban quarters, both of which shunned and excluded outsiders. Correspondingly, the *ashrāf* served as the unofficial spokesmen of the established urbanites, Arabic-speaking Sunnis. This was aptly demonstrated by their center of power, the quarters within the city walls.[25]

To return to the question, was there then some basis for restructuring our understanding of Aleppo's society based on economic class lines? The sometimes class nature of the janissary-*ashrāf* rivalry gives some cause for agreement with those who wish to revamp the "mosaic" theory. At the same time, we must also recognize that this possible nascent class identity was hidden behind other labels that were more easily admitted by the culture's understanding of itself. Poor craftsmen living in the inner walled city might have had common economic interests with those who lived in the janissary-dominated quarter of Bānqūsā, which transcended the divide. But except in times of extreme crisis in the city, such as famine or siege, these were largely subsumed by loyalties that were defined more broadly by ethnicity, religion, or tradition.

ALEPPO'S MERCHANTS

Having reviewed the question of the nature of class identity in Ottoman Aleppo, we are presented with a possible reason why merchants in Syria did not evolve into the same sorts of political and economic pressure groups as did their counterparts in western Europe. Unlike either the *ashrāf* or the janissaries, Aleppo's merchants were not recognized as being a separate corporate body by either Muslim law or Ottoman practice, and lacking such an identification, they seldom acted in a unified manner with uniform goals. Instead, the leading merchants (referred to as *fakhr al-tujjār*, literally "pride of the merchants") were mentioned as belonging to a more broadly based group of urban notables, the *aʿyān*, who constituted the ad hoc civilian leadership in the city, usually called together only in times of crisis.

Such a case occured in 1656, when Sidi Ahmed Paşa was appointed governor of Aleppo. He mistreated the local populace, and the retiring governor, Kara Mustafa Paşa, refused to vacate the citadel with his retinue, giving the city in effect two governors at once. A period of anarchy and looting in the city followed, during which some of the prominent merchants of the city appealed to Istanbul to revoke Sidi Ahmed's appointment. It seems to have worked, as shortly thereafter Sidi Ahmed was appointed to the governorship of Sivas, and Kara Mustafa was reappointed to his old post in Aleppo.[26] But such occasions of concerted action undertaken by the merchants were rare. In contrast to the situation in western Europe, where merchants saw a community of interests to be promoted, the merchants of Aleppo spoke with one voice only in times of the direst necessity and then usually in consort with other members of the civilian elite, such as the *ʿulamā*. Thus the delineation of that group's membership is not as apparent as it might at first seem.

Commerce played a major role in the economic life of almost every level of Aleppo's society. The nature of Aleppo's economy, tied as it was in the Ottoman period to the transit trade, and the traditions of Syrian economic life in general created an environment in which the buying and selling of merchandise was an almost ubiquitous endeavor for the city's citizenry. It might seem, therefore, that a listing of those elements of the urban population that comprised the merchant "class" would be useless, for it appears that almost all Aleppines who had any excess capital were at one time or another engaged directly in trade or in credit relationships involving commerce. This is the pattern presented in the court records, where we find among those engaged in trade Muslim judges, Greek Orthodox bishops, members of the Ottoman military bureaucracy, women, and beduin tribesmen.

Clearly, not all of these people were merchants, that is, people who were primarily engaged in commerce for their livelihood. But this broad participation by various individuals from differing social groups emphasizes the importance of trade in the popular imagination as a means to create wealth. Unlike many other preindustrial cultures where merchants were segregated by caste, ethnicity, or social prejudice from the population at large, merchants in Ottoman Syria could become folk heroes, something to be boasted of and to emulate.

This societal attitude is reflected in the popular culture of the period, preserved in the tales retold over and over in the coffee shops of the city. In these stories, military heroes were either remote in time, such as the pre-Islamic ʿAntar, or place, the Banū Hilāl of North Africa, or they were not Arabs at all, Ṣalāḥ al-Dīn (the Kurdish hero of the Crusades) and Ẓāhir Baybārs (the Mamluk sultan who finally drove the Franks out of the Middle East), representing a trend early established by which the urban Sunni Arabs abdicated military and political authority to outsiders. Enshrined instead as contemporary local heroes were the characters of the picaresque *Thousand and One Nights,* with Sindbad the merchant prince a prime example. In the popular imagination, if a person was clever enough and could travel to distant lands, he could use his wit and luck to turn poverty into enormous wealth. It was a theme often repeated. Rarely did a hero fight if he could cajole his way out of trouble. Good business sense, then, and not valor, was the trait most often glorified and extolled. The rich merchant was the society's paragon of success, but more than that, he represented a universal everyman on whom fortune had smiled. And in many individual cases, life imitated art.

The pinnacle of commercial success in Aleppo was personified by those individuals who had become the "pride of the merchants." These were men who had amassed considerable capital and no longer had to travel with the caravans to earn their profits but could stay at home and let others work for them. As described by Russell:

> The merchants of Aleppo are numerous, and a few of them are esteemed opulent. Some have travelled, in their youth, to Bagdat, Bassora, or even to India, and continue though advanced in years, to make a journey now and then to the capital, in the caravans which transport their merchandize: when they do not go themselves, it is usual to comit the care of their goods to some trusty slave.[27]

In fact, it seems rarely to have been a slave at all, but rather a young, enterprising Aleppine who sought to become one of the fabled merchant princes in his own right.

The process by which an aspiring merchant might achieve his ambitions is clearly articulated in the court records. As the cases involving contracts in long-distance trade reveal, the most common format for such ventures was the *commenda* (in Arabic, *muḍāraba*) agreement. Simply put, the *muḍāraba* consisted of a verbal agreement sworn by two parties before a judge and two witnesses, the terms under which one party would provide the capital to finance the operation while the other would do the traveling and the trading. At the completion of the venture, the active trader would repay the investor his capital, and the remaining profit would be divided according to a prearranged formula. As a legal contract, it was identical both to the Venetian *colleganza* and the *muḍāraba* described by Muslim classical legists, and closely related to mercantile practices found throughout the Mediterranean basin.[28]

In Aleppo, two-thirds of the profit would usually go to the investor and one-third to the trader. In a *muḍāraba* agreement, the investor alone was responsible for absorbing losses. The living and traveling expenses of the agent were deducted from the net returns before the profit was calculated, as were any other expenses deemed legitimate for the conduct of trade.[29]

The conditions under which the agent was to operate, including the amount of money he was to carry, his destination, and the commodity he was to purchase, were usually stipulated in a verbal contract. The judge would then issue a written statement of the contract *(ḥujja)* to the investor, outlining the agreed-upon terms. That document carried the burden of proof in any dispute that might later arise. To insure that the agent would not simply abscond with the money, a guarantor was usually named in the agreement. Should the trader not return, the guarantor, who was most often a relative of the agent, was responsible for the sum invested. The fact that the guarantors were rarely obliged to pay off such debts testifies to the general high level of good faith and integrity that permeated these contracts. Needless to say, without that level of trust and honesty, long-distance trade would have been extremely difficult in an era that had neither rapid travel nor easy long-distance communication.

The advantage of the *muḍāraba* agreement to a potential investor was that it seemingly allowed a relatively high rate of return on his or her capital in a way that was sanctioned by Muslim law as interest-bearing loans were not. The actual rate of return an investor in this period might expect is not, however, clear. Although there are numerous such cases in the court registers of Aleppo, few present the entire set of details—including the original amount invested, the time period of the contract, and the profits received—to allow us to ascertain with any certainty the average rates of profit accruing from *muḍāraba* ventures. Nonetheless, from the cases we do have, it would seem that profits of one hundred percent over the original investment were clearly possible.

A dissolution of one such agreement registered on March 7, 1708, demonstrates their potential profitability. In that case, Abū ʿAbdullah Muḥammad b. ʿAbd al-Ghānī, who was the guardian of the children of the deceased Ḥājj Ibrāhīm b. Ḥājj Muḥammad al-Sāmirlī, brought to court two agents to whom Ḥājj Ibrāhīm had entrusted 15,000 *ghurūsh* in *muḍāraba* before his death. The first agent, a certain Khiḍr Celebi b. Ḥājj ʿUthmān, was given 10,000 *ghurūsh,* from which he returned a profit of 12,500. The childrens' share was calculated as being 8,333 and 2/3 *ghurūsh,* or two-thirds of the total. Khiḍr stated, however, that he had contracted with Ḥājj Ibrāhīm to go only as far as "Gilan and Iran" when he had in fact gone all the way to India. He claimed, therefore, that his percentage of the profit should be higher, as he had taken greater risks than were authorized in the contract.

The judge ruled that the extra travel did not change the conditions of the contract, and Khiḍr was ordered to hand over the childrens' stipulated share, as well as the principal, to their guardian. The other agent, Muḥammad b. ʿUthmañ (it's unclear whether he was Khiḍr's brother) had been given 5,000 *ghurūsh* and returned a profit of 6,550 *ghurūsh.* Again, the children received two-thirds, in this case, the principal plus 4,366 and ⅓ *ghurūsh.* Thus the total profit Ḥājj Ibrāhīm had earned posthumously from his investment was 12,700 *ghurūsh,* or a return of approximately 85%.[30] We do not know from the cases how long a period had elapsed between the setting up of the contract and the final accounting, but nevertheless this example testifies to the potential long-distance trade had for generating wealth, not only for the investor, but for the agent as well.

Not all *muḍāraba* agreements ended so favorably for the investor, as the risks of the caravan trade could be as formidable as were its profits. Banditry, war, or the death of the agent were all possibilities that could wipe out the investment capital with little recourse for compensation if it were ruled the agent was not at fault, as in such cases, the agent did not have to return the investment capital from his own resources to the investor.[31] Even when no calamity befell the agent, bad luck or poor judgment could produce pitifully small returns, as in a case registered on January 16, 1656, where we learn that the agent, ʿIsā w. Jirjīs, returned to ʿAbd al-Raḥman b. ʿAbdallah only 40 *ghurūsh* profit from a capital investment of 500 *ghurūsh* in *muḍāraba* to buy silk.[32] Presumably, an agent who had engineered such a fiasco would soon have little reputation left as a reliable partner for such ventures, but there was little recourse open to the investor to recoup his or her losses.

Despite these possible risks, it must be recognized that the *muḍāraba* offered a framework through which investors could expect higher returns than were obtainable elsewhere. In a case registered on April 4, 1641, a Jewish widow stated she had entrusted 250 *ghurūsh* to her brother-in-law with the understanding that the profits accruing from the investment would go to support her children. He complied with the agreement for two years, providing the support of 6 *ghurūsh* per month, or an annual return of 28.8%. But according to the widow, he had stopped paying any money to her four years before, and she demanded the accumulated profits. In his defense, the brother-in-law stated that the widow had, in fact, dissolved the *muḍāraba* agreement between them four years previously and that he had returned the principal at that time.[33] This case demonstrates that the *muḍāraba* was perceived as being both a profitable and a relatively safe investment by the widow, especially since support for orphans was one of the exceptions allowed by the Muslim courts in Aleppo to the general prohibition on usury.

Even though it often saw sophisticated applications, the *muḍarāba* did not represent an equivalent to the principle of joint-venture capital as it had developed at about the same time in Europe.[34] In cases where a set of partners would form a *muḍāraba* agreement with another individual or individuals, the capital for the venture would be termed the capital of partnership *(māl al-sharika),* and each partner would gain in profits or share in the loss in relation to the percentage of the capital he or she contributed. This was similar to a joint-venture-capital agreement, but the partnership was not considered to be a legal entity in its own right, and individual liability remained the underlying principle in all business arrangements covered by Muslim law.[35] There could be no corporate bankruptcy, only individual debt.

Still the *muḍāraba* arrangements provided the means by which young

Aleppines could achieve the goal of being a merchant prince like Sinbad of the fables. The system was designed to reward initiative, and it seems to have been a relatively effective way of handling the rigors of long-distance trade in the premodern era. Employing it, local citizens set off to Egypt, Iran, and India to make their fortunes. Once wealth was made, however, as we shall see in chapter 5, there were often more preferred ways to invest it, but trade, undoubtedly, offered the most available way to create wealth in the first place.

In addition to the agents of the merchant capitalists discussed above there was a second category of traveling merchants, of less exalted status, within Aleppo's mercantile community—the peddlers. These were the itinerant traders with diverse trading goods and small overhead who conform to the stereotypes of traditional Middle Eastern commerce suggested by Steensgaard's thesis of the Asian trade revolution.[36]

Although the volume of trade of an individual peddler might be small, as a group peddlers played a vital role in merchandizing imported products to the towns and villages of Aleppo's hinterlands and in the return transport of the products of those regions, notably soap, *khām* cloth, gullnuts, and Angora wool to Aleppo. In Aleppo, these goods were either consumed locally or exported beyond Syria, by the agents of the large-scale merchants or the European trading companies. Representatives of various ethnic groups were represented in the peddling trade, although there appears to have been some areas of specialization. Jews, for example, played an important role in the transport of Angora wool from Anatolia,[37] while the trade in *khām* produced mainly in the towns of southeastern Anatolia was typically controlled by Anatolians, either Turks or Armenians.[38]

A good example of the diversity of products, as well as the small volume of any given article handled by these peddlers, is a case registered on September 29, 1707, in which a translator for the French merchant community, a Maronite named Ḥiyūb w. Badrūs, brought charges against Ḥannā w. Dawūd of Antioch, for a settlement of goods Ḥiyūb had sent Ḥannā to sell in Antioch. The total value of the shipment was large, 785 *ghurūsh,* and it included thirty-two different items—a virtual catalog of textiles produced in Syria and southeastern Anatolia—but no individual item was represented in bulk.[39]

The distinctive feature of the peddling trade, then, was not its value but rather the small volume and diversity of goods handled, as well as the peddlers' apparent willingness to travel anywhere. These characteristics of the peddling trade are illustrated by a case registered in 1728, which settled the estate of a peddler, Mikhā'īl w. ʿAṭallah Jirdī, who had died while on his way to Istanbul. His total worth, consisting of various trade goods and outstanding debts owed him, came to 2,028 *ghurūsh*, an amount that would have probably put him into the upper brackets of the city's population in terms of net worth (see chapter 5 below). In addition to his trade goods and his debts, our peddler left three surviving daughters named, appropriately, Hindīya (Indian), ʿAjamīya (Persian), and Baṣra, an indication of the scope of his travels.[40]

Finally, the largest but least influential segment of Aleppo's merchant community were the retailers who formed the last link between the wider international markets and the local consumer in Aleppo itself. This category included those persons who either owned their own shops or rented them from others. In either case, the retailer sold merchandise brought into the city by the agents of the wealthy merchants and/or the peddlers, or they were craftsmen who sold their own wares and were thus members of the various craft guilds of producers.

Typically, those retailers who did not sell their own products were much more tightly controlled by a formal corporate structure than were merchants who dealt in the wholesale importation of foreign goods. There were marketing organizations of spice sellers, coffee-shop owners, sellers of *khām*, and so on. These petty merchants operated out of their own shops, usually located in or near a market specializing in their particular product. They were free to keep the profits of individual sales, in contrast to members of guilds specializing in services, such as dyers and bleachers of cloth, where the membership usually pooled income and apportioned it out to individual members based on their standing in the guild. (The guilds will be discussed in more detail in chapter 6.) Nevertheless, the corporations of retailers each had their own individual head, or *shaykh*, who enforced regulations concerning the quality and prices of merchandise.[41]

As regards freedom of action, the retailers stood midway between the independent merchants and the craft corporations. Obviously, effective price controls were less a possibility among those retailers who sold imported goods subject to wildly fluctuating prices than for those who sold locally produced crafts. For example, the price of coffee was dependent on the safe passage of the caravans from Mecca, which brought not only returning pilgrims but coffee from Yemen. It was also subject to the competition of coffee coming from the Americas. As a result of these external influences on market conditions, the price of a camel load of coffee could fluctuate as much as fifty percent over the space of a year in the wholesale market of Aleppo. Such wild variations made uniform price control difficult, if not impossible, to enforce.[42]

Furthermore, unlike the service and craft guilds, whose membership was limited, the retailers' associations were open to anyone who possessed or rented a shop, and individual shopkeepers were free to enter into financial arrangements with outsiders, without the consent of their fellow shopkeepers.[43] Strictly speaking, although referred to as *taife*s, the shopkeeper organizations were not technically guilds in either the European or the Ottoman understanding of the term. They were, however, subject to the market price controls *(ḥisba)* set by their organization and institutionalized by the state.

MERCHANTS AS FREE AGENTS

As we have seen, Ottoman society has often been characterized as a corporate one, or alternatively, as a mosaic. In this view, an individual's place was defined by membership in various corporate groups recognized as tax units by the central administration. These might be occupational, religious, ethnic, or residential in nature. In that society, for example, a Christian Arab silk weaver inhabiting the Judayda quarter, a largely Christian suburb of Aleppo, would be considered as being a member of the Greek Orthodox *millet (millet-i Rum),* although not an ethnic Hellene, a member of the silk weavers' craft guild, and an inhabitant of his quarter. He would be responsible to all three corporate groups for taxation owed by them collectively to the central government and subject to the internal regulations of each. These were to be enforced, in turn, by the legally constituted leaders of each unit. In the case of our weaver, these would have been, respectively, the patriarch of the Orthodox church in Aleppo, the head or *shaykh* of the weavers' guild, and the quarter headman. All of these officials had recourse to the Muslim judges in the city and the legal and moral force they could muster to ensure conformity. In this way, the smooth and orderly functioning of society could be maintained. Furthermore, the individual weaver had little or no recourse to the government, nor it to him, other than through the structure of the various corporate entities to which he owed his allegiances. A private individual could, it is true, petition the government directly in unusual circumstances and was individually liable should he run afoul of the law, but such actions were rare and exceptions to the general collective face individuals in Ottoman society presented to the outside world.

But was this corporate character distributed evenly throughout, including members of all occupations? By all accounts, merchants, or at least the peddlers and long-distance traders, were largely outside the boundaries of any corporate groups recognized by the government. This contention is supported by several facts. First, the traveling merchants, unlike members of the craft guilds and retailers, were apparently never taxed collectively by occupation. For example on April 14, 1635, Aleppo's governor announced the collection of a special tax to help finance the imperial campaign *(imdad-i seferiye)*. Although the various craft guilds were collectively assessed set amounts of cash, the merchants were not liable as a corporate group; rather, taxes were assessed on specific markets *(sūqs):* the *sūq al-dahsha* (a proper name), the *sūq al-qumāsh* (cloth market), and the *sūq al-bāzīstān* (the *bedestan;* see chapter 4).[44] The implication is that the tax was assessed on the location in which the merchants were active and not necessarily on the commodities in which they dealt, although in the case of the cloth market one would assume the two coincided.

A further indication of the absence of a mercantile corporate structure is the manner in which taxes were levied on goods brought into the city from outside. These taxes on imports were levied directly on the individual merchant at the official government customs station when the goods entered the city, and not at time of sale.[45] In contrast, taxes on local production were paid collectively by the guild through its *shaykh* to the government tax collectors at defined intervals, usually once annually, unless extraordinary taxes were required. Furthermore, while the rate of taxation on imports owed by an individual merchant was carefully stipulated in the province's law code *(kanun-name)* and were enforced by the judges, the craft corporations' chiefs could and did change the level of taxation that fell on a particular craftsman according to circumstances that affected the group at large.

Additional evidence for the absence of a formalized structure lies in the fact that the only price control facing the traveling merchants was the expected one of supply and demand, whereas for the guilds there were price and quality controls mandated by the citywide regulation of trades, the *ḥisba*. Quality control was governed by the buyer's discretion, although incidents of outright fraud could be taken to court for redress. Unlike members of producer guilds, merchants were free to set prices individually and to enjoy their profits, without sharing them with less successful competitors. The apparent impetus for this uncharacteristic permissiveness on the government's part was its realization that price controls could drive the traveling merchants away (see below in chapter 6).

In the absence of an organization with a *shaykh*, many of the functions he would have performed fell to the office of the *shāhbandar* (a term of Persian origin meaning "master of the port"). The *shāhbandar* was usually appointed from among the ranks of the wealthy merchants of Aleppo.[46] He held an imperial patent *(berat)* granting him his office, but his actual authority seems to have been limited. D'Arvieux asserted that the *shāhbandar* often acted as a judge in cases involving commerce,[47] while Aigen added that he was consulted in all disputes involving weights and measures.[48] While cases in the Aleppo court records do not support d'Arvieux's assertion, they do show that the *shāhbandar* served as an expert witness before the court in cases involving trade, as Aigen contended.

For example, in a case registered on September 13, 1636, the *shāhbandar,* at the request of the tax collector of the city, testified as to what gifts were given to the tax collector and the customs agent by the chiefs of the two caravans that had arrived that year from Baghdad.[49] Furthermore, the *shāhbandar* served as a spokesperson for the merchants before the government, either in presenting candidates to fill a post important to the merchants, such as the heads of the corporations of weighers or brokers, or in voicing complaints about the abuses of the military bureaucracy. More commonly, he witnessed various legal proceedings, including the government appropriation of property of merchants who had died without apparent heirs, and in the investiture of leaders of the craft guilds.

Figure 2 presents a list of the persons who held the office of *shāhbandar* between the years 1610 and 1751, reconstructed from the extant documents. Although there are gaps in the list, it allows us to make several important generalizations concerning the men who held the post. First, most were civilians, although the next to the last name on the list, Osman Ağa, even though a son of a former *shāhbandar,* was a member of

Figure 2. *Shāhbandars* of Aleppo, 1610–1726

1610	ᶜUmar Çelebi b. Ḥājj Muṣṭafā
1635	"
1636	"
1640	"
1644	ᶜUmar Çelebi replaced by Muḥammad Çelebi b. Ḥājj ᶜAbd al-Raḥman al-Baghdādī
1655	Muṣṭafā Çelebi b. ᶜUmar Çelebi
1660	"
1672	Sīdī Yūsuf Çelebi b. Ḥājj Ṣalāḥ al-Dīn
1673	Mustafa Paşa, *mütesarrif* of Maᶜarrat al-Miṣrīn
1679	Ali Çelebi
1680	Mustafa Paşa
1682	"
1686	ᶜAbd al-Raḥman Çelebi Abū-Shukūrzādah
1688	*shāhbandar*'s office taken away from Ahmed Payaslıoğlu and returned to Ḥājj ᶜAbd al-Raḥman Abū-Shukūrzādah
1707	Ḥājj ᶜAbd al-Raḥman Abū-Shukūrzādah
1720	"
1726	Osman Ağa b. Ḥājj ᶜAbd al-Raḥman Abū-Shukūrzādah
1751	Faris Ağa b. Osman Ağa

the military establishment. The eighteenth century witnessed a growing participation of the military in all aspects of economic life in Syria.[50] In the case of the office of *shāhbandar,* that process had already begun with the split term held by Mustafa Paşa and the short term of Payaslıoğlu Ahmed in the seventeenth century. Osman Ağa's obtainment of a post traditionally held by established merchants was not to be unexpected. His combination of military rank and civilian origin (he was after all the son and grandson of merchants) seems to be yet another indication of the merging of interests and family ties between the local elites and members of the military who were putting down roots in the city.[51]

The second feature that emerges is that although the post was not necessarily passed from father to son, in at least two cases sons did succeed fathers to the post eventually. Finally, most of the men serving in this capacity had long terms of office. We can assume, therefore, that the post of *shāhbandar,* like that of *muftī,* was one of the provincial institutions that was filled with local notables. As such it helped to give the Ottoman provincial administration, faced as it was with highly impermanent provincial governors and judges, a degree of continuity, as well as providing a voice by which local interests could be aired.

The records of the Ottoman central administration present two examples of the process by which a *shāhbandar* was replaced, which further clarify how the office reflected local mercantile interests. In the first, dated January 6, 1645, the commander of the city's citadel *(dizdar)*, requested that the Porte replace the current *shāhbandar*, Ḥājj ʿUmar Çelebi, with the son of a former *shāhbandar*, Muḥammad Çelebi b.ʿAbd al-Raḥman. The petition stated that Ḥājj ʿUmar had become senile, and as a result of his unspecified actions, caravans were avoiding the city. On the other hand, Muḥammad Çelebi was described as being an upright and highly moral individual, acceptable to all. In response to the petition, the government appointed Muḥammad to the post. It remains a mystery why the garrison chief formally submitted the petition in the first place.[52] Perhaps his revenues were being affected by the drop in caravan traffic.[53]

In the second case, dated September 22, 1689, the chief judge of Aleppo forwarded a petition from a delegation made up of the city's notables, which asked that the office of *shāhbandar* be taken away from Payaslıoğlu Ahmed and given to Ḥājj ʿAbd al-Raḥman Abū-Shukūrzādah. In that petition it was stated that while Ahmed knew next to nothing about trade, Ḥājj ʿAbd al-Raḥman was a merchant who had learned the trade from his father and was thus competent to administer the post. This request was also granted.[54] The significance of this case was that it demonstrates that late into the seventeenth century, local merchants were still strong enough to block the encroachment of the military into what they considered their sphere of power. This would not be the case for long. It also provides a rare example of merchants acting in concert to promote their interests, an indication of how crucial they felt the office of *shāhbandar* to be to them.

After its militarization in the eighteenth century, the fate of the office in unclear. Alexander Russell stated that in his time, the mid–eighteenth century, the *shāhbandar* routinely was included as a member of the provincial council.[55] The office is also mentioned in other English sources. A Levant Company factor wrote in 1740 that fees that were routinely paid at the weighing of silk, 5 *ghurūsh* per *qinṭar*, of which 2 and 1/6 *ghurūsh* went to the brokers and the warehousemen and the rest to the *shāhbandar*.[56] On September 30, 1755, another factor stated that a bill was payable to the "Bazargeen bashy" *(bazirgan başı)*, chief merchant, a title which is suggestive of the office of *shāhbandar*, if not exactly identical.[57]

By the mid–eighteenth century, the office holder had ceased being as active in commercial cases and where mentioned at all seems to have been involved in litigation involving his own interests. We can assume, therefore, that the post had become a sinecure for someone with connections in the government and that it no longer represented purely merchant interests. Whether it was purchased as a *malikane* (tax farm), as were so many other posts at the time, we have no evidence. Merchants had never had a guild to promote their interests and were not recognized as a tax group *(taife)* by the Ottomans. Thereby lacking any formalized solidarity, they had only one institutionalized office, the *shāhbandar*, to promote their interests. By the middle of the eighteenth century, however, even it was no longer of much use to them.

THE PRACTICE OF COMMERCE IN ALEPPO

Having established the social and legal position of merchants in Aleppo, we must now attempt to see to what degree we can identify the individuals, or at least the type of individuals, who engaged in the long-distance caravan trade. Many have written of the anonymity of Asian merchants, conservative in their lifestyles, unrecorded by contemporary observers, and an enigma to the modern historian.[58] To a large extent this characterization holds true for the merchants of Ottoman Aleppo.

The European consular and company records are largely silent about all but their own direct competition, the Armenians and, to a lesser extent, the Jews of Livorno. With very few exceptions, European visitors never overcame the barriers of language and culture that separated them from their hosts, and while they might write of the conspicuously powerful in the city, the military and the *ʿulamā*, they largely ignored the Muslim merchants, with whom they rarely dealt. Likewise, Muslim sources such as chronicles and the ever-popular biographical dictionaries of Ottoman Syria are unsatisfactory. Trade was a socially acceptable profession, but a record of commercial activity alone was rarely considered worthy enough to be preserved for posterity. Thus while it might be mentioned that a particular notable family had acquired its wealth through trade, the actual ancestor who established the fortune would not have been included in the compendium of the notables of his own time. This absence of merchants in the literature of the elite contrasts markedly with the position they held in the literature of the popular culture where they were often the heroes.

Faced with these obstacles, we are forced to rely on what can be learned about the merchants from the court records of the city, even while recognizing that these, too, are far from a completely satisfactory source. The Muslim courts, as constituted in Aleppo, were empowered both by tradition and Ottoman political authority to regulate virtually all aspects of commerce as it was conducted in the city. It was not necessary, however, to register all contracts formally before a judge. A contract was legally binding if it had been verbally affirmed before two witnesses. As long as those two witnesses could be produced before the court to testify as to what they understood the terms of the contract were, no written documentation was necessary.

It would appear therefore that the vast majority of day-to-day transactions were the products of verbal agreements, and if they did not later engender litigation over the terms of the contract, they were unrecorded by the courts. As a result, the court records have preserved a very selective sampling of commercial transactions. We have, for example, a very high proportion of cases involving the settlements of the estates of deceased merchants from which litigation arose over the terms of unfulfilled contracts.

In an attempt to lessen any randomness in registration, a sample was drawn from only those cases where the transactions involved commodities that were valued at 500 *ghurūsh* or over. With such large sums at stake, it is presumed that the participants would have been more inclined to register the transaction or contract with the courts than in the cases involving pettier sums. Second, a sum of 500 *ghurūsh* represented a small fortune for Ottoman Aleppines. Thus we can be sure that anyone involved in these transactions was wealthy and a candidate for being considered as one of the *fakhr al-tujjār* rather than a peddler. He would, therefore, be of use in identifying the actors in the long-distance trade. Third, no sample was taken from the middle decades of the eighteenth century, when it becomes clear that there was a sharp drop-off in commercial contracts so registered.

What emerges from these cases is a picture of commerce in Aleppo that conforms to a large degree to the broad outline presented in chapter 1, at least as regards the caravan trade eastward. The trade with the West, on the other hand, seems to be singularly underrepresented, with regard both to cases in which Europeans actively participated—only four of the cases abstracted here involved European participation—and to those that involved the exchange of the principal European trade good, broadcloth. But before discussing possible reasons for this omission, a discussion of what can be learned from these cases is necessary.

The registration of the various *muḍāraba* agreements provide us with the evidence that Aleppo natives were actively engaging in the silk trade with

Figure 3. Abstract of Commercial Cases

	1632–65	*1678–86*	*1706–26*
A. Type of Transaction			
1. *Muḍāraba*			
Christian agents	6	2	8
Muslim agents	3	2	3
Christian investor	3	1	5
Muslim investor	6	3	6
Total	18	8	22
2. *Simple Partnerships*	6	9	8
3. *Purchases* (method of payment)			
Credit	11	7	7
Cash	1	1	3
Barter	1	0	0
Total	13	8	10
B. *Destinations* (where listed)			
Iran	2	1	3
Anatolia	4	1	8
Egypt	3	0	2
Other	1	0	3
Unlisted	27	23	24
C. *Commodities* (where listed)			
Silk	8	9	10
Broadcloth	4	4	1
Indigo	2	0	3
Soap	6	2	0
Indian cloth	0	0	3
Other	6	2	4
Unlisted	11	8	19

Iran as capital investors and occasionally as agents, and the important role of such transactions for the long-distance trade with Iran. The total number of such trading expeditions to Iran was not high, although it was undoubtedly higher than figure 3 indicates. We can assume this for the simple reason that many of the cases in which Anatolian destinations were given involved cities such as Erzurum or Van, waystations to Iran. But even if few in number, the amounts involved in deals involving Iran often dwarfed those expended in other areas of trade. A *muḍāraba* agreement, financed by a partnership between Ḥājj Maḥmūd al-Jūkhī and ʿAbdallah Çelebi al-Shukūrzādah in 1717, with a certain Manuk w. Bedros acting as agent, involved the capital sum of 40,200 *ghurūsh*, with which Manuk purchased 35 *qinṭars* and 88 *raṭls* of silk in Iran, which he then transported back to Aleppo.[59]

In the cases in which Iranian destinations are mentioned, or those in which silk was the commodity traded, the overwhelming role played by the Armenians is striking. Of the total 102 cases abstracted, Armenians participated in 20, all involving silk. Although some of these Armenians had the obviously Iranian identification of "Julfalı" as toponyms *(laqab)*, many more were associated with Ottoman towns—"Arabgiri," "Vanlı," "Erzurumi"—an indication that while the trade may have been an almost exclusive Armenian monopoly, it was not necessarily an Iranian Armenian one, and that formerly semirural Anatolian Armenians were entering into international commerce in significant numbers.

The role of local Syrian Christian agents in these agreements is also noteworthy. While there were the occasional Muslim agents, largely involved in the trade to Iraq and India, Christian agents predominated, while the majority of the investors in *muḍāraba* agreements were Muslim. A typical *muḍāraba* agreement thus involved a Muslim putting up the capital and a Christian acting as the agent. The reverse seems never to have occurred. In part, the preponderance of Christians acting as agents can be explained by the participation of the Armenians in the Iran trade, but it also may have resulted from a greater willingness on the part of local Arab Christians to engage in trade, as other profitable occupations were not always open to them. As Russell states:

> The sons of Christians in any tolerable circumstances are taught to read and write the Arabic, and usually follow the profession of the father, in some branch of trade; or they serve in quality as scrivans, or agents to the Turkish merchants. They are more accustomed to travel with the

caravans than the Aleppeen Turks, but few in proportion leave their native town.[60]

In addition to what they tell us about the Iran trade, these cases also demonstrate the continuing importance of commerce with Egypt, consisting of Syrian soap and silk traded for linen, ammonia, and safflowers; and with India, represented by indigo and Indian cloth. The trade in Indian cloth actually seems to have picked up greatly in the eighteenth century.[61] In both cases, there was a large degree of ethnic specialization apparent among the merchants so engaged, in much the same way as trade with Iran was dominated by Armenians, as agents if not as investors. The trade with Egypt, for example, witnessed in the eighteenth century an increasing participation by Syrian Christians, to be discussed in more detail in the following chapter, while the trade with India was virtually a Muslim monopoly, although members of the Baghdad Jewish community were also represented.

Unfortunately, while these cases reveal that Muslim Aleppines were engaged in trade involving large capital amounts, we are still left with precious little information about their identities. A few family names occur often enough over the century and a half—al-Shammālī, ibn al-Mishṭ, ibn al-Labaq, al-Sāmirlī—to enable us to identify those families as having most probably constituted merchant dynasties, but there is little evidence to verify the intuition. Alternatively, the prominent *ᶜulamā* families featured in the biographical dictionaries—the Baylūnīs, the Kawākibīs, the Kūrānīs—are significant in their absence. There was, however, one individual merchant, Niᶜmat Allah Çelebi Arīḥāwīzādah, whose activities were recorded often enough for us to sketch his career over the course of the seventeenth century and it might serve to elucidate those of his cohorts.

Niᶜmat Allah Çelebi first appears in the registers in the year 1632 in a couple of small-scale loan agreements and real-estate deals.[62] We don't hear of him again until 1654, when he appears in a partnership agreement that has all the earmarks of the peddling trade.[63] By 1660, however, he was identified as being one of the *fakhr al-tujjār* in a case in which it was stated that he had hired twenty camels to carry goods from Cairo to Mecca and then another fifty camels to carry goods from Mecca to Aleppo.[64] Unfortunately, there is no indication of what was being carried, nor whether Niᶜmat Allah owned the goods or was simply acting as the agent. The absence of anyone else's name being registered in the case points to the former interpretation, but it is not conclusive. We also learn that Niʿmat Allah had a brother, Luṭfī, whose son Zayd al-ʿAbidīn worked on occasion as a factor for Niʿmat Allah. Niʿmat Allah's own son, Muḥammad, was identified by the more exalted title of *fakhr al-aʿyān* ("Pride of the Notables") in a *muḍāraba* agreement registered in 1678.[65]

It is not clear what the family's origins were, although from the name *(laqab)* Niʿmat Allah bore, we can assume they started in the village of Arīḥā to the southwest of Aleppo. Niʿmat Allah's father was alternately identified as having been a solider or a merchant. But whatever his own origins, Niʿmat Allah confirms the common belief that trade could transform a family from insignificance to prominence in one lifetime, if not magically, as in the café stories, at least through luck and effort.

We don't know how much wealth the collective efforts of the Arīḥāwīzādahs were able to acquire in the seventeenth century, but the family built a caravansary *(khān)* in the city as a pious endowment *(waqf)* in the eighteenth century.[66] A contemporary of theirs, the merchant Sayyid Aḥmad b. Sayyid Muḥammad al-Ghazzāl, who died in 1678, left the fantastically large estate of 87,947 and ¼ *ghurūsh* to his still-infant children.[67] Sayyid Aḥmad's is sadly the only such registration of a merchant's estate to have survived in the archives, but it points to the considerable wealth that commerce could generate for Niʿmat Allah's contemporaries.

Having seen what these cases can tell us, we must return to what they cannot, the role of the Europeans in Aleppo's trade. In contrast to the almost total absence of cases involving Europeans in which sums of over 500 *ghurūsh* changed hands, there are frequent transactions in which Europeans participated, involving exchanges worth less than 500 *ghurūsh*, registered in the courts in the sample time periods. But before jumping to the conclusion that the Europeans favored small-scale transactions, we have to look at the attitudes of the European agents toward the Muslim courts.

Despite the occasional praise of the level of justice and honesty prevalent in the Muslim courts voiced by some travelers,[68] the Europeans resident in Aleppo seemed to have been generally wary of Muslim justice. They, therefore, sought to avoid recourse to the Muslim courts except when absolutely necessary. This was especially true for the English. As early as 1625, the Venetians, who did resort to the Muslim courts although they were suspicious of them as well,[69] reported that the English consul in Aleppo had ordered his countrymen to avoid the courts at all costs, justifying his actions to the Venetians, the old Levantine hands, by saying, "I will not follow the example of your consul and appeal to corrupt Turkish justice, as we have sworn on the Gospels to have no litigation before the infidels."[70] There may, in fact, have been other reasons. In a letter written by George Dorrington, the English vice-consul in Aleppo in 1596, the following apprehensions were stated:

Lastlie, your defence against Turks we cane in no case alow of; condemninge your abilitie therin, both in the order of your proceadings, in the manner of your behaviour, and your unorderlie speakinge, or not speakinge at all. And to your waunt therin you have taken a turchman so simple of witt and ignorant of languadges that what you speake amisse he makes it wourse; whearby, when you come before a magistrate, you ar a laughinge stocke to all the audeince.[71]

Nevertheless, in the cases where the Europeans did resort to the local courts, there seems to have been no apparent pattern of discrimination against them. But as these are relatively few in number, they might only represent situations in which the Europeans were confident of victory and so consented to litigation.

In a letter written in 1704, an English factor mentioned that a local Muslim merchant who was engaged in a dispute with the English dragoman (translator) had boasted that he could produce fifteen Mulsim witnesses to testify to anything he said as being true.[72] Whether or not this was, in fact, what the Muslim in question had actually claimed, it underscores the English perception that the scales of justice were weighted against them in the Muslim courts. This attitude toward the local judicial system was as often as not, however, as much a result of cross-cultural misunderstanding as of any actual intent on the part of the authorities to defraud the Europeans.

An example is supplied by a case brought by an Englishman in 1660 against the son of a deceased Muslim for an outstanding debt owed by the father. The Englishman, named in the document as Harry the son of Likārdū (Richard?), produced a written document containing the seal of the now dead Sayyid Ḥusayn, which verified that he owed Harry 267 *ghurūsh* remaining from the price of 550 *ghurūsh* for an unspecified quantity of broadcloth. The son denied that the letter was valid, shifting the burden of proof to the Englishman, who asked for three days' delay in the proceedings to produce witnesses who could verify his story. Three days later, the Christian translator for the English merchants appeared at court and said that Harry had failed to find the witnesses, and the case was dismissed. To the English, used to the validity of a written contract from their own legal tradition, such a case must have seemed like Muslim collusion to deny a debt. But for the Muslims, the testimony of a living Muslin who swore that he was telling the truth could only be outweighed by other living witnesses who were also willing to swear to the validity of their testimony.[73]

As a result of the mistrust that emerged from such cases, the English devised two strategems: to rely increasingly on commercial relations with local Christians, who lacked any perceived advantage in the courts, and to avoid the courts completely. The latter approach could create problems of enforcement, as the English were obviously limited to what measures they could bring on their own against an Ottoman subject. On the one hand, they could resort to diplomatic pressure at the Porte. This approach, however, usually involved an investment in gifts that made the process prohibitively expensive in all but the most important cases.[74] Alternatively, they could institute a boycott of any individual who refused to repay an outstanding loan or who had reneged on a contract. The boycott, known as "battalation" (apparently from the Arabic *baṭṭal,* "to negate"), was enforced upon the entire English trading community by the consul and effectively cut the offending party off from the lucrative trade with the West.[75]

The English were able to avoid the Muslim courts to a large degree due to the extraterritoriality they enjoyed in the Ottoman realm (under the terms of their capitulatory treaties they were exempted from being tried in criminal cases by Muslim law) and their economic might. This exemption was expanded further in the capitulatory agreement of 1675, under which commercial disputes between Englishmen and local residents were to be referred directly to the Porte, where the resident English ambassador would present the case. As such we should not be surprised that the court records do so little to document their presence in the city. Similarly, the records of the Levant Company reveal little about Muslim involvement in the caravan trade, and we are left wondering whether in fact there could have been such two distinct, almost parallel trading worlds existing at the same time in the same place with so little contact between them. Our suspicions are that this was, in fact, not so. In the estate left by Sayyid Aḥmad al-Ghazzāl, there were outstanding debts owed him by Europeans amounting to thousands of *ghurūsh,* and occasionally merchants bearing distinctly Muslim names are mentioned in letters sent back to London by Levant Company factors.[76]

In conclusion we return to the question of whether merchants in Aleppo, or any other Ottoman city, comprised a distinct social class. While merchants were an influential component of Aleppo's economic elite, they rarely viewed themselves as a separate social group with specific class interests. As such their political interests often lay with other groups much more broadly defined. This lack of a clearly articulated identity was undoubtedly derived in part from the status of merchants in Islamic society at large, which neither condemned nor segregated them. Rather, almost anyone who had capital, engaged at one time or another, in trade. More important, as we shall see in chapter 5, once capital was raised through commerce it was almost always invested in alternative spheres of the economy.

As such merchants in Aleppo, unlike those in western Europe, did not necessarily feel that commerce was their unique preserve or, alternatively, that it was the only medium open to them for investment. Therefore, they did not have the intense interest of their counterparts in Europe in encouraging trade. Still it seems from the abstract presented above that much of the long-distance trade for which Aleppo became famous in a wider world was in fact handled by trading diasporas of merchants from outside Syria, even if some of the capital supporting the trade was local. For these outsiders, trade was not simply one possibility among many to make their fortunes; rather for reasons of religious and cultural prejudice and sometimes legal discrimination, trade was the only road to fortune that was open to them. It is to those communities of foreign merchants that may have comprised a nascent merchant class along the lines of the Western European model that we must now turn our attention.

NOTES

1. Berchet, p. 102.
2. Aigen, p. 39.
3. Rabbath 2:186.
4. Russell 1:97–98.

5. Ömer Lütfi Barkan, "Essai sur les donées statistiques de registres de recensement dans l'Empire Ottoman aux XVe et XVIe siècles," *JESHO* 1:9–36.

6. Charles Issawi, "Comment on Professor Barkan's Estimate of the Population of the Ottoman Empire, 1520–1530," *JESHO* 1:329–31.

7. Barkan, "Essai sur les donées statistiques."

8. André Raymond, "The Population of Aleppo in the Sixteenth and Seventeenth Centuries According to Ottoman Census Documents," *IJMES* 16:447–60.

9. Raymond, "The Ottoman Conquest and the Development of the Great Arab Towns," *International Journal of Turkish Studies* 1:84–101; Jean-Claude David, *Le waqf d'Ibšir Paša à Alep* (Damascus, 1982); Heinz Gaube and Eugen Wirth, *Aleppo* (Wiesbaden, 1984).

10. Constantine Volney, *Travels through Syria and Egypt in the Years 1783, 1784, and 1785* (English trans.) (London, 1787), 2:147.

11. For a critical discussion of Volney's work, see Albert Hourani, "Volney and the Ruins of Empire," in his *Europe and the Middle East* (Los Angeles, 1980), pp. 81–86.

12. Raymond, "The Population of Aleppo."

13. Russell 2:33; Rabbath 1:121.

14. Pococke 10:530.

15. Aleppo 21:225; Aleppo 34:6; Aleppo 43:312.

16. Abdel-Nour gives a figure of 10% for the Christians out of a total of 100,000 persons living in the city (pp. 66–72). Given the *jizya* totals, this percentage seems too low.

17. Bryan Turner, *Marx and the End of Orientalism* (London, 1978), among others.

18. For what has become the classic presentation of this formulation, see H. A. R. Gibb and Harold Bowen, *Islamic Society and the West* (London, 1957).

19. Turner, p. 43.

20. Inalcik, "Filāḥa," *EI*[2].

21. Damascus, National Archives, Awāmir al-Sulṭānīya series from Aleppo (henceforth AS) 1:196, 229.

22. Rafeq, "Changes in The Relationship between the Ottoman Central Administration and the Syrian Provinces from the Sixteenth to the Eighteenth Centuries," in *Studies in Eighteenth Century Islamic History*, ed. Thomas Naff and Roger Owen (Carbondale, 1977).

23. Būlus Qarā'lī, *Ahamm ḥawādith Ḥalab* (Cairo: n.d.), 64.

24. AS 2:88; Istanbul, Başbakanlık Arşivi, Maliyeden Müdevver (henceforth MM) 2727:55, 24 Recep 1124/27 Aug. 1712; MM 2960:207, 16 Cemaziyelevvel 1118/26 Aug. 1706.

25. For a different interpretation see Rafeq, "Changes in the Relationship," pp. 65–66.

26. Naima, 6:119–25.

27. Russell 2:56.

28. Braudel, *The Prespective of the World*, pp. 127–32; Abraham Udovitch, *Partnership and Profit in Medieval Islam* (Princeton, 1970).

29. Aleppo 17:339.

30. Aleppo 2:117.

31. Aleppo 3:287.

32. Aleppo 3:845.

33. Aleppo 22:331.

34. For example, for the Aleppo merchants' competitors, the Levant Company, see Wood; for the East India Company, see Chaudhuri, *The English East India Company: The Study of an Early Joint-Stock Company* (London, 1964).

35. Aleppo 37:108; Inalcik, "Capital Formation in the Ottoman Empire," *JESHO* 29: 101.

36. Steensgaard, *The Asian Trade Revolution*, pp. 22–59.

37. Aleppo 18:27; Aleppo 20:290.

38. Aleppo 43:104.

39. Aleppo 2:81.

40. Aleppo 53:273.

41. Typically, the craft corporations in a Syrian city during the Ottoman period could be divided into three generalized categories: service corporations such as dyers; those involved in actual craft production, such as the silk weavers; and corporations involved in marketing, such as the sellers of *khām*. Rafeq, "Maẓāhir min al-tanẓīm al-ḥirāfī fī bilād al-Shām fī al-ʿahd al-ʿUthmānī," *Dirāsāt Tāʾrīkhīyah* 4:30–62.

42. SP 110/22:337, 5 August 1702.

43. An indication of this is the free sale of shops without the consent of the membership of the shopkeepers' associations, and various financial arrangements between individual shopkeepers and outside investors. Aleppo 78:153, 215.

44. Aleppo 16:280. A century later a similar assessment was made on thirty-seven individual *sūqs* found within the city walls for the upkeep of the Umayyad Mosque in the city. Aleppo 85:4.

45. MM 7326:44, 1 Cemaziyelahır 1070/13 Feb. 1660.

46. Ḥājj Muṣṭafā Çelebi, for example, registered a loan he made to the villagers of Arāmnāz of 6,000 *ghurūsh*. Aleppo 28:362.

47. d'Arvieux 6:372.

48. Aigen, p. 40.

49. Aleppo 20:98.

50. Rafeq, "Changes in the Relationship."

51. A similar process was occurring in Damascus, Karl Barbir, "From Pasha to Efendi: The Assimilation of Ottomans into Damascene Society," *International Journal of Turkish Studies* 1:68–83.

52. MM 2475:44, 7 Zilkade 1054/6 Jan. 1645.

53. MM 9841:191, 12 Zilkade 1065/14 Sept. 1655; MM 3613:6, 26 Şevval 1073/4 April 1663; MM 2915:168, 27 Zilhicce 1092/7 Jan.1682.

54. MM 9871:377, 7 Zilhicce 1100/22 Sept. 1689.

55. Russell 1:323.

56. SP 110/27:251, 27 April 1740.

57. SP 110/32:160, 30 Sept. 1755.

58. Chaudhuri, *Trade and Civilization in the Indian Ocean: An Economic History from the Rise of Islam to 1750* (Cambridge: 1985), p. 204.

59. Aleppo 45:308.

60. Russell 2:56.

61. Inalcik, "Ḳuṭn," *EI*[2]; Chaudhuri, *The Trading World of Asia,* p. 247.

62. Aleppo 17:350; Aleppo 19:57.

63. Aleppo 3:648.

64. Aleppo 28:206.

65. Aleppo 36:32, 132; Aleppo 34:5.

66. Margaret Meriwether, "The Notable Families of Aleppo, 1770–1830: Networks and Social Structure" (unpublished Ph.D. thesis, University of Pennsylvania, 1981), p. 278.

67. Aleppo 33:129–31. There was also the Amīrīzādah family, who rose to prominence in the city in the eighteenth century from seemingly humble origins in much the same way that the Arīḥāwīzādahs had in the seventeenth century. Gaube and Wirth, p. 226.

68. Aigen, p. 37; d'Arvieux 6:370–71, 384–85; Teixeira, p. 116.

69. Berchet, p. 60.

70. Venice 19:174.

71. *The Travels of John Sanderson in the Levant, 1584–1609*, Hakluyt Society 2nd ser., no. 67, (London, 1931), p. 152.

72. SP 110/23:33–34, 28 Jan. 1704.

73. Aleppo 28:159.

74. SP 105/116: 225–26, 23 July 1718.

75. SP 105/117:56, 28 March 1732; SP 105/118:95, 17 Nov. 1748.

76. SP 110/27:120, 28 June 1735; SP 110/27:146, 5 June 1736.

CHAPTER III

Merchant Diasporas and Trading "Nations"

The story of the Levant trade appears inextricably bound to the fates of the various trading communities who were its principal actors: the British and the Armenians in the seventeenth and early eighteenth centuries; from the mid–eighteenth century onward, the French and Christian Arabs. The existence of such merchant "diasporas," as they have been dubbed by Curtin and others,[1] is not unusual in the history of the world at large. Long-distance trade in the premodern world required complex arrangements of trust and the sharing of information if it were to function at all. These prerequisites were most often shared within an extended family, but when trading networks traversed a continent or a sea, an individual family was hard pressed to manage. The same needs, however, could be met within a kinship group, whether it be based on religion, tribe, caste, or ethnicity. The development of such specialized classes of traders was aided in many societies by the mistrust, fear, or contempt that was often accorded individuals who handled money and, seemingly, made profits from the labor of others.

In the Middle East, such patterns of mercantile specialization were historically not as prevalent as they were elsewhere. Although the Phoenicians and the early Hellenes had provided the virtual paradigm of trading diasporas, by the Roman and Byzantine periods commerce was in the hands of a mulitiplicity of peoples who dwelt in the Mediterranean basin, with no group predominating to the exclusion of the others. Rather, the region itself had become a cradle of merchants, with its sons establishing trading networks in western Europe, across the Sahara to Africa's Sahel, down the east coast of Africa, and eastward to China and the Indies.

It was into this complex trading world that Islam was born. Its early centuries saw the prosperity of the core Muslim lands linked to long-distance trade. Trade, in turn, became a vehicle for extending the new faith, and Islamic society reciprocated in its attitude toward commerce. Almost alone among the civilizations of the medieval Old World, it accorded to mechants a place of prestige and influence, a reflection perhaps of its origins. The tribe into which the Prophet Muhammad was born, the Quraysh, had been, after all, a trading diaspora in its own right, transporting the exports of the Yemen *(Arabia Felix)* to the Mediterranean via Syria.

The political and cultural unity of Islam created a conduit for trade between East and West, and the Muslims used their geographical good fortune to their advantage, dominating the ancient silk road to China and opening up trading relations with expanded areas of Africa and Southeast Asia. Within this vast world there were of course individuals who specialized in commerce, but with the exception of peoples on the fringe of the *Dār al-Islām* ("the house of Islam," i.e., the Muslim world)—the Berbers of Sijilmassa, the Uygurs in Chinese Turkestan, and the Omanis with their descendants, the Swahili of the East African coast—trade was not the monopoly of any particular ethnic group, sect, or tribe.

By 1500, however, the opportunities for long-distance trade in the Muslim lands were beginning to contract. In part, this was due to the expansion of European commercial and military interests into the Indian Ocean. Imbued with the religious fervor of the *Reconquista,* the Portuguese, like the Spaniards in the Mediterranean, could only see the Muslims as enemies. Undoubtedly this religiously based antagonism was intensified, as well, by the fact that Muslims offered the Portuguese their main commercial competition for the control of the trade of the Indies.[2] Similarly, in the Indonesian archipelago itself, the aggressive Dutch competition for the spice trade led oftentimes to war, with the Muslim sultanates gradually losing out to better technology and organization.[3]

Simultaneously, Muslim merchants who had earlier established a presence in Venice began to curtail their activities as the Italians more aggressively sought to control the Levant trade for themselves.[4] Unfortunately, this part of Mediterranean economic history has yet to be elucidated, and the reason for the Muslim commercial retreat from the West remains an enigma. There are several possible reasons: an increase in Christian corsair activity against Muslim shipping, a hardening of Venetian intolerance toward Muslim merchants in their midst, or simply a lack of interest on the part of Muslim merchants (coupled with a traditional contempt for the West) in going to the lands of the Franks. But for whatever reason, by the time of the Ottoman conquest of Syria the Venetians and the Genoese clearly dominated the trade of the Levant to Europe, to the exclusion of participation by any of the indigenous Middle Eastern peoples.

Accompanying these global shifts in trading patterns, the situation in the Middle East was changing as well, to the detriment of the Muslim merchants. But this blow came not so much as a result of Western incursions as from the calcification of the historic mistrust between Sunnis and the Shi'a, personified in the rivalry between the Ottoman sultan and the Iranian shah over which one was entitled to lead the community of the faithful, the *umma*. This campaign degenerated into a propaganda war, accompanied by an insistence on "right-think" on both sides of the frontier with the unfortunate adherents to the nonestablishmentarian sect in either realm subjected to brutal persecution. While an iron curtain did not descend to separate the Ottoman Empire from that of the Iranians, the ideological conflict was reduced to a fundamental mistrust of believers who followed the "wrong" sect on either side of the border.

In the sixteenth century, this hostility led the Ottomans to impose an embargo on Iranian goods and to prohibit Iranian merchants from entering the empire.[5] The policy only succeeded in weakening the Ottoman economy and was apparently not evoked again during the wars of the seventeenth century, although individual Iranian merchants occasionally had their goods confiscated as war booty.[6] Nonetheless, Shi'a mechants must have felt a certain unease in a land whose official policy called for the extirpation of the *kızıl baş* heresy, while Sunni Ottoman merchants, whether Turks or Arabs, must have shared similar trepidations about traveling into the lands of the shah. The Muslim world had become irreparably torn asunder as political considerations limited the horizons of trade, as well as cultural and intellectual exchange. Trade might continue to follow the old caravan routes from Iran to the Mediterranean, but it was a trade, as we shall see, increasingly in the hands of the Christian subjects of either the sultan or shah, and not in the hands of Muslims.

THE EUROPEAN TRADING COMMUNITIES

Enmity bred of competition was not unique to the Muslim world. While the Ottomans and Safavid Iranians were locked in a struggle to claim the spiritual mantle of the Prophet, the European states battled each other for the control of an emerging world economy. Although the stakes were higher in other parts of the world, such as India and the Americas, the same competitive spirit that was forging a new world system was evident in the Middle East, where the dowager of the Levant trade, Venice, was challenged by the commercial Johnny-come-latelies, Britain and the Netherlands.

There were similarities in the reasons behind the triumph of the northern Europeans over their southern European rivals in both the Levant and the Indian Ocean, including their aggressive marketing of new products and the strength of their commercial trading companies.[7] But there were also significant differences in the nature of the competition, which was overcome in the two arenas of trade.

The Portuguese trading empire in the Indian Ocean rested to a large extent on coercion supplied by their fleet, with trade being handled under the rubric of a state enterprise monopoly. Venice, by contrast, oversaw a trading diaspora of its citizens in the Mediterranean, providing wherever possible consular protection to individual family merchant houses who operated in the fashion of the renowned Polos. The Venetians had maintained their position through diplomatic guile, by occasional military force, and by supplying the wealthy elite of the Middle East with luxury goods on which they had come to rely. Nonetheless, their tenuous hold over the Levant trade was constantly being challenged both by other Italian commercial city states and by the growing political power and ambitions of the Ottomans, who saw Venice as a regional rival to be reduced.

To combat Venice, the Ottomans favored the French and the English in their commercial dealings, thereby hastening the demise of the republic's trading network. Although the Ottomans were wary of all Franks, a response conditioned by history, the sultans were shrewd enough to understand that commercial contacts with the wider world were of benefit to their realm. Despite the general axiom that the unbelievers constituted one nation *(milla)*, it was not always wise to treat them as if they did. The ideology of statecraft as it had evolved in the Muslim lands over the centuries recognized the need to promote trade for the general wealth and prosperity of the realm. This understanding involved an awareness on the part of Muslim legal scholars of the need to work out an official status for the Western merchants living in the House of Islam that would distinguish them both from native Christians and from subjects of the Christian powers with whom the Muslims were at war.

By the Ottoman period, the legal groundwork had already been established, and the western Europeans, although technically subjects of enemy powers, were granted a special dispensation that allowed them to trade and travel relatively freely in the Ottoman state. This status was formalized by the sultans through a series of written commercial agreements with the Western states they favored. These were the treaties known in the West as the Capitulations (*imtiyazat* in Ottoman Turkish), about which much has already been written. Although they later came to symbolize the degradation imposed by Western military and political might on the Muslim peoples in the nineteenth and twentieth centuries, in their original form these treaties were an acknowledgment by the Ottomans of the usefulness of trade with the West for the furtherance of state interests. The Ottoman sultans and their advisers carefully chose which Western powers would be honored by such treaties, in order to cultivate potential allies such as England and France, or to deny the benefits of trade to states, such as Venice or Russia, with which they were in conflict.[8]

The implications of the capitulatory agreements for the subsequent political and economic history of the Middle East are outside the boundaries of this study. But it should be noted that the Capitulations granted an extraterritoriality to the European merchant trading communities, in effect making them mininations in the Ottomans' midst. These agreements, which were perceived by the Ottomans as constituting a sound foreign and economic policy, nonetheless contained the seeds of the empire's dissolution. By introducing the concept of a legal status based on nationality for the European merchants into a society where such ideas could only be disruptive, they had established a standard to which indigenous trading diasporas would aspire.

For Muslims, as has often been stated, the idea of nationality in the premodern eras seemed at best irrelevant and at worst irreverent. The ideology of the fundamental unity of believers, despite the disunity of competing dynasties, helped for centuries to open the borders of the Muslim world to trade. A traveling Muslim merchant would not be considered or treated as a subject of an alien power when he left home. Rather, he would be entitled to the same rights in court as a local merchant, and the courts, being Muslim, would administer a code of law with which he would be familiar. Furthermore, our traveling merchant would be subject to the same standards of behavior and legal obligations in the city in which he was trading as if he were a native, which, as a member of the *umma,* he in fact was. Neighborhoods of ethnically distinct Muslim merchants might exist. Indeed, we know they were to be found in seventeenth-century Aleppo, but the legal status of those merchants residing within them was indistinct from that of their neighbors.

Similarly, non-Muslims from Muslim lands were assumed to be *dhimmī*s (Christians or Jews who had accepted the political, if not religious, authority of Islam) with the same rights, or lack of rights, as Ottoman non-Muslims and subject to the same extra taxes that they were. Simply put, there was nothing in the tradition that would permit regulations favoring Ottoman subjects over those of any other Muslim state. Loyalty to a particular Muslim state was defined as obedience to its dynastic house, and that could change. Witness the very real challenge posed to the Ottomans by the movement they labeled the *kızıl baş* heresy.

Although the same could be said for almost all premodern state systems, there was an added volatile dimension in the Muslim world, which arose out of an acknowledged political bond that legally, as well as morally, superseded the question of to which dynastic house individual Muslims owed their temporal, if not temporary, allegiance. Evidence of a recognition of this lack of distinction among individual subjects of the *Dār al-Islām* can be found in the customs regulations issued by the Ottoman state in which Muslims or *dhimmī*s, from any Muslim state including the empire itself, were all taxed at the same rate, usually 2.5% and 5% respectively.[9]

The Europeans, by contrast, were not only distinguished by the sobriquet of Franks but were invariably ascribed a nationality as well, *Efrenk-i Ingiliz* or *Efrenk-i Filemenk,* English and Dutch. This reflected their own use of the term "nation" to describe the network of European merchant communities, a clear evolution from the individual family trading houses of the earlier centuries.

Each of these "nations" jealously guarded its separate identity, commercial successes, and relationship with the Ottoman authorities. At times individual Ottoman officials might view all Europeans as being the same and act accordingly, but it is clear that for the most part the Ottoman state appreciated the differences between the nations as well. The internal organization of each nation might differ in its structure, but all were autonomous bodies, headed by consuls who were appointed from the home country and whose authority was supported by the Ottoman state.

In the case of the English nation, the consul was directly responsible not to the king but rather to the board of directors of the Levant Company who had appointed him. No Englishman could engage in commerce unless he was a member of the company, and part of the consul's function was to insure compliance with company directives. Merchants who disobeyed were disciplined and could be fined or, in more serious cases, ordered home. The consul was, furthermore, entitled to collect consular dues from his countrymen and all others seeking the protection of his flag, and to administer all the internal affairs of the community. While the consuls of France and Venice, and apparently the Netherlands as well, were appointed by their governments directly, they enjoyed the same autocratic administrative rights as did their English counterparts.[10]

The European trading communities in Aleppo, like those that were being established throughout the world at roughly the same time, were undoubtedly isolated and lonely places for the young men who manned them. While not legally confined by the host country in the way that their compatriots were in Japan or China, the Europeans in the Ottoman Empire were still less than welcome guests in a strange land where immense barriers of language and culture, as well as fear and mistrust, separated them from the people among whom they dwelt. With very few exceptions, they were content to let those barriers remain. Russell, one of those who was not so complacent, said: "Of the Europeans, even those who live long in the country, very few acquire more knowledge of the Arabic than is barely sufficient for familiar conversation, and it is very rare that any of them take the trouble of either learning to read or write it."[11]

It is important to note, however, that this isolation was not imposed by Ottoman law, although the society at large unquestionably held prejudices against the Franks. In addition, conservative attitudes about alcohol and sex in Aleppo made easy social mixing for the Europeans difficult, but not impossible. While in the eighteenth century the Europeans in the main confined themselves to a monastic existence in the khans in the commercial heart of the city, cut off from all but their own social company, in the seventeenth century there were cases of Europeans buying large houses in various quarters of the city.[12] Similarly, no restrictions prevented the Europeans from dealing directly with the Muslims, but a general mistrust of Muslims, as evinced in the preceeding chapter in reference to the court system, kept those contacts to a minimum. As Russell stated, "The Europeans have little or no social intercourse with the Turks. They seldom see them but in the way of business, which is usually transacted through an interpreter, though the Frank himself happens to understand the language."[13]

The factors' lack of acquaintance with their surroundings is easily confirmed. One can read through the various letter books of the Levant Company factors and get very little sense of what life in larger Aleppo was like. What we do see is their homesickness, desperation, and dispair. Alcoholism and disease seem to have been recurring problems, and there is an overwhelming preoccupation with procuring the comforts of England: books, cider, tea, cheese, and ham.[14]

What we also learn from this correspondence are the apparent advantages of a commercial company organization over the traditional family-run Levantine commercial houses that were being superseded. The most important of these was an increased access to information on the almost current world prices of various commodities. Although it took several months for letter packets to arrive from home, the information they contained enabled factors to know, for example, what the London, Amsterdam, and Lisbon prices for coffee were and, therefore, whether it would be wise to buy coffee in Aleppo to ship to Europe or, alternatively, to order it from the West Indies for the Syrian market. A similar process seems to have been at work in the indigo trade.[15] In today's world of instant international communication, such information networks seem almost unbelievably inefficient, but in that age, they represented in effect a quantum leap in communications that provided the company factors with a distinct edge over their competition.

TRADING DIASPORAS FROM WITHIN THE *UMMA*

Despite the transformation of the trading world of the Middle East during the seventeenth century, the traveling Muslim merchants, familiar holdovers from an earlier era, still plied the caravan routes even if they no longer retained their pride of place in the great trans-Asian trade. As indicated in the previous chapter, the young men of Aleppo still set out as merchants to trade in the East and Egypt, and similarly Aleppo was visited by traders coming from the opposite directions. Most who aspired to the title of *fakhr al-tujjār* were agents in *muḍāraba* agreements, but there were also merchants who set out to India or Iran with what seemed to have been goods worth only a trifling capital investment. These could only have been peddlers in the classic Asian model, little changed in the practice of their trade from their predecessors in Islam's golden age.

We cannot be sure how large a group these international peddlers within the *umma* comprised. The suspicion is that the commercial dealings of most small-scale traders were never registered, and, indeed, it is usually only with their deaths away from home and family that we learn of their individual existence at all. The total volume of trade they handled is equally an unknown factor in assessing their importance to the overall economic life of the period. But that they, as a group, continued to exist, despite the changes in the ways Middle Easterners were defining their group loyalties and despite growing and often hostile competition from the West, we have no doubt. Whether peddlers or commercial agents, the continued existence of both categories of traveling merchants from within the *umma* challenges the notion that a fundamental change had occurred in the seventeenth century in the ways western Asians conducted their commerce.

Leaving aside merchants coming from within the boundaries of the Ottoman Empire, there were two distinct groups of non-Ottoman Muslim merchants from within the *umma* who had a substantial presence in Aleppo in this period: the Iranians and the Indians. Egyptian, Anatolian, and Iraqi merchants were much more significant as regards their number and the volume of trade they handled than either of these other two groups. But unlike the non-Ottomans, they never achieved the status of being recognized by Ottoman officialdom as constituting a *taife*, and so have remained largely anonymous.

The Iranian Muslims were few in number, but they are important for what their presence tells us about the continuation of trade along its ancient routes through the Middle East despite growing sectarian hostility. Although they came from the camp of what was, along with the Russians and the Austrians, one of the Ottoman's greatest enemies, the Safavi shah, there is no indication that they were discriminated against, officially or unofficially, in Aleppo. Yet the fact that the central Asian merchants in the city were carefully distinguished from other Iranians by the designation *Buharalı Acemiler* ("Bukharan Persians"),[16] seemingly carried the implicit understanding that a distinction was recognized between Persian speakers who came from the lands of an ally of the Ottomans, the Uzbek khan, and those who were from Iran. We cannot know whether the Iranians were Sunni or Shi'a, but whatever their sect, the amount of trade carried on by Iranian Muslims was insignificant when compared to that of their Armenian countrymen. Their importance lies, therefore, in the fact that they were to be found at all, given the various factors that were at work against their presence.

The Indian merchants did not face the same potential political problems as did the Iranians. Yet difficulties of travel for Indian merchants in the face of the Western naval dominance of the Arabian Sea and the increasing attempts by Westerners to monopolize the trade of the Indian Ocean must not have made their pursuit of profit easy. Still, there was a persistent, if not necessarily large, Indian presence in Aleppo throughout the seventeenth century. For the most part, the Indians were peddlers operating on a small scale. They would stay in Aleppo for periods up to a few years and then travel on to other places. Ironically, it was their mobility that alerts us to their presence, as we know of them largely through the occasional divorce suits brought by their wives in Aleppo on charges of desertion.[17]

Other Indians seemed to have had a more permanent presence in the city than the cases of the transient peddlers would imply. There was a residential area named the Zuqāq al-Hunūd ("the alley of the Indians") in the quarter of Khandaq al-Balūj and a membership list of the guild of the bleachers of *khām* included five individuals who were identified as being Indian.[18]

Unlike the situation in Iran, where Hindu merchants were often present,[19] the Indian merchants in Aleppo were exclusively Muslim. Despite their undeniable Muslimness, at least one overzealous tax collector of the *jizya* in Aleppo tried, in 1639, to have them classified otherwise. The Indians, however, were able to prove that they had paid the taxes levied on their quarter, establishing that they were citizens in good standing. Additionally, they produced a *fatwā* from the chief *muftī* of Aleppo saying that they were Muslims. This led the judge to issue an injunction to the tax collector to desist from his harrassment of the community.[20]

In addition to the small-scale peddling trade conducted by these almost anonymous Indians, there is evidence of commerce on a much larger scale between the subcontinent and the Ottoman Empire. In 1645, an Indian merchant named Muḥammad Nāṣir was involved in lengthy negotiations over the customs duties he was to be assessed in Aleppo. From the testimony registered locally and the final ruling on the case registered in Istanbul, we learn that Muḥammad Nāṣir was a commercial agent for an Indian prince, identified simply as Mīr Ẓarīf. In that capacity, he had shipped a quantity of Indian goods for his patron to the Ottoman realm. These included 50 loads of indigo worth 12,5000 *ghurūsh,* which were sold in Istanbul, and 40,000 *ghurūsh* worth of unspecified goods, which were shipped through the port of Iskenderun to Venice. In return, Muḥammad Nāṣir imported 60,000 *ghurūsh* worth of European goods, which he intended to take by caravan to Basra.[21]

Muḥammad Nāṣir's story is interesting for a couple of reasons. First, it confirms that, despite the Europeans' concentrated efforts to divert India's trade, commerce at times still followed the old trade routes, not only to the Middle East but to Mediterranean Europe beyond. Unfortunately for us, such trade would only be registered in the courts of Aleppo if it involved sales in the city's markets. It is impossible, therefore, to know, in the absence of the city's customs registers, whether this case represented a trend or was simply an extravagant exception. The second interesting point presented by this account is that it illustrates the role of individual merchants handling state commerce.[22] While this type of activity is absent in Aleppo, at least as far as the Ottoman ruling house was concerned, it was an option often employed by the Iranian shahs to the east who chose as their agents the Armenians of Julfa.

Armenians had played a significant role in the trade of the Levant for several centuries. Before the conquest of the Cilician Armenian kingdom by the Mamluks in 1375, they had dominated the East-West trade through the port of Ayas. With the fall of the kingdom and the growth of the importance of Iranian silk for the European market, Armenians were again in position, in their ancient homeland astride the Turkish-Iranian border, to act as brokers for the trade. By 1600, the preeminence of the Armenians in the silk trade of Iran had been firmly established. Muslim merchants still engaged in the trade, but their numbers had diminished in comparison to what they had been a century before.[23]

Most of the Iranian Armenians who participated in the silk trade of the sixteenth century were from one town, Julfa, located on the Araxes

(Araz) River. Responding to this, the English merchants in Aleppo indiscriminately called all Armenians Chelfalines, regardless of their actual place of origin. For the English the Julfa Armenians were an exotic group, but even in 1600, they were already recognized as being the key to Iran's silk trade, described by William Biddulph as follows:

The Chefalines are Christians, dwelling upon the borders of Persia, betweene Mesopotamia and Persia, at a place called Chelfa. These bring Silke to Aleppo to sell. They are a plaine dealing people. If a man pay them money, and (by over-reckoning himselfe) give them more then their due, though there be but one piece over, so soone as they perceive it, though it bee many dayes after, they will bring it backe againe, and restore it, and thinke they shall never returne safely into their Countrey, if they should not make restitution therof. These people perswade themselves, and report unto others, that they dwell in that place which was called Eden, whereinto Adam was put to keepe and dresse it.[24]

Despite its seeming strengths, Julfa suffered a major setback as a commercial center in 1604, when Shah Abbas ordered the evacuation of the region in the face of an advancing Ottoman army and removed the entire population to the Iranian interior. The Julfa Armenians, however, were able to make a remarkable recovery through the patronage of the same shah who had ordered their deportation. Shah Abbas resettled the refugees outside his capital of Isfahan, in a suburb named New Julfa, and gave the community a monopoly over his country's silk trade. That monopoly was abolished by his successor Shah Safi (1629–42). Nonetheless, the Armenians still effectively managed to control Iran's export trade even without an official monopoly, through an expanding network of their countrymen that extended into Poland and eastward to India.[25]

Armenian merchants from Julfa also established themselves in Amsterdam, where their merchant community at times reached one hundred members and boasted its own fleet, which sailed between the Levant and the Netherlands.[26] The Armenians, like the Levant Company, represented an evolution in the patterns of trade from the ways in which it had been conducted in the preceding centuries. The Armenians may have never developed venture stock financing as did their English competition, but they possessed a commercial network that had strong links between its members, supported schools for merchants-to-be, and published manuals to serve as guides to aspiring young merchants. In short, they developed into a trading diaspora as sophisticated as was their western European competition.[27]

Although the impetus for this commercial network came largely from Iranian Armenians, their success could not help but have had an impact on their ethnic cousins who lived within the boundaries of the Ottoman state. Still, it seemingly took several decades for the changes to be felt. In 1600, the most influential members of the Aleppo Armenian community came from Julfa, and the Iranian Armenians may have even comprised a majority of the community's total numbers. In a study made of Armenian tombstones extant in the city, it was found that of those preserved from the years 1571 to 1659, twenty-nine out of forty-five were for individuals who had come originally from Julfa.[28]

The presence of these Iranian Armenian merchants in Aleppo triggered a cultural flourishing of the city's Armenian community as a whole. Supported by the silk merchants, new churches were constructed and illuminated manuscripts were commissioned. Concomitant with Aleppo's growing economic and cultural role in the Armenian diaspora, Azaria, the Catholicos of Sis (1581–1601), himself originally from Julfa, moved his see to the city. It is not clear whether his immediate successors followed his example, but by the middle of the seventeenth century the city had become the de facto residency of the office, challenging the historic center of the faith in Ejmiacin (near Yerevan in the present-day Armenian SSR).[29]

The growth of Aleppo's economic and cultural importance for Armenians in the early seventeenth century, coupled with unrest in Anatolia,[30] attracted a wave of migration of Ottoman Armenians into the city. We are able to trace this migration in no small part because of the problems it posed for the Ottoman collectors of the *jizya*. Under Ottoman law, no doubt a reflection of the underlying theoretical ideal of a united *umma* despite the reality of a very real fissure between Sunnis and Shi'a, there was no legal distinction between an Ottoman Armenian and one coming from Iran. The Ottomans recognized, however, that a traveling Christian merchant should only be required to pay the tax once, in his home town, as to ask more was unjust.

Nonetheless, this policy, however open-minded it had been in its formulation, began to break down when the Christians arriving in Aleppo came to stay permanently rather than simply to trade. One of the earliest *taife*s of migrants to be constituted in the city consisted of Armenians from the Sasun region, located to the west of Lake Van in Turkey. On January 26, 1661, representatives of that community registered the names of seventy-seven adult male Sasuni Armenians who had left their villages, as the land there could no longer support them.[31] Once in Aleppo, many of these migrants would claim, as did a group from Arabgir in 1637, that they were exempt from paying the *jizya* in Aleppo, having sent such taxes as they owed back home regularly.[32]

Suspicions that the migrants were not always being so scrupulous in meeting their legal obligations in their native towns led the central government by 1653 to implement a new tax called the *yave cizye* (literally, "the *jizya* on those who had strayed"), to be collected by the governor of Aleppo on all new Christian immigrants to the city.[33] Interestingly, the order issued in that year contravened an order registered only five years earlier that stated that Christians coming to Aleppo from Van and Erzurum had to remit their *jizya* taxes to the governor in Diyarbakır.[34]

The new law stated that a migrant to Aleppo, whether he came to stay permanently or for only an extended residency, would be registered as owing the *yave cizye* in Aleppo for a period up to ten years, after which time he would become a legal Aleppo *dhimmī*. Theoretically, under the new system the same amount of money from all the Empire's potential *jizya* payers would end up in the central treasury as before, and the apparent loophole of being able to claim to have paid the tax elsewhere would be closed. We are not told in these orders whether the *yave cizye* was assessed at a different rate from the ordinary *jizya* levied on native non-Muslims, but the absence of any mention of a differentiation leads to the suspicion that there was none.

As might be expected, the confusion over who was legitimately covered by the categories of the *yave cizye* led often to an overly ambitious application of the new rule by Ottoman tax collectors, as the repeated complaints of Ottoman Armenians going on pilgrimage to Jerusalem and Armenian merchants from Iran that they were being forced to pay it attest.[35] In such cases, the governor was reminded that the tax could only be collected from those who had resided in Aleppo for more than seven months.

The institution of the tax indicates that a significant migration was taking place, but it is much more difficult to ascertain from where the migrants were coming and what their total numbers were. Orders issued in 1653 and 1663 mention variously Isfahan, Mardin, Erzurum, Van,

Sasun, Arabgir, and Diyarbakır as being the points of origin for the migrants.[36] In a *jizya* listing for Aleppo made in 1695, in which 5,391 adult Christian males were registered, 1,234 individuals were indicated as paying the *yave cizye*, an indication of the impact migration had on Aleppo's Christian population in the period. Of these *yave cizye* payers, roughly half had identifiably Armenian names, while of those listed simply in the *jizya* category, the ratio of Arab to Armenian names was better than four to one.[37]

The Iranian Armenian merchants did not, however, find the innovation of the *yave cizye* to be any real improvement over their former status. In addition, they found irksome the practice by which Ottoman officials would confiscate for the treasury *(bayt al-māl)* property belonging to Iranian merchants who had died in the empire without any apparent heirs. This practice did not differ from the way in which the estates of all Ottoman subjects were handled, but the grace period of six months for heirs to make themselves known to claim the estate of a dead relative was much too short for families of traveling merchants.

An example of the hardship this could create is found in a case registered on April 14, 1679, in which a certain Avak w. Mugerdiç of Nakçevan claimed the estate of his nephew, Mirican w. Garabid, who had died in the khan of Khayrbek in Aleppo. He was, however, too late. His nephew's worldly possessions had already been confiscated and sold by the *bayt al-māl.* The uncle was given a listing of what Mirican owned—4 bundles of furs, 26 pieces *(top)* of silk cloth, 5 *kilims,* a musket, a sword, plates, and a pot—but was told it was impossible to restore the goods to him. Neither was any mention made of restitution of the cash value of the goods.[38]

Incidents such as that sparked a lobbying campaign by the Iranian Armenians to obtain recognition that their status was not, in fact, the same as Armenians who were subjects of the Ottoman sultan. In 1690, a decree was issued exempting them from the *jizya,* and in 1724, the Ottoman government agreed to allow a representative of the Iranian shah *(şah vekili)* to handle the deposition of estates of Iranians who had died in the Ottoman Empire.[39] While this exemption from general Ottoman practice did not grant them extraterritoriality corresponding to the rights contained in the Ottoman-European capitulatory agreements, the Iranian Armenian diaspora had won an important recognition of their distinct status as traders in the Ottoman Empire.

While the Ottomans may have eventually come to distinguish between Iranian and Ottoman Armenians for purposes of taxation and legal status, it is not at all clear whether the Armenians themselves made such distinctions. The identification of subgroups within the Aleppo Armenian population—the Sasuni *taife,* for example—seems to have largely been a seventeenth-century phenomenon. It was not maintained after the wave of migration to the city had peaked, although a distinct guild of Sasuni bakers continued well into the next century.[40]

Furthermore, as discussed in the previous chapter, by the end of the seventeenth century both Aleppo Armenians and Armenians with Anatolian *laqab*s had moved into the silk trade, further blurring distinctions between Ottomans and Iranian Armenians insofar as the arena of their commercial endeavors was concerned. Thus while it is safe to say that the silk brought by caravan to Aleppo was for the most part handled by Armenians, the trade was no longer an exclusive preserve of those of New Julfa.

The English factors operating in Aleppo viewed the near monopoly of the Armenians, local or otherwise, with ambivalence. It did not take a great deal of perspicacity on their part to realize that the Armenians were all that stood in the way of the rival East India Company's ability to steal the silk trade of Iran away. This was coupled with the realization that Englishmen were ill-suited to travel into Iran directly on any sort of a regular basis. The Levant Company had attempted that option, establishing a factory in the town of Erzurum in 1689 to trade with Iran. The factory began operations in 1691 but was closed two years later as it was said that its operations were injurious to the company's operations in Izmir and Istanbul.[41]

Despite the general order of 1693 mandating a general withdrawal of English operations to the coast, a factory was maintained for several more years in Ankara to buy mohair. This exception proved to be ill-conceived, however, as in March of 1706 a mob attacked the English merchants there and forced them to take refuge in one of the city's khans. For several months, rumors reached Aleppo of the factors' massacre at the hands of a fanatic mob, but by summer they had been rescued by the Ottoman army.[42] Nonetheless, the experience seems to have soured any English idea of maintaining a commercial presence in the Ottoman hinterlands, and the trade of the interior was relinquished completely to the Armenians, adding to their seeming indispensibility.

Economic reasons also may have conditioned a coastal policy. In a letter written in 1750 that discussed the feasibility of opening a factory in Baghdad to counter the one opened by the East India Company in Basra, the British consul in Aleppo stated that in the past, goods carried by English merchants from Erzurum and Baghdad had been ruled by the Ottoman government to have constituted internal trade. English merchants traveling those routes, therefore, were exempted from the privileges of the *imtiyazat* (the capitulatory agreements) and were subject to the same rate of taxation as were Ottoman Christians.[43] Given this Ottoman policy, it was hardly cost-effective for Britons to attempt traveling into potentially hostile territory, as local Christians could handle the transit trade much more cheaply and safely.

While the Levant Company factors were forced to accede to the necessity for the Armenians in the scheme of things, even going as far as to write prominent merchants of New Julfa in 1719, inviting them to bring their goods to Aleppo,[44] they were wary of their potential for competition. The Armenian merchants were not barred from entering England, but neither were they given the same freedom of action that they enjoyed in the Netherlands.[45] There were individual Armenians present in London, but their commercial activity was circumscribed by the monopoly enjoyed by the Levant Company over the importation of Levantine products to England and the export of English goods of the Ottoman Empire.

That monopoly made it necessary for Armenians wishing to trade with England directly to use the subterfuge of bribing English factors to load their goods on company ships under the factors' own names. Such illegal operations were apparently a real temptation for a number of factors, as the repeated orders forbidding the practice demonstrate.[46] One Armenian in particular, a certain Arutin George, or alternatively di Giorgio, based in London, seems to have been a repeated offender. He was a former translator for the Levant Company in Izmir and, together with a brother still operating in Izmir and a brother-in-law in Livorno, formed a syndicate and used their contacts with Levant Company factors to illegally ship goods to and from London. In response to one such charge against him, in 1710, the company set a fine of twenty percent of the value of any of his goods caught and confiscated to be imposed on the Englishmen who aided the nefarious practice.[47] But as orders banning Armenians from English ships continued to be issued after that date, it seems unlikely the practice was effectively checked.

In addition to the Armenians, another trading diaspora, that of the Sephardi Jews, offered at least limited competition to the ambitions of the Levant Company. Like the Armenians, the Jews who had fled or been expelled from the Iberian peninsula following the *Reconquista,* formed an extended community with members found in many cities throughout the Mediterranean basin. Although the primary cultural and commercial centers of the Sephardi diaspora were located in Italy, from the sixteenth century onward they established an important presence in the Ottoman Empire, with large communities in both Izmir and Salonica,[48] and by 1600, in Aleppo as well.

In 1672, there were 380 registered Jewish *cizye hane* ("households") in Aleppo, of which 73 were identified as being *Efrenc Yehudileri* ("Frankish Jews," i.e., Sephardi), and the others as *Araban-ı Halep Yehudileri* ("Arab Jews").[49] While the *jizya* households were not identical with the actual number of adult males,[50] we will assume that the ratio between "Frankish" and "Arab" households roughly corresponded to the percentage of the total Jewish community each comprised, leaving the Sephardis a large minority of the total.[51]

Unlike the Armenians, the Sephardi Jews did not enjoy the control of any specific commodity or trade route, so they were largely reduced to serving as middlemen for various European merchants. This could present problems for the community, given the general mistrust of outsiders held by most trading diasporas. The English, in particular, seemed to have been loath to have any business dealings with them. In part this was based on a suspicion, voiced by a factor in Aleppo in 1671, that no Jew would testify on behalf of an Englishman if it meant another of his community would be adversely affected.[52]

Reflecting English mistrust, general orders were issued by the Levant Company in 1713 to its membership in Istanbul, Izmir, and Aleppo, stating that no Jew could be hired to serve as a company translator, effectively barring Jews from obtaining the coveted position of *beratlı* (one exempted from Ottoman law and taxes through the protection of a foreign signatory to a capitulatory agreement).[53] As in the case of banning the Armenians from importing Levantine goods into England directly, this prohibition undoubtedly represented a fear of potential competition as well as mistrust, as demonstrated by reports sent to London in 1694 and 1696, warning of the activities of "Portuguese Jews" who were undermining the company's commerce between the Ottoman Empire and various Mediterranean ports.[54] But there also can be little doubt that this less-than-friendly attitude was tinged by anti-Semitism as well. A letter dated October 19, 1722, written by the British consul in Aleppo, stated bluntly that Italian Jews should be granted the protection of his office, only "providing they prove to be more sincere than they have been in the past."[55]

Denied the patronage of the most important Western trading nation in Aleppo, the Sephardi Jews turned to France. Ironically, in the same year that the Jews were ordered expelled form Marseilles, 1682, they were granted French protection in Aleppo.[56] It was clear from the start, however, that this protection did not mean equality. The French had won as a part of their capitulatory agreement, signed in 1673, a reduction of the customs rate assessed on them from 5% to 3%, the rate always enjoyed by the English.[57] But the Jewish merchants under their protection continued to pay the rate of 5%.[58] This was, in effect, the same rate charged on Ottoman Jewish subjects. The benefit of French protection, therefore, was restricted to the exemption the "honorary" Frenchmen gained from Muslim law. Nonetheless, even this limited patronage was resented by the French merchants, who endeavored on several occasions to have the privilege rescinded.[59]

Given this hostility, many of the Jewish merchants sought other protectors. Russell reports that by 1750 many were Venetian subjects, and there was even an occasional Jewish merchant who enjoyed British protection as well.[60] Nonetheless, the Sephardi Jews, facing the wall of mistrust from the Europeans and with the Ottomans' growing inability to award them any specical considerations, were unable to break into the trade of the Levant effectively. They were forced, therefore, to move into those sectors of the trade, such as Angora wool, which the Europeans were either not interested in or unable to exploit. Their opportunities were clearly limited and, by the middle of the eighteenth century, their economic position in Syria was being eclipsed by the rising commercial star of the Syrian Christians.

THE SYRIAN CHRISTIANS: A NEW TRADING DIASPORA

The emergence of a distinctive Syrian Christian trading diaspora in the Levant is one of the more dynamic subplots of Aleppo's history in the Ottoman period. For it was the Christians alone among the various local peoples of Aleppo who emerged as clear beneficiaries of Aleppo's position as an emporium of the East-West trade. When by the nineteenth century the Levant Company stock had been liquidated among its shareholders and the halcyon days of New Julfa were a faded memory, Syrian Christians were pursuing the ambitions awakened in the seventeenth century in their old centers of Aleppo and Damascus, as well as in newly established ones, such as Beirut and Cairo. Yet in 1600 it had appeared to most outside observers that the native Aleppo Christian community was so sunk in poverty, indolence, ignorance, and filth that it could never amount to anything. Nonetheless, over the course of the century, that community, or at least a significant part of it, was transformed, and the key to understanding the change seems to lie in the evolving face of Aleppo's commercial relations with a wider world.

In 1600, the Aleppo Christian community was divided into at least four sects: Greek Orthodox (also referred to as Melkites in the Syrian context, or in Ottoman Turkish, *millet-i Rum*), Maronite Catholics, Syrian Orthodox (alternatively Jacobites, or Suryani in Arabic and Turkish sources), and the Armenians. The largest group was undoubtedly the Greek Orthodox.[61] They were indiscriminately referred to as "Greeks" in the European sources, although from the local evidence, including personal names encountered in the court records, it appears that this group, with the exception of its clergy and an occasional errant Cypriot, was almost exclusively Arabophone and not Hellene.

Greek Orthodox Arabs were a ubiquitous part of the urban demographic mix of Ottoman Syria. They were the Christian community most assimilated into the cultural and economic mainstream of the Arab Muslim majority, but they were also apparently the poorest. According to both Biddulph and Teixeira, who visited Aleppo at the beginning of the seventeenth century, the community was destitute. Biddulph added the derogatory description that the men worked as porters, while the women were the city's prostitutes.[62] We have to be cautious of these characterizations, however, as the Orthodox Christian community was often more wary of the Franks, whom it considered to be steeped in theological error, than were Muslims. The dislike was reciprocated by the Europeans, who described the Greek Orthodox Christians as superstitious and backward. Still, it seems safe to assume that the community's membership had little economic influence and less political power.

The Syrian branch of the Greek Orthodox church, with its patriarch established at the see of Antioch but physically located in Damascus throughout the Ottoman period, had enjoyed a great degree of autonomy, if not actual independence, from the mother church in Constantinople during the centuries when Syria and Anatolia were under different, and usually antagonistic, political regimes. With the Ottoman conquest of Syria, however, that independence ended as the Greek patriarch in Istanbul was able, with Ottoman support, to assert his authority over what he considered to be his Syrian flock. In practical terms, the new order meant that a largely Arabic-speaking laity was placed under the control of a clergy that was largely Hellenophone.[63]

This reunion was viewed with resentment by Aleppo's Orthodox Christians, who on occasion went before the Muslim court to complain of mistreatment by their priests and bishops. Interestingly, they were the only religious minority community to use that forum to seek redress from their clergy, a symptom of their assimilation, or perhaps of their frustration. In one such case, registered on September 3, 1678, a group of Greek Orthodox Arabs asked that the Porte remove their bishop because he could not even speak Arabic, a sign of the linguistic rift that separated the community from its leadership.[64]

In contrast to the Melkites, who had always been in Aleppo, the other three sects were largely immigrant communities. The Maronites originated in northern Syria, but over the centuries had migrated into the Syrian and Lebanese coastal mountains. Early in the sixteenth century, they had reestablished their links to the West, which had lapsed after the Crusading period. By 1600, they had become prominent as agents and translators for the various European communities, as well as being active in the Levant trade in their own right through their domination of the cultivation and marketing of silk in Mount Lebanon. We cannot be sure to what degree Aleppo's Maronites were immigrants drawn into the city by the trade with the West or simply descendants of those early followers of Saint Marun who had steadfastly remained in northern Syria. But whatever their origin, their numbers were never high, although the community was clearly the most prosperous of the four Christian sects in the city.

If we have trouble ascertaining the origins of Aleppo's Maronites, we have fairly good documentation for the migration of Suryanis and Greek Orthodox Arabs that accompanied the major influx of Armenians into the city in the seventeenth century. Figure 1, above, shows that between

1640 and 1740 the number of adult Christian males in the city of Aleppo more than trebled, which, when compared with the overall population trends of the century, indicates a major migration was taking place. In the early part of the century, the migrants seem to have consisted largely of Melkite Arabs from Hama, Homs, and Tripoli. Just as there was a separate *taife* of Sasuni Armenians, there were groups of Orthodox Arabs from Homs and Hama who maintained a corporate identity separate from that of the larger Aleppo Orthodox community.[65] But like the Sasunis, mentioned earlier, these communities seemed to have been absorbed by the larger community over time.

By the latter part of the century, however, the tide of immigration had shifted and was coming largely from Anatolia, including not only Armenians but Suryanis from the towns of Mardin and Diyarbakır. The migration of such large groups of people undoubtedly created social and economic problems for both the migrants and the host community. Like the Armenians, however, the Suryanis managed to create a specialized niche for themselves, in their particular case, in Aleppo's famed textile industry. By the middle of the seventeenth century, they had established their own guilds for making the striped cloth, called *ʿirāqī*, for which they became famous.[66] Aigen tells us the Suryanis dominated the silk-weaving industry as well. This industry was largely centered in the new Christian suburb of Judayda, which had expanded north of the city's wall in the seventeenth century and in which both Suryanis and Armenians resided.[67]

The relationship between the various communities was far from harmonious, however, even if they often shared the same quarters of the city. This was due in part to the natural mistrust a true believer has for someone considered to be a heretic and in part to the linguistic differences that separated some of the communities. But it was also derived from Ottoman policy toward the Christian sects. Although much has been made of the functioning of the *millet* system (the officially sanctioned autonomous religious bodies within the empire), neither the term nor the concept seems to have been much in use by Ottoman officialdom in Aleppo. On the contrary, the usual attitude was summed up in the expression "al-Kufr kullu milla wāḥida" ("unbelief constitutes one nation"), voiced by the judges in several intercommunal disputes taken to the city's courts for ajudication.[68] In practice, this meant that the Ottomans levied the special taxes (*avarız, tekalif,* and so on) on the Christians of the city as a whole and left it up to them to determine the breakdown of how much each community would pay.

When the extraordinary taxes were first imposed, there seems to have been a certain degree of equanimity among the sects, as representatives of the Greek Orthodox, Armenian, and Suryani churches stated in 1642 that all extraordinary taxes would be divided equally among them. But as the taxes increased and were imposed with greater frequency, the goodwill broke down and disputes arose over the fairness of the apportionment of the shares each time a new tax was levied. It would seem that the Ottomans themselves eventually had to intervene to separate the bickering communities and established a schedule that put the largest share of the taxes on the Greek Orthodox community.[69]

The compromise imposed from above seemed doomed from the start, however. While the Orthodox leadership acknowledged their community's superior numbers, they said these were offset by the large number of indigent Melkites and by the fact many of their flock had evinced the the propensity to "turn Frank."[70] The complaints registered by the Orthodox representatives concerning the defection of their membership underscores an underlying theme of the history of Christian Aleppo in the Ottoman Empire: the growing defection of Christians from the Eastern-rite churches to ones that were in communion with Rome during the course of the seventeenth and eighteenth centuries. But despite the claims of the Melkites, this shifting of allegiances affected all the three traditional churches.

As early as 1625,[71] French Catholic orders had sent missionaries to Aleppo with the expressed purpose of winning adherents to Catholicism from the established Eastern-rite churches. This movement was strengthened during the reign of Louis XIV, when the number of Catholic priests assigned to the French consul in the city rose from eight in 1670 to twenty-eight in 1681.[72] This missionary activity produced impressive results. By the third quarter of the seventeenth century, it was estimated that three-quarters of the Suryani population of Aleppo had become Catholic. There were significant numbers of converts from the other sects as well, but in the lists of converts kept by the French missionaries in the second half of the seventeenth century, the overwhelming majority were Suryanis. This impression is supported by a British estimate in 1750 that only ten percent of the Melkites had become Catholic.[73]

The Uniate movement, as this change in religious identity has come to be called by the Vatican, was revolutionary in the way that it affected Aleppo's Christians. Like the Protestant movement in Europe, it called on each individual believer to make a personal commitment whether to accept the new dispensation or not, offering an option for change that might carry with it economic advancement, if some degree of social isolation. In part, the movement's attraction was rooted in the frustration of the Greek Orthodox laity with their Greek clergy. This was recognized by the Catholic missionaries, who allowed the local communicants to use their vernacular, Arabic, as their liturgical language, three centuries before Vatican II would allow other Catholics to use theirs. But the fact that the movement also drew on Suryani converts undermines an interpretation based solely on a linguistic rift between laity and clergy in the see of Antioch.[74]

The older established churches viewed the growth of the Uniate movement among their communicants with alarm, and they petitioned the Ottoman authorities to help them stem its tide. The Ottoman government responded to their petitions by issuing orders forbidding the Christian *raʿāyā* from changing their sect. Typical of such decrees was an order from the Porte to the governor of Aleppo registered on May 3, 1709. It reported that the French were converting members of the Melkite, Jacobite, and Armenian sects to that of the Franks, although this had been implicitly forbidden by imperial decree. It went on to order the governor to investigate the matter further and to appoint a representative from each of the three sects affected. His duty was to inform on any cocommunicant who had turned "Frank." Any who did so would be banished from the city.[75]

In spite of the belief that all infidels were united by their unbelief, the Ottoman authorities chose to support the established traditional church hierarchies in the interest of preserving order. In at least one case, Suryanis who had been apprehended attending a Latin mass were ordered imprisoned in Adana.[76] Despite this dramatic retribution for the practice of freedom of conscience, there seems to have been more than a bit of benign neglect coloring the government's response, however, as the growth of the number of Catholics under its nose attests. This was partly a result of counterpressure exerted by the French on behalf of their protégés. But it was also due, in no small part, to a genuine lack of concern on the authorities' part for the internal divisions of the Christian communities, as long as those communities continued to pay the taxes assessed on them.

This government policy of noninvolvement, however, was undermined by one of the prime incentives that the French were willing to offer some Catholic converts: the legal protection of the consulate signified by an imperial decree *(berat)*. This patent exempted the holder from the taxes and other obligations imposed on Ottoman subjects. The European consuls in the Ottoman Empire had long received the right of having their local employees exempted from taxation under the provisions of the capitulatory agreements. Originally this exemption only included the consular interpreters, or dragomans as they were called in the Levant, who were a necessary part of conducting business in the Ottoman Empire for the knowledge they had of both the local languages and business practices. The dragomans serving the various consuls were largely recruited from the local Christian community, although Jews and Levantine Italians sometimes held the post as well. The primary requirement for a candidate for the post, called a *Giovanni di Lingua* by the English factors, was knowledge of Turkish, Arabic, and Italian, the commercial lingua franca, although literacy was also sometimes a prerequisite. Although the English factors frequently complained that the Italian spoken in Aleppo was almost incomprehensible to anyone who knew correct Italian, it served its purpose as a trade language.[77]

As the consul's activities expanded in the Middle East, however, the exemption was also extended to include local agents who worked for the Europeans in smaller commercial centers. For the most part these agents were local Christians, such as the Jauna family, who served as agents for the English in both Cyprus and Tripoli, and Jean Cheloub and later Paul Maashouk in Acre and Ramla,[78] who handled English commercial affairs, as well as their own private trading operations.

While the French used the granting of *berat*s to win friends among the Christian population of Aleppo, the English were extremely reluctant to follow a similar policy. Nonetheless, in a letter written on September 30, 1737, their consul in Aleppo discussed the policy of granting the title of honorary dragoman to local merchants by the Dutch and the French. He said there were many such cases and that it did not seem to harm either country's interests.[79] This ambivalence was unique, however, and most letters from the company factors show a clearly articulated fear that such practices could in the end only be injurious to English merchants, who would invariably find themselves in competition with the "honorary" Englishmen. It was not until 1749 that the English consulate in Aleppo even expanded its staff of dragomans from two to three, although after that date the numbers seem to have increased beyond that. By comparison, the Tuscans and Venetians, much smaller trading communities, sponsored in 1752 ninteen honorary dragomans between them, all merchants.[80]

We cannot be sure how many Christians in Aleppo were able to achieve this special status, but according to al-Ghazzī, the Ottomans, concerned about the possible defection of Christian taxpayers to the Frankish camp, sent an inquiry in 1796–97, only to find that there were 1,500 Christians exempted by *berat* in Aleppo.[81] These numbers were undoubtedly inflated, however, as consular reports submitted by the British consul in the city in 1847 stated that there were 19 honorary Britons, 13 honorary Russians and Prussians, 10 honorary Austrians and Swedes, 13 honorary Sardinians, and 54 honorary Frenchmen at that time. This census had come after another complaint from the Porte concerning the inflated number of dragomans who were working for the Europeans.[82]

We suspect that the figures for the late eighteenth century weren't so different. It would seem unreasonable that without strong Ottoman action, the number of those holding *berats* would have shrunk so dramatically in the space of fifty years. Families, after all, were loath to surrender the priceless *berat* even after the letitimate holder had died.[83] Nonetheless, whatever their total number, the honorary Franks were almost invariably merchants able to take advantage of consular protection to promote their business interests, and as such, their economic impact on the city was undoubtedly much greater than their numbers indicate.

Proof of this contention was the rise to prominence during the eighteenth century of several important Christian merchant families in Aleppo, all of whom enjoyed the privilege of being *beratlı* (possessing a *berat* establishing them as being protected by the foreign flag under which they served). With this improved status came a new title employed in the court records, *ḥawāja*. This term, an Arabic corruption of the Persian honorific *kh^{w}aja*, first appears in its original Persian form in the seventeenth century, when it was applied to the Armenian merchants from Iran by the European sources. Interestingly enough, that form of address was not employed by the court records themselves when referring to the

Armenians. By the middle of the next century, however, the title was attached by those who kept the court records to the names of prominent non-Muslim merchants in Aleppo, corresponding to the use of *fakhr al-tujjār* for prominent Muslim merchants. Although the majority of those to whom this form of address was applied were, in fact, local Christian *beratlıs*, those so honored also included Jews and Christians who did not enjoy *beratlı* status and even the Europeans themselves. Subtly, the language had expanded to indicate the new social and economic status the local minorities had won for themselves.

Two of the most successful Christian merchants of the period, Shukrī ʿĀʾida (Aide, Aidy, or Aidur in the English sources) and his son Jirjīs (Giorgio to the English), were both *beratlıs* and *ḥawājas*, proof of the economic advantages a *berat* conferred on its possessor. The father first made his appearance in the Levant Company records in 1734,[84] and soon after became one of the leading merchants in Syrian silk with whom the company dealt. In 1747, the son Jirjīs was appointed to be a dragoman for the English consul in Aleppo,[85] but soon after ran afoul of the Ottoman authorities. On June 3, 1750, he was arrested by them on the charge that he had aided the governor of Baghdad in the sale of goods the governor had appropriated illegally from the Baghdad customs house.

The consul in Aleppo suspected, however, that behind the arrest lay the machinations of one of the consulate's other dragomans, Yūsuf Dīb. Dīb was a Melkite who in 1749 was able to effect the arrest of several members of the city's Catholic clergy and laity. The consul had reprimanded him for doing this, even though the group was only held for forty-eight hours, but the consul, in turn, had been overruled by the English ambassador in Istanbul, who informed him that it was not necessarily to the disadvantage of English interests to have a check placed on the "Papists." Dīb had earlier written to the ambassador questioning the loyalty of Jirjīs, who was Catholic, and apparently planted a seed of doubt about the advisability of having Catholics in the employ of England. It was seemingly the ugly specter of Catholic-Melkite rivalry that lay at the bottom of Jirjīs's arrest, or at least that is what the consul feared. He may have been right, as the English embassy, despite repeated requests from Aleppo, was slow to effect Jirjīs's release. It was only after the consul promised to make good the fine/bribe of 7,500 *ghurūsh* on his own, should the company's board of directors fail to approve the expenditure, that the ambassador interceded and effected Jirjīs's release in Istanbul in June of 1751.[86]

After his release, Jirjīs returned to the company's employ, although the rivalry between him and Yūsuf Dīb continued to simmer. The conflict between the two families seems to have had economic as well as religious causes, however. The ʿĀʾida family, besides serving the English, had an extensive network of trade that included the operations of Shukrī's brother Ṣafar, and Jirjīs's cousin ʿAbdallah in Istanbul. In addition, Jirjīs was one of the most extensive property owners in the city of Aleppo in the mid–eighteenth century.[87]

Yūsuf Dīb was also active in various endeavors, including the subletting of the *malikane* of the village of Baṭīyā in Darkūsh for a number of years,[88] and he most probably was envious of both the ʿĀʾidas' wealth and Jirjīs's position as head dragoman for the Levant Company. Clearly the position as head dragoman for England opened the door to many a commercial opportunity of which Yūsuf could rightly be jealous. The English consul had written in 1752 that the reason there was a need for an expanded number of dragomans was that no one was willing to devote himself full-time to working for the English, as anyone who might be qualified was sure to have outside business interests to which he would want to attend first.[89]

The court records amply demonstrate that this was, in fact, truer than perhaps the consul even suspected. It was not only the dragomans for the English who were able to use their position to advance their commercial ventures, as the dragomans for the French and the Dutch consuls were also prominent in the court records as merchants and financiers, yet those serving the English were undoubtedly the most successful. But then England was the leading Western commercial presence in the city in the years before 1750.[90]

It was not just the Christians with *berat*s who moved into commerce in the seventeenth century, however, but Syrian Christians in general. As seen in Figure 2 above, Christian Aleppines were increasingly important as commercial agents working for Muslims capitalists. The reason for this transformation is not entirely clear, but it undoubtedly did not lie with the Europeans alone. In part, it may have been conditioned by the tensions between Iran and the Ottoman Empire discussed above. Nonetheless, as many of the agents were Syrian Christians rather than

Armenians, the factor of being favored by a merchant diaspora, or the Iranian shah, should be at least partially discounted. Also, Syrian Christians were to be found in *muḍāraba* arrangements that sent them to India, Anatolia, and Egypt, areas where if anything they would have faced the disadvantage of being subject to a higher rate of taxation than were Muslim commercial agents.

But for whatever reason, a once-disadvantaged community had apparently developed astounding business acumen to the degree that by the middle of the eighteenth century, Syrian Christians were assuming many of the commercial roles formerly filled by Muslims, due in part to their willingness to adapt to new commercial realities and perhaps in part to a better education. The Jesuits had established a school in the city in the seventeenth century in an attempt to win converts away from the traditional churches. The school's curriculum included Arabic, Greek, and Italian, all of which would have equipped its students for the changing face of Syria's commercial life, which increasingly involved Europeans.[91]

In addition, trade with Egypt provided a sector in which the Christians emerged with a clear-cut advantage that enabled them to surpass their Muslim competition. Throughout most of the seventeenth century, the eastern Mediterranean had remained a largely Ottoman lake insofar as the control of coastal shipping was concerned. While European vessels had a virtual monopoly over commercial shipping between the Middle East and Europe, the coastal trade along the Syrian coast to Egypt, Cyprus, and Anatolia was in the hands of Ottoman subjects. The small coastal freighters that plied this trade were largely manned by Cypriot Greeks, but participation by Syrian sailors, as well, was not uncommon.[92]

An incentive for the continued domination of the trade by local seamen was provided by Ottoman law. From a case registered in Aleppo on October 23, 1640, we learn that an Armenian merchant from Julfa, on his return from Europe, first stopped in Cyprus and then transported his merchandise from there to the Syrian port of Payas on an Ottoman vessel. The reason for this seemingly roundabout itinerary was that the tax rate was lower than if he had come straight to Syria on a European ship.[93] Along those same lines, a provision in the customs regulations for Aleppo, issued on April 2, 1702, stated that henceforth Venetian merchants arriving in the city from Istanbul, Izmir, Cyprus, Tripoli, or Alexandria would have to pay customs duties in Aleppo, as if they were arriving from outside the boundaries of the empire. The implication was that previously they had been exempt.[94] Yet a further incentive to using Ottoman ships, before the tax code change in 1702, was that the European consuls were given the right to place an additional tax on merchandise arriving in Iskenderun on ships flying the flags of their nations. On the other hand, European merchants on Ottoman vessels were subject only to Ottoman internal taxes, which in some cases were lower.[95]

By the early eighteenth century, this situation had been reversed. References to Ottoman ships plying the coastal routes cease in both the travelers' accounts and the Aleppo court records, to be replaced by indications that the sea transport of the eastern Mediterranean had largely become dominated by ships flying various European flags. If it had been economically advantageous to employ Ottoman ships in the seventeenth century, it must be asked what considerations led to the erosion of their previously paramount position.

A prime reason for the change in preference, insofar as Ottoman merchants were concerned, may have been fear of piracy. The travelers of the previous century had often remarked on the danger posed to sea transport by corsairs, and one English factor had even likened the danger of the beduin on the desert to the corsairs on the sea.[96] By the eighteenth century, this reality of the sea trade had not improved, but those participating in the plundering had changed.

In the seventeenth century, the pirates were just as likely to have been North African as Tuscan, and a European flag offered no real protection. In the eighteenth century, the corsairs were almost exclusivly European, preying on Ottoman vessels as an extension of a holy war for glory and booty. This gave the Ottomans even less leverage in dealing with pirates than they had previously held, being reduced to checking European vessels in their ports for stolen merchandise and enslaved Muslims.[97] At the same time, the advantage of ships flying European colors improved dramatically. The English, in particular, developed a reputation for dealing sternly with piracy, and it did not take long for Middle Eastern merchants to realize that their goods had a better chance of making it to port if they traveled under the Union Jack.[98]

Coupled with this incentive was the growing awareness on the part of the Levant Company factors that a profit was to be made in the coastal trade. As early as 1635, the English consul in Aleppo had won the right from the Porte to collect consulage fees from Ottoman Muslims and *dhimmīs* who shipped their goods on English vessels, an indication that the use of English boats in the coastal trade was already established.[99] At the time, the practice provided an economic incentive for the English by earning money for the ships, which had come with broadcloth from England, in the slack time while they were waiting to take silk back to London.

This coastal trade, within the Ottoman economic demiworld, included the transport of olive oil and soap from Tripoli and Iskenderun to Istanbul, where either could demand double the price it cost in Syria;[100] of tobacco (which had become a major agricultural product of the Latakia region) and raw silk to Egypt; and of rice, cotton, and coffee from Egypt to Syria. These products were bulky, relatively low-priced staple items, for which ships were particularly well suited. Previously such goods had been carried by caravan, and it is obvious that the increasing use of European shipping affected not only Ottoman coastal sailors' livelihood but the internal caravan trade as well.

The Ottomans perceived a possible threat in this shift in transport patterns. But this concern was not for the livelihood of the local transportation workers; rather, they feared that once loaded on to European ships, commodities such as rice and coffee, which were forbidden by imperial decree from being exported out of the realm, would end up in Europe. Orders were issued in 1716, for example, expressly forbidding the shipping of those two commodities within the empire by European vessels.[101] Significantly, the document listed the reason why European ships were being chosen in the first place: the local merchants' fear of pirates. Prohibitions such as that, however, seemed to have been largely ignored, and the decline of Ottoman commercial shipping continued more or less unabated.

The growth of a European presence in the coastal shipping of the Levant in the early eighteenth century offered unprecedented opportunities for Syrian Christian merchants. The French undoubtedly favored their protégés, the Catholics, above all others,[102] but even English captains looked with more favor on Christian passengers than on Muslim ones. This was due to their fear that any contract entered into with a Muslim would be struck down in a Muslim court. Citing this apprehension, a general order was issued by the Levant Company on December 23, 1673, explicitly forbidding the transport of Muslims or their goods on English ships.[103] Yet as orders were issued—for Iskenderun in 1698 and for

Damiette in 1704—to the effect that consulage fees were to be collected from Muslim merchants boarding English ships,[104] we would assume that Muslims were not in fact effectively banned from English shipping. There was, nonetheless, a clear-cut preference for Christian merchants, as the English felt, rightly or wrongly, that local Christians had even less chance of getting a favorable hearing in the Muslim courts than did the Europeans.

According to the English, the Syrian Christian merchants felt a corresponding preference for the Levant Company as shipping agents over the French, as is stated in a letter written September 17, 1725:

We have been often solicited by some Christian merchants of substance and reputation for a good ship to be employed in the tobacco trade between Latichea and Damieta which would not fail of constant employment, but then it is absolutely necessary that the commander be a man of ability and probity, for 'tis that they want chiefly, for shipping they have enough but the French, they can put no confidence in. . . .[105]

This trust engendered many a contract between Syrian Christian merchants and British shippers. A good example of such was registered by the Levant Company factors on February 23, 1732. In it, two Syrian Christian merchants, identified as Samʿān Qaṣṣāb and Naṣr Allah w. Sulaymān, hired a ship to transport 100 bales of tobacco from Latakia to Damiette and then to ship an unspecified cargo back to either Latakia or Payas. The cost of the hire was 2,000 *ghurūsh,* 500 to be paid at the beginning of the trip and 1,500 upon the return, plus an additional charge of 10 *ghurūsh* for every day over 70 that the trip entailed.[106] Despite all this apparent goodwill, the English found that their ships were too large to be of use to most merchants who plied the coastal trade, and it became increasingly harder for them to compete with the smaller French vessels. By 1735, they had decided to withdraw from the competition altogether, leaving coastal transport to French and Aegean Greek boats.[107] This development gave local Christian merchants an even greater advantage, as the French preference for Christians over Muslims had already become a feature of their national policy in the Middle East.

Besides the obvious boon that the reversal of patterns of shipping in the eastern Mediterranean brought to them, the local Christians were aided by the changes in the nature of the Levant trade that occurred over the first half of the eighteenth century. The decline in the export of

Iranian silk and the rise of exports of locally produced cotton and silk required merchants who would buy from the producers—almost invariably Muslim in the case of cotton, often Christian in that of silk—and then sell it in Tripoli, Sidon, and Aleppo to the Europeans. This contact did not necessarily militate against participation by Muslim merchants, as one has only to glance at the ledgers kept by the Levant Company factors to find Muslim merchants involved in the trade. Nonetheless, it is also clear that, partly because of the inclination of local Christians to go into commerce, now that the doors had seemingly been opened, and the corresponding disinclination on the part of many Muslims to deal directly with the Franks, coupled with a European mistrust of doing business with Muslims in the first place, all produced a favorable climate for Christian Arab participation.

Christian Syrians had begun going to Egypt to trade in the seventeenth century, but from the evidence supplied by the court records, it would seem that they did not dominate the trade at the time. By the next century, this had changed. While Muslim Syrians continued to trade with Egypt, their activities were outpaced by those of their Christian countrymen.[108] Similarly, purchases of Syrian silk by Levant Company factors in Syria in the first half of the eighteenth century show a preponderance of Christian names, although not to the exclusion of Muslims. Due to their willingness to do business with the Franks, Syrian Christians found themselves in a new position of economic importance that no one would have considered possible a century and a half before.

The Armenians, Sephardi Jews, and Syrian Christians, Catholics and otherwise, all represent trading diasporas in the sense of the term suggested by Curtin. To them might be added the English Levant Company factors, who supply an illustrative example of the metamorphosis of a traditional trading diaspora, supported by the bonds of religion or ethnicity, to one built on strictly profit motives, the forerunner of the multinational corporation as it were. But whatever their composition, the fact that these diasporas became crucial to the trade of the Levant at all seems to indicate that changes were occurring in the trading world of the Levant.

To be a successful merchant in the Levant trade in the eighteenth century it was no longer quite enough to be a member of the *umma*. Barriers had been erected that no longer allowed Muslims to trade freely in the House of Islam, and alien ships increasingly controlled the transport of both the eastern Mediterranean and the Arabian Sea. A change in the trading patterns engendered by European competition and the decline of Iran's economy meant that trade had to be carried on with the Franks. While this did not necessarily prohibit Muslims from engaging in commerce, it did give the individuals who knew the Franks' languages and business methods a distinct advantage. While Syria's Christians found a brave new world that offered them opportunities of which they had not dreamed before, Syria's Muslims found their world growing ever smaller and more circumscribed.

NOTES

1. Philip Curtin, *Cross-Cultural Trade in World History* (Cambridge, 1984).
2. For accounts of these developments, see Chaudhuri, *Trade and Civilisation in the Indian Ocean,* and C. B. Boxer, *The Portuguese Sea-Borne Empire, 1415–1825* (London, 1969).
3. Discussed in M. A. Meilink-Roelofsz, *Asian Trade and European Influence in the Indonesian Archipelago between 1500 and about 1630* (The Hague, 1964).
4. S. Turan, "Venedik'te Türk ticaret merkezi," *Belletin* 32:247–83.
5. Inalcik, "The Ottoman Economic Mind," pp. 213–14; Andras Riedlmayer, "Ottoman-Safavid Relations and the Anatolian Trade Routes: 1603–1618," *The Turkish Studies Association Bulletin* 5:7–10.
6. Venice 11:317.
7. Among others, Chaudhuri, *The Trading World of Asia and the English East India Company;* Om Prakash, *The Dutch East India Company and the Economy of Bengal* (Princeton, 1986); Niels Steensgaard, *The Asian Trade Revolution.*
8. Inalcik, "Imtiyazat," EI^2.
9. MM 2475:76–78, 20 Ramazan 1054/20 Nov. 1644; MM 7326:43, 1 Cemaziyelevvel 1070/14 Jan. 1660; MM 2742:93–94, 18 Ramazan 1076/25 March 1666.
10. For a comparison of the internal organization of the different nations," see Steensgaard, "Consuls and Nations in the Levant from 1570 to 1650," *Scandinavian Economic History Review* 15:13–55.
11. Russell 2:2.
12. Aleppo 2:108; Aleppo 42:130–31; Aleppo 50:275.
13. Russell 2:3.
14. SP 110/25:132, 22 Dec. 1725; SP 110/25:138, 24 Dec. 1725; SP 110/72:28ff., 20 Sept. 1753.
15. SP 110/32:73, 27 June 1754.
16. MD 79:408, 17 Şevval 1019/2 Jan. 1610.
17. Needless to say, it was not only Indians who were deserting their wives but Egyptians, Iranians, Iraqis, and Türkmen as well. Aleppo 17:32, 41, 61, 70, 99, 187, and Aleppo 18:827.
18. Aleppo 23:351.
19. W. M. Floor, "The Merchants *(tujjar)* of Qajar Iran," *Zeitschrift der Deutschen Morgenländischen Gesellschaft* 126:101–35. Abbé Carré, *The Travels of the Abbé Carré in India and the Near East, 1672 to 1674.* 3 vols., The Hakluyt Society, 2nd ser. nos. 95–97, 3:825.
20. Aleppo 21:213.

21. Aleppo 24:202, 212; MM 2765:100, 4 Ramazan 1055/24 Oct. 1645.

22. Inalcik, "Capital Formation in the Ottoman Empire," p. 111.

23. Fahri Dalsar, *Türk Sanayi ve Ticaret Tarihinde Bursa'da İpekçilik* (Istanbul, 1960), pp. 133–36.

24. William Biddulph, cited in *Purchas His Pilgrimes* ed. Samuel Purchas, The Hakluyt Society Extra Ser. vol. 8 (1905):274–75.

25. R. W. Ferrier, "The Armenians and the East India Company in Persia in the Seventeenth and Early Eighteenth Centuries," *Economic History Review*, 2nd ser., 26:38–62; Vartan Gregorian, "Minorities in Isfahan: The Armenian Community of Isfahan 1587–1722," *Iranian Studies* 7:652–80.

26. Keram Krevonian, "Marchands Arméniens au XVIIe siècle," *Cashiers du Monde Russe et Sovietique* 16:199–244; Silvio van Rooy, "Armenian Merchant Habits as Mirrored in the 17th–18th Century Amsterdam Documents," *Revue des Études Arméniennes* 3:347–57.

27. Curtin, pp. 182–206.

28. Kevonian, endnote 93, p. 231. Polonyalı Simeon, an Armenian resident of the Polish city of Łwow, visited Aleppo in 1617 and confirms this impression, saying that the Julfa community comprised the majority of the three hundred Armenian households in the city at that time. Polonyalı Simeon, *Polonyalı Simeon'un Seyahatnamesi, 1608–1619* (Istanbul, 1964), p. 155.

29. Avedis Sanjian, *The Armenian Communities of Syria under Ottoman Domination* (Cambridge, 1965), p. 261; J. M. Rogers, *Islamic Art and Design, 1500–1700* (London, 1983), pp. 41–44; Rabbath 1:54; Aleppo 22:429.

30. Polonyalı Simeon, p. 93; see also Ronald Jennings, "Urban Population in Anatolia in the Sixteenth Century," *IJMES* 7:21–57.

31. Aleppo 2:234.

32. Aleppo 20:284.

33. MM 9838:21, 12 Müharrem 1064/3 Dec. 1653.

34. Aleppo 25:210.

35. MM 9850:141, 16 Zilhicce 1073/23 July 1663; Aleppo 34:206.

36. MM 3774:38, 24 Müharrem 1074/29 Aug. 1663; also MM 9838:21 cited above.

37. MM 3498:45, 1107/1695–96.

38. Aleppo 34:206.

39. AS 1:10; MD 100:133, Evail-i Şevval 1101/July 1690; AS 2:100.

40. Aleppo 31:170; Aleppo 85:185; Aleppo 3:673 (an agreement among the Armenian community dated 1655, by which the Sasuni bakers were exempted from contributing to the *tekalif* taxes assessed on the community as a whole); Sanjian, pp. 52–53, although his assertion that the guild "practically monopolized the sale of wheat as well as the baking and distribution of bread and confectionary" seems overstated, given the evidence of both extensive grain trade handled by Muslims and the existence of largely Muslim bakers' and confectioners' guilds in the city. Aleppo 27:116 (Muslim millers); Aleppo 27:463 (Muslim confectioners); Aleppo 3:334 (millers and bakers).

41. SP 105/114:411, 27 Nov. 1693.

42. SP 110/23:317, 2 March 1706.

43. SP 110/29:167, 23 March 1750.

44. SP 105/116:337, 29 April 1719.

45. An agreement between the Netherlands and Shah Safi in 1631 guaranteed extraterritorial privileges to subjects of the shah in the Netherlands. J. C. Hurewitz, ed., *Diplomacy in the Near and Middle East: A Documentary Record, 1535–1919,* (New York, 1972), pp. 20–21.

46. SP 105/114:185, 21 June 1699; SP 105/115:103, 21 May 1697; SP 105/117:162, 13 Jan. 1735; SP 110/22:89, 22 July 1701.

47. SP105/115:116, 31 Oct. 1716; SP 105/116:89, 25 Feb. 1713.

48. For a more complete discussion of the Italian and Ottoman Jewish communities, see Jonathan Israel, *European Jewry in the Age of Mercantilism, 1550–1750* (Oxford, 1985); Aryeh Shmuelevitz, *The Jews of the Ottoman Empire in the Late Fifteenth and the Sixteenth Centuries* (Leiden, 1984).

49. MM 9849:127, 9 Şevval 1082/8 Feb. 1672. This marks one of the earliest usages by the Ottomans of the term *araban,* usually associated with the beduin, to mean simply Arabic speakers.

50. McGowan, pp. 82–83.

51. A similar distinction was made in Palestine. Amnon Cohen and Bernard Lewis, *Population and Revenue in the Towns of Palestine in the Sixteenth Century* (Princeton, 1978), p. 156.

52. SP 105/113:263, 23 June 1671.

53. SP 105/116:89, 25 Feb. 1713.

54. SP 105/114:639, 11 May 1694; SP 110/20:89, 5 July 1696.

55. SP 105/116:446, 19 Oct. 1722.

56. Israel, p. 162; François Charles-Roux, *Les échelles de Syrie et de Palestine au XVIIIe siècle* (Paris, 1978), p. 48.

57. Necdet Kurdakul, *Osmanlı Devleti'nde Ticaret Antlaşmaları ve Kapitülasyonlar* (Istanbul, 1981), pp. 77–83.

58. SP 110/23:115, 16 Aug. 1704.

59. Charles-Roux, p. 48.

60. Russell 2:8–9; Aleppo 95:28.

61. Russell gave breakdowns for the various communities as follows: Greeks (sic), 13,500; Armenians, 6,750; Syrians (sic), 3,750; Maronites, 3,030 (Russell 2:28). These proportions compare favorably to the *jizya* totals for the city listed in a court case in 1754: Greek Orthodox, 3,418; Armenians, 1,730; Suryani, 1,109; Maronites, 956 (Aleppo 85:130–31).

62. Biddulph, p. 275; Teixeira, p. 116.

63. The most satisfying discussion of the Uniate movement remains Robert Haddad, *Syrian Christians in a Muslim Society* (Princeton, 1970); see also Robert Betts, *Christians in the Arab East* (Atlanta, 1975), and Charles Frazee, *Catholics and Sultans: The Church and the Ottoman Empire* (London, 1983).

64. Aleppo 34:39.

65. Aleppo 20:289; Aleppo 22:121.

66. Aleppo 21:210.

67. Aigen, p. 75.

68. Aleppo 20:28; Aleppo 80:179.

69. Aleppo 23:147.

70. Aleppo 45:75; Aleppo 85:131–32; Aleppo 87:216–17.

71. Frazee, p. 132.

72. Warren Lewis, *Levantine Adventurer: The Travels and Missions of the Chevallier d'Arvieux, 1653–1697* (New York, 1962), p. 41.

73. John Joseph, *Muslim-Christian Relations and Inter-Christian Rivalries in the Middle East* (Albany, 1983), p. 40. Rabbath 2:87–88; SP 110/29:25, 18 April 1749.

74. While a process of Arabization was undoubtedly going on among the Suryani migrants in Aleppo (Russell 2:33), there is no indication that there was the same sort of linguistic and cultural friction in the community as among the Melkites. Rather, it would

seem that the solidarity offered by the new faith was attractive to newly displaced persons. This interpretation is supported by the fact that while large numbers of Suryanis in Aleppo switched their allegiances to the Uniate church, the movement made little headway in the migrants' ancestral villages in the region of Mardin province. Frazee, pp. 207–09; Betts, p. 95.

75. Aleppo 2:27.

76. Aleppo 51:95.

77. SP 105/116:487–88, 16 Dec. 1724, approval of funds to buy books for the young dragoman in training, "the Greek Anastius," with which to learn to read and write Turkish and Arabic; SP 105/117:41, 16 Nov. 1731; SP 110/23:322, 6 April 1706.

78. SP 110/20:50–51, 3 June 1702; SP 110/22:307, 29 June 1702; SP 110/23:73, 3 May 1704; SP 110/23:139, 12 Oct. 1704. Amnon Cohen identifies Maashouk as a Dutchman, but this seems improbable. Holland did not maintain a national as consul in Aleppo in the first decade of the eighteenth century, and it would seem unlikely it would have done so in the much less significant trading center of Acre. Also, the family name indicates a local rather than a Netherlands origin for the merchant. Cohen, *Palestine in the 18th Century* (Jerusalem, 1973), pp. 12–13.

79. SP 110/26:246, 30 Sept. 1737.

80. SP 105/116:487, 13 Dec. 1722; SP 110/23:131, 17 Aug. 1704; SP 110/29:36, 3 June 1750; SP 110/29:116, n.d. In volume 78 of the Aleppo court registers, which covers the year 1751, there are five individuals identified, in various cases, as being dragomans for the English consul.

81. al-Ghazzī 3:311. This figure is supported by documents preserved in the Istanbul archives. Ali Bağış, *Osmanlı Ticaretinde Gayri Müslimler* (Istanbul, 1983), p. 44. The court records provide some indication that perhaps some individuals were being registered as *beratlı* without the consuls' knowledge. In a case heard in 1753, a dragoman for the Netherlands consul claimed that an individual was exempt from taxes as he was his servant. Other Christians, however, testified that the man was, in fact, a weaver, who earned his livelihood from that trade and was, therefore, liable to contribute to the taxes levied on the Christian community. The court asked the dragoman to produce evidence from the consul to confirm his story. When he could not do this, the weaver was denied tax-exempt status (Aleppo 80:259). This contrasts to other cases where when proof was produced that an individual was indeed employed as a servant by the dragoman, and hence a foreign consul, that individual was granted tax-exempt status (Aleppo 85:44, 50). Interestingly, it was the coreligionists of the persons claiming *beratlı* status who lodged the challenge in these cases.

82. FO 861/2: p. 3, no. 3, 14 Feb. 1846; p. 50, no. 11, 19 June 1847. Compare this to the eighty-four names listed in Ottoman documents in 1793 as being *beratlı* in Aleppo. Bağış, pp. 111–15.

83. SP 105/118:96, 17 Nov. 1748.

84. SP 110/27:111, 29 Dec. 1734.

85. SP 105/118:46, 18 Sept. 1747.

86. SP 110/29:25–29, 18 April 1749; SP 110/29:34, 25 Sept. 1749; SP 110/29:40, 3 June 1750; SP 110/29:49–51, 11 July 1750; SP 110/29:86, 14 June 1751; see also Abraham Marcus, "People and Property in Eighteenth Century Aleppo" (unpublished Ph.D. thesis, Columbia University, 1971), p. 158.

87. Marcus; Aleppo 78:106.

88. Aleppo 78:108, 121; Aleppo 80:162.

89. SP 110/29:116, n.d.

90. Aleppo 78:215; Aleppo 80:257; Aleppo 90:53.

91. Frazee, p. 133.
92. Polonyalı Simeon, p. 103; Aigen, pp. 115–16; d'Arvieux 1:237, 247.
93. Aleppo 22:17.
94. MM 3598: 29–30, 4 Zilkade 1113/2 April 1702.
95. Aleppo 20:115.
96. SP 110/12:11, 5 Jan. 1670.
97. SP 110/16:113, 20 Nov. 1689.
98. Haddad, p. 41.
99. Aleppo 20:115.
100. SP 110/15:12, 19 Feb. 1686; SP 110/15:50, 25 Jan. 1687.
101. Istanbul, Başbakanlık Arşivi, Cevdet. Maliye 2644, 25 Ramazan 1125/13 Sept. 1716.
102. Haddad; Thomas Philipp, "Jews and Christians: Their Changing Position in Politics and Economy in Eighteenth Century Egypt and Syria," in *Egypt and Palestine: A Millenium of Association (868–1948)*, ed. Amnon Cohen and Gabriel Baer (New York, 1984), and *The Syrians in Egypt*, Berliner Islamstudien 3 (Stuttgart, 1985).
103. SP 105/113:376, 23 Dec. 1693.
104. SP 105/114:45–46, 19 Oct. 1676; SP 105/114:175, 15 Feb. 1698; SP 110/23:32, 28 Jan. 1704.
105. SP 110/25:51, 17 Sept. 1725.
106. SP 110/27:72–73, 21 Feb. 1732.
107. Ralph Davis, *Aleppo and Devonshire Square* (London, 1967), p. 185.
108. Philipp, "Jews and Christians"; André Raymond, *Artisans et Commerçants au Caire au XVIII*[e] *siècle* (Damascus, 1973–75), pp. 482–96.

CHAPTER IV

The Commercial Institutions of a Caravan City

The markets of the Levant often appeared to the Western visitors of the seventeenth and eighteenth centuries as they do to the casual tourist today: tumultuous, disordered, and chaotic. Nonetheless, trade in Aleppo, as elsewhere in the Middle East, rested upon firmly established and, generally, well-organized commercial institutions. In turn, these institutions were crucial in providing a practical application of an Islamic theory of an economy, just as those of seventeenth- and eighteenth-century England were in implementing mercantilism.

Each of these institutions in Aleppo's commercial network contained its own set of internal rules and regulations that were enforced by the Muslim courts and the imperial Ottoman administration. So arrayed, they had provided for centuries a durable infrastructure for the conduct of trade. Most had their origins in the urban mercantile traditions of the region stretching back for millennia, but others gained new functions and responsibilities, or were given the force of legal writ, during the Ottoman period. Indeed, the highly centralized nature of the Ottoman state bureaucracy mandated a standardization of Aleppo's commercial life to such a degree that at least on the surface it came to resemble that of a dozen other major urban centers throughout the empire. There remained, however, one institution that was largely untouched by Ottoman regulations: the caravans.

THE CARAVANS

It has become a somewhat tired metaphor that the camel is the ship of the desert. Yet the image is useful in conjuring up the complexities involved in the cravan trade for peoples whose traditions are linked more to the sea than to the desert. After all, the beduin (used here to mean only Arabic-speaking nomads) often compare their desert to a sea, and as with the sea, travel across the desert required in premodern times a body of people who had expertise in its ways and in handling the vehicle of its traversal, the camel. Parallel to the freedom provided by the sailing ship, the camel provided its master with a liberty and mobility that made him an object of fear to those who did not possess that knowledge and at the same time rendered him indispensable to the city dwellers for interurban transport and communication. The beduin, like their free-booting maritime contemporaries, may have deserved their reputation for lawlessness, but as the technology of their trade remained a mystery to all others, they were a nuisance that had to be tolerated.

Given the monopoly held by the beduin on all things related to the desert, it comes as no surprise that the caravan trade in Aleppo was intricately linked to the nomadic tribes, beduin and others. Typically, Middle Eastern cities in the premodern period had a market zone outside the central area, where caravans were organized. These quarters have in most cases maintained their former aura of transience in the twentieth century by becoming the location of the intercity bus depots and garages, maintaining their function if not their exact appearance from the Ottoman period. Then, as now, these quarters were where formerly, or some cases still marginally, nomadic peoples, had settled.

In Aleppo, most of the activity generated by the caravans—the rental of animals, the making and marketing of tents, saddles, packs, and so on—was conducted along the eastern fringe of the town in the quarters of Bānqūsā, Tātārlar, and Qārliq.[1] As we have seen, the eastern suburbs grew extensively during the Ottoman period as Türkmen, Kurds, and beduin were drawn into the urban environment. Once there, these nomadic peoples often turned to trades relating to the caravans, as befit their traditions. The Türkmen and beduin, in particular, seem to have had a virtual monopoly over the rental of pack animals to travelers, with the Türkmen in control over the trade to the north and the beduin, naturally enough, dominating the routes to the east and south.

The actual size of the caravan depended, in large part, on the destination and the season of departure. Those traveling the desert routes, to either Iraq or the Hijaz, were much larger than those going into Anatolia. Tavernier's caravan in 1638 from Aleppo to Baghdad consisted of

600 camels and 400 men,[2] while one traveling in the opposite direction arrived in the city in 1610 with over 1,000 camels and 120 merchants,[3] and caravans reaching 2,000 camels were apparently not unusual.[4] Although large, the transdesert caravans going to Iraq only departed twice a year, while the Hijaz caravan timed to coincide with the hajj occurred only once annually.

The departure of the Baghdad caravans was linked to the seasons, with the most favored times being December and then again in late April or early May. The late spring departure season had the disadvantage of coming at a time when the daytime heat was already beginning to climb to unbearable highs, but it avoided the dangers of winter flash floods, which could be devastating.[5] A late spring departure also had the advantage of coming after the camels had foaled, but while there was still minimal pasturage remaining after the winter rains. The caravans originating in Baghdad left at roughly the same times as those leaving Aleppo, and travelers often reported meeting a caravan along the route, coming from the opposite direction.[6] The usual crossing time between Aleppo and Baghdad was forty-five days,[7] so that the beduin involved in the renting and care of the camels could make one return trip a year.

In contrast to the desert routes, the Anatolian caravans at times consisted of no more than a dozen animals, but they left the city at all times during the course of the year, not waiting for a large caravan to form. As the Anatolian caravans passed through inhabited areas, the procurement of supplies was not as great a problem as it was in the desert, so travelers did not require as many animals to carry their provisions. In addition, except in times of general unrest and insecurity, the traveler along the Anatolian routes faced only small bands of brigands, usually Kurds in the mountains to the north and east of Aleppo, as opposed to the large tribal contingents that the beduin were able to muster. As such, security of numbers was not as essential in Anatolia, although merchants often saw fit to hire armed guards to accompany them when traveling there.[8] In addition to being smaller and more frequent, the Anatolian caravans relied on mules as well as camels for portage, as mules were generally better suited to the mountainous terrain. Oddly, given the fact that a camel could obviously carry more weight, the cost of renting a mule for transport in the seventeenth century paralleled relatively closely the rate for camels.

Figure 4 contains examples of various fees charged for animal rental in the seventeenth and early eighteenth centuries as contained in the Aleppo court records. Although the evidence presented here is anecdotal at best, lacking consistent figures for either destination or time, it presents us with some idea of the approximate cost of caravan transport in the period.

The relatively low cost of such transport demonstrated by these examples, as well as by the testimony of European travelers,[9] and the fairly consistent price structure over the century are significant. Given that a merchant might load merchandise worth well over a 1,000 *ghurūsh* on a single animal,[10] the transportation costs he incurred were equal to less than 1% of the merchandise he was transporting. Conversely, bulky low-value merchandise such as grain was almost prohibitively expensive to transport by caravan. As grain prices throughout the period ranged between 10 and 20 *ghurūsh* a *qinṭar* in Aleppo, transportation costs could almost double the price to the consumer.

This cost differential was, in turn, reflected in the dietary habits prevalent in the cities of the Levant in the premodern period. While Egyptian rice was commonly eaten in Aleppo, especially by the wealthier classes, the city being only three days away from the coast and cheaper sea transport, it was an extreme luxury in the inland towns of Mosul and Diyarbakır. There the traditional *pilav*s were often made of bulghur wheat produced locally. Aleppo's easier access to seaborne grain provided it with a benefit in times of famine, as foreign grain, either from Italy or Egypt, could be imported to avert major calamity,[11] something not as easily done for towns such as Damascus that were less accessible to the coast.

The caravan, like a ship, had its internal dynamic of operation. Once a caravan had been organized, the animals rented, and the merchandise loaded, the merchants would choose one of their number to serve as the caravan master (Arabic: *ra'īs al-qāfila;* Turkish: *kervan başı*). Tavernier reported that the post was usually filled by one of the wealthier merchants in the caravan and was chosen from whichever ethnic group comprised the majority of the merchants traveling with it: if Armenians predominated, it would be an Armenian, and so on.[12] Others stated that while the caravan master was always a wealthy merchant, he was often someone who had close ties to the beduin tribes.[13]

The latter was an essential qualification, for the caravan master negotiated with the beduin as to the fees that would be charged for safe pas-

Figure 4. Sample Rental Costs for Pack Animals from Aleppo

Destination	*Animal*	*Number*	*Weight*	*Rate*	*Date*
Erzurum	mule	15	12q	17g/q	1631
Erzurum	camel	8	8q	10g/q	1636
Diyarbakır	mule	4	NA	18g	1636
Diyarbakır	mule	7	4q	53.5g total	1636
Mosul	mule	45	NA	9.5g/m	1674
Mosul	mule	52	36q	12g/q	1726
Birecik	camel	NA	530q	2.75g/q	1727
Birecik	mule	NA	NA	2.75g/m	1727
Baghdad	camel	NA	NA	40g/c	1638
Jerusalem	mule	3	NA	43g total	1640
Jerusalem	mule	3	NA	20g/m	1640
Damascus	mule	3	NA	20g/d RT	1631
Üsküdar	camel	24	21q	12g/q	1645
Üsküdar	camel	NA	NA	15.5g/q	1662
Üsküdar	camel	NA	NA	13g/q	1665
Mecca	camel	5	50r	60g/c	1632
Mecca	camel	9	50r	91g/c	1632
Mecca	camel	6	60r	50g/c	1632
Mecca	camel	7	NA	47g/c	1639
Mecca	camel	1	P	58g/c	1639
Mecca	camel	8	NA	46g/c	1639
Mecca	camel	1	P	57.5g/c	1639
Mecca	camel	2	NA	39g/c	1642
Mecca	camel	3	NA	48g/c	1642
Mecca	camel	5	50r	42g/c	1655
Mecca	camel	2	1q	42g/c	1655
Mecca	camel	1	P	10g/c	1672

Abbreviations: NA, not available; c, camel; m, mule; g, *ghurūsh;* P, passenger; q, *qintar;* r, *raṭl;* RT, round trip

sage. Honesty would also seem to have been at a premium. In 1701, for example, the caravan master on the hajj, a highly prestigious and politically important office, pocketed the fees he had collected from the merchants to serve as gifts for the beduin, with calamitous results.[14] In addition, the caravan master regulated such mundane affairs as the hours of traveling and rest for the caravan and served as judge in disputes that arose while the caravan was on the move, a role analagous to that of wagonmaster in nineteenth-century North America.

Although the caravan master possessed a great amount of personal authority, criminal cases that developed while the caravan was in route between cities had to wait until the caravan reached a city where a judge presided to be settled. Theft seems in particular to have been a recurring problem, and there was an occasional murder as well.[15] In such cases, the charges had to be verified by the testimony of two responsible witnesses. This was often a problem because of the mobility of most of those who might serve as potential witnesses.

Nonetheless, there was a conscious effort on the part of those involved to follow the regulations of Muslim law as regards the operation and policing of the caravans, with apparently no special considerations given to the institutions's peculiar circumstances. Thus, in response to a report from the governor of Mosul that the beduin of the Shāhwān tribe (a subtribe of the Āl Shammār) were plundering caravans in his province and selling the merchandise openly in the markets of Mosul, the central government issued an order that the incidents were to be investigated and the culprits punished. But this was to be done only if the statutory fifteen years from the time the crimes had been committed had not elapsed already, and after an investigation to prove that the merchandise the beduin were selling was indeed stolen had been conducted.[16]

Thus the beduin were not only the mainstay of the caravan trade, they were also the chief threat to its security. A caravan, no matter how large would have been hard put to defend itself from a concentrated raid by the tribesmen. As a simple expedient to avoid this disastrous outcome, the caravans routinely paid protection money to the paramount *shaykhs* of the tribes through whose territory they would pass. For further protection, the Ottoman government maintained a network of caravansaries (*khāns*) along the main caravan routes to provide travelers with a safe haven in which to spend the night. One of these, located in Maᶜarrat al-Nuᶜmān, was described by an eighteenth-century English traveler:

It is a large strong and built of free-stone, not unlike the Leaden Hall or rather the Exchange in London, being a square edifice with rooms, which are reserved for the principal merchants and officers of the karawan: Underneath which is a portico or colonade with mastabez, or floors raised two or three feet from the ground, and there the common travellers are lodged. In the middle of the court stands a little masjed or mesku, vulgarly called by us a mosk, the dome whereof is covered with lead, as well as the roof of the khan: To it belongs a lovely fountain and well, which is of vast depth before one comes to water. The khan is capable of lodging 800 passengers and their horses with a great deal of ease. It is of that sort of inns which are endowed by their founders, where a traveller may have bread, pilaw and mutton gratis; adjoining the khan is a bagnio and a street containing a coffee-house and five or six shops on each side. . . .[17]

Obviously, not all the caravansaries were quite as commodious, and along the open desert road to Baghdad, they often did not exist at all. But where the system was in place, along the routes to Anatolia, the Hijaz, and the northern desert route (via Urfa, Mardin, and Mosul), it was scrupulously maintained in times of strength. But as the empire became increasingly beset by internal and external challenges, gaps in the network developed. The decay of the caravansaries was deemed critical by the central government, which sought to treat the problem by refurbishing or, in some cases, regarrisoning strategically positioned caravansaries along the main routes.[18] Still, it must be recognized that by the end of the seventeenth century, the great interlocking system was in trouble. Raids on the caravans became more frequent as the political configurations in the desert shifted.

In addition to the military option represented by khans and garrisons, the Ottomans attempted to maintain order among the tribes through the time-honored Middle Eastern tradition of bribery and cooptation of the tribal leadership into the ruling establishment. In the case of the beduin this was accomplished through institutionalization of the office of the "Prince of the Arabs," as it was referred to by the Europeans (in Arabic, the title was *amīr al-ᶜArab,* "commander of the beduin"; in Ottoman, *çöl beyi,* "lord of the desert"). The Prince's authority was recognized by imperial decree, which allowed him to collect transit taxes from passing caravans. In return, he maintained order in the desert and when necessary provided tribal auxiliaries and camels for Ottoman military expeditions.[19]

Although the office seems to date back at least to Ayyubid times (thirteenth century), the Ottomans were slow to acknowledge its utility. But after several campaigns without result to control the Mawālī beduin (their *shaykh* traditionally held the office), the Ottomans decided in 1574 to follow the practice of their predecessors. The tribal *shaykh* of the Mawālī, invariably called in the seventeenth century Abū Rīsha ("Possessor of the Plume"), was assigned a gift of 6,000 ducats a year and the hereditary nature of the office was acknowledged.[20]

The Abū Rīsha's responsibilities were outlined in an agreement registered in Aleppo in 1735, in which the current holder of the office, listed simply as Shaykh Efendi, agreed to protect both peasants and travelers from beduin and bandits along the Euphrates River caravan route from Birecik to Ridwaniya (opposite Baghdad) and to follow all orders issued from the Porte.[21] In addition to the formal agreements made with Istanbul, the Abū Rīsha was free to make private arrangements with the various European trading nations to provide special protection for their goods.[22]

Although there were occasional lapses of the treaty (reported, for example, by Teixiera in 1605 during the course of a dynastic struggle between two nephews of the current Abū Rīsha for succession[23] and by Naima in 1644 when the garrison of Aleppo was devastated by Assāf Abū Rīsha's forces after a misunderstanding),[24] in general, the agreement held down through the end of the eighteenth century.[25] Unfortunately, by the end of the seventeenth century, the Mawālī beduin were no longer in a position to provide security in the Syrian desert as they once had done, and the office was no guarantee of peace.

In times of peace, the relationship between Aleppo and the nomadic and seminomadic peoples who lived in the city's hinterlands was beneficial to the city's economy. The urban population depended on the tribes for almost all the meat they consumed; pack animals and drivers for the caravan trade; secondary animal products such as wool, cheese, and rugs; and products from the few remaining forests, including gallnuts and firewood. This symbiotic relationship was not always benign, however, as in times when the tribal groups began to assert their power as that of the central government waned. Typically, these nomadic groups would not attack villages simply to plunder and kill, although such incidents did occur. Rather, they would demand tribute from the villagers or pasture their herds in the villagers' fields, destroying their crops.

The usual response of the peasants to such attacks was to flee either to the mountains or to the cities. In the case of the caravans, outright raiding and looting, as opposed to the petty thievery in peacetime, became common once the tribes were convinced that there would be no reprisals and the temptation that the wealth of the caravans offered became too much to bear. The process of nomadic incursion, followed by peasant flight and the accompanying increased insecurity of the caravans, occurred in many parts of Syria, including the coast. But it was especially acute in the region surrounding the cities of Homs and Hama, in the province of Raqqa along the Euphrates, and Jabal Samʿān. In the first two regions, the transgressors were invariably beduin, while in the latter they were Kurds.

For reasons that are not entirely clear, the seventeenth century witnessed the outward migration of the ʿAnāza confederation from the Arabian peninsula into the Syrian desert. This migration, in turn, exerted pressures on the tribes already in Syria, most notably the Mawālī, who were forced to move into the cultivated areas along the desert's fringe to find pasturage.[26] The newer arrivals from Arabia were less inclined to accept passage fees from the caravans. Consequently, the eighteenth century was a time of increasing attacks, especially on the hajj caravans, with devastating effects for Aleppo's merchants.[27] Fortunately for Aleppo, conditions did not deteriorate as completely along the eastern routes. While the Abu Rīshas did not seem to care very much about protecting the peasants under their sway, the Baghdad caravans were largely untouched by raiders throughout that troubled period, in marked contrast to those of the hajj.

In the region to the north and west of the city, the tribal problems were largely with various Kurdish groups. The situation was exacerbated by the trend of gradual migration of Kurds into northern Syria, which had begun most probably in the eleventh century. The Kurds, unlike the beduin, were not true nomads, and their presence often meant direct competition with the sedentary population, largely Arabic-speaking, for control of the agricultural lands.[28] In particular, the Kurds were able to establish themselves in the region surrounding the town of ʿAfrīn, known today in Syria as Jabal al-Akrād ("the Mountain of the Kurds"). These tribally organized Kurds, although not as totally uncooperative as the ʿAnāza, were nevertheless seen by the provincial administration as a threat to the stability of Aleppo's control over its hinterlands as witnessed by the Canpulatoğlu revolt and, in 1750, even to the city itself.[29]

In a last desperate attempt to deal with the nomad problem, the central government tried a solution long familiar in imperial China, to fight nomads with nomads, or more precisely to pit Türkmen—who it was hoped would be more manageable in a Syrian context than they had been in Anatolia, where they were the troublemakers—against beduin and Kurds. Such a policy of forced migrations of people to meet state needs *(sürgün)* was not new in the seventeenth century. It had been employed effectively by the Ottomans to bring Muslim settlers into the Balkans and Cyprus and to populate their capital of Istanbul after its conquest in 1453.

In Syria, the Ottomans had settled Türkmen tribespeople, headed by the Sayfās whom we met earlier, along the coast in the sixteenth century in an attempt to control the mountain strongholds of the various heterodox religious groups who inhabited Mount Lebanon and the Jabal al-ʿAlawīyīn (Syria's coastal range). As such, it most probably seemed to the Ottoman authorities that the resettlement in Syria of Türkmen was a logical and potentially effective way of checking the incursions of other nomadic groups while reducing those tribes' ability to make mischief in their traditional grazing areas.

In 1691, Istanbul ordered the settlement of several Türkmen tribes (including the İlbeklü and Bekirli Türkmen) in the province of Raqqa, on the edge of the great Syrian desert, in response to persistent reports from the provincial governor that the peasants in his charge were abandoning their lands in the face of repeated beduin attacks. The Türkmen were given fields that had been abandoned and were exempted from any taxation for thirty-two years in return for their promise to secure the caravan routes.[30]

From the start, the plan had flaws. Many of the tribesmen had been deported from their original homeland in the vicinity of Maraş because of misconduct, and it was not long before the Bekirli Türkmen, in particular, were adding to the general level of lawlessness that already plagued the province of Raqqa. Perhaps it was to be expected, after all. The tribes had been pastoralists themselves, and the transition to agriculture in a region where the climate was unfamiliar could not have been easy. Consequently, in areas that were only marginally productive at best, banditry offered a means of livelihood clearly preferable to farming.[31] Still others sought to leave Raqqa and migrate with their herds to the region around Amık Gölü, where conditions were more favorable for their traditional style of transhumance and other Türkmen were already long established.[32]

The government had more success in permanently settling the İlbeklü Türkmen in the province of Raqqa, but even in their case, it had to frequently monitor the tribe to insure that it did not return to Anatolia.[33] Istanbul made similar attempts to settle Türkmen in the strategic Homs-Hama region in 1693, 1698, and again in 1713.[34] After the first decade of the eighteenth century, however, these efforts came to a halt with seemingly little long term effect.

With these failures, the government seems to have accepted the permanent deterioration of security along the caravan routes as unavoidable and there were no more government-sponsored attempts to restore order. Rather, it looked with favor on local forces that could act as the central government's proxy. This explains, in part, the long-lived success of the ʿAẓm family in controlling the governorship in Damascus, in the eighteenth century, as they had repeatedly proved their ability to maintain order on the hajj route.[35]

No such local power group emerged in Aleppo, however, and northern Syria remained unsettled, with even the Mawālī beduin resorting to raids. But as this anarchy along the caravan routes coincided with a general decline of the long-distance caravans' overall economic importance, it might be argued that the government no longer felt that order was worth the cost it would require to restore tranquility along the routes. So much of the region was allowed to drift into anarchy. In fact, it was not until the decades of the Tanzimat, most particularly after the sectarian unrest in Syria in 1860, that the government had either the will or the ability to suppress the tribes finally in northern Syria and restore some modicum of security for travelers and peasants alike.

In addition to the long-distance caravans we have been discussing, which linked Aleppo to far-off fabled cities, trade in Aleppo was dependent on the short-distance local caravans that plied their way between the city and its port of Iskenderun. As Aleppo lay some three days distant from the sea, these caravans were necessary to transport the goods the European had shipped to the port of Iskenderun and those they had bought in Aleppo and wished to export. This was a specialized type of caravan, as the vast majority of the clients were Europeans. As such, the caravans were organized whenever there was a need. In the seventeenth century, the managing of this service was entirely in the hands of a Türkmen tribe, but by the eighteenth century it had passed to the control of one of the many service guilds that seem to multiply expotentially in the Ottoman period.

The incentive for a guild organization on the part of the muleteers who handled the trade was the large amount of money that could be earned from the Europeans. Teixeira reported, at the beginning of the seventeenth century, that the amount paid annually by the Franks for the service was 80,000 *ghurūsh,* while in 1756, the fees paid by the English alone came to 109,417 *ghurūsh,* a figure the consul thought was excessive.[36] The Europeans sought to break the power of the monopoly of the guild by employing outside muleteers in 1737. This resulted in large-scale attacks on the caravans by Kurds, whom the Europeans believed were being paid by the former muleteers.[37] Although these raids, in turn, provoked the Ottomans to retaliate, the stolen goods were only recovered when the dragoman working for the English was able to effect their ransom from the Kurds in Kilis.[38]

Similar labor disputes with the French led to violence again in 1743 and 1744,[39] and the message became clear to the Europeans. They returned shortly thereafter to the former muleteers for a service contract. Following this episode, there were no further attempts at union busting, and perhaps as a result there were no more Kurdish raids. Although the European were obviously unhappy with the arrangement, they were forced to maintain an uneasy truce with the mule skinners.

KHANS, *SŪQS*, AND COFFEEHOUSES

Once a caravan arrived at Aleppo, it would halt outside the city walls until the merchants were registered by the Ottoman customs officials. With the formalities over, the merchants would be met by drivers with donkeys or camels, competing with each other to transport the merchandise to one of the *Dār al-Wakāla*s (literally, "The House of Agency") for weighing and taxation if the goods were bulky and of low value, or to the official customs station if the merchandise were of high value. There were several places where the bulkier goods could be weighed. We know that in 1712, for example, an imperial order listed locations at the Damascus *[sic]*, Antioch, and Nayrāb Gates, at the khan of Ibşir Paşa, and in the quarter of Bānqūsā.[40] In other words, there was a station located at almost every access point to the city. There was, however, only one central-government customs station in the city for such luxury goods as European broadcloth or Iranian silk. The handlers of the animals for local transport, like most of those in the caravans themselves, were beduin who retained their tribal organization in lieu of a guild. The competition between tribes for this trade was often intense and led to conflict between them, occasionally affecting the merchants' ability to get their goods into the city.[41]

When the merchandise had been weighed and taxes paid, the merchants hired porters to carry their goods to the khans in which they would stay while they were in Aleppo. Due to the narrowness of most of the city's streets and the congested condition of the central market area, animal transport was necessarily kept to a minimum and used only for the most bulky of objects. An army of porters was needed, therefore to keep the commerce of Aleppo running smoothly. The porters, like all other service workers, were organized into labor guilds that either specialized in the transport of a particular product such as yoghurt,[42] or monopolized the location in which it operated. Wages for these services were low. We learn that in 1711, for example, the porters at the *Dār al-Wakāla* in Bānqūsā were paid 10 *ʿuthmānīs/akçe* for each *qinṭar* of solid goods carried and 5 *akçe* for each liquid *qinṭar*.[43] Nevertheless, the desirability of belonging to a guild, with the guarantee of an income such membership entailed for the various rural people who had migrated to the city, was great, and there was no shortage of those who would take even niggardly wages.

Most of the nonresident merchants who arrived with the caravans stayed in one or other of the city's khans or caravansaries. Typically, these were massive stone structures consisting of two stories built around an open courtyard. They were described by Russell as follows:

> The khanes are spacious solid stone buildings, usually constructed in a quadrangular form, and one story high; of which the ground floor on each side is divided into apartments, arched above, and lighted only by window in front, and the door. The story above, instead of windows, presents an open gallery, or piazza, from which is a range of rooms like the back rooms below. The stair cases leading to the first story are on each side of the gateway; and the roof, as in most buildings, is flat and terraced. The ground floor serves for warehouses, counting houses, lodgings, and sometimes for stables; the other floor is chiefly for the reception of travellers, who find lodging there at a very moderate expense. Most of these apartments are still worse lighted than the ground rooms, there seldom being windows backward. Matts are all the furniture provided by the khane; travellers bring the rest with their baggage.[44]

The khans were not elegant, but they were functional, convenient, and secure. As such, local merchants often used them to store their merchandise and even conducted business out of the rooms on the ground floor rather than in shops.[45]

The actual number of khans in existence in the seventeenth century seems to be a matter of some confusion. The total was given by Tavernier in 1637 as 40, by d'Arvieux in 1687 as 68, by Polonyalı Simeon in the second decade of the same century as 40, and by the Turkish traveler Evliya Çelebi as 70, of which 47 are described as being lead-roofed and two as being *bedestans*.[46] In an entry of the Aleppo court records in the year 1631, 35 khans are listed, while Russell wrote that there were over a century later only 20 major khans in the city. Russell's indication of a decline in the number of khans is supported by an entry from the court records from 1754 in which 20 khans are listed as existing within the city walls, five of which were designated as not being in use.[47]

Part of the discrepancy in the various figures undoubtedly lies in the apparent confusion between markets and khans, on the one hand, and between what was technically a khan and what was merely a *qaysārīya*, on the other. In Aleppo, the term *qaysārīya* (local spelling *qasārīya*) referred to a structure smaller than a khan that sometimes only consisted of a few rooms and that could be used for either workshops or places of residence for traveling merchants. By Russell's time they were often simply low-cost tenements for recently arrived migrants.[48]

Whether khan or *qaysārīya*, any commercial structure in the city was most probably financed through the institution of the *waqf*, or pious endowment. While the Ottoman central treasury often paid for the construction of caravansaries on the open road, bridges, port improvements, and so on, the construction of markets and khans in urban areas was left largely to the private sector of the economy. In Aleppo, there was a noticeable increase in the construction and the endowment of such commercial buildings in the sixteenth century, as the city expanded to the north and east. The establishment of a pious endowment had obvious investment potential for the endower in that it saved the wealth from the fractionalization that was mandated by Muslim inheritance laws. Moreover, it preserved the endower's name for eternity (or at least as long as the structured endowed survived) as a pious Muslim and a doer of good deeds.

The beneficiaries of the income generated by the pious endowments varied. The revenues of the *khān al-ḥarīr* in the quarter of Farāfira were assigned to a Sufi *tekke,* as were those of the khan of *Qāḍī al-Hāwī;* those of the *khān al-ṣabūn* went to help feed the poor of Madina, while the revenues accruing to the *khān al-shaykh* went to support a hospital (the *dār al-shifā al-Nūrī*).[49] The revenues involved could be considerable. The *khān al-ṣabūn,* for example, was rented in 1636 for a period of a year for 1,000 *ghurūsh;* the *khān al-jadīd* in the quarter of Jubb Asad Allah, consisting of twenty-one stores and a coffee shop, rented also in 1636 for 1,200 *ghurūsh;* and the *waqf* of Kara Mustafa Paşa, to be discussed below, was rented in 1691 for 2,300 *ghurūsh.*[50]

Despite the large revenues they could produce and the obvious luster that their construction gave to the city, it might be argued that money invested in the pious endowments might have been more profitably used elsewhere. Indeed the founding of a *waqf* often represented a siphoning off of capital into what would become economically unproductive institutions. Furthermore, the revenues they produced were more often than not directed to charities outside of the city itself. Although the growth in the city's commercial infrastructure, in the form of markets and khans, was of major benefit to the mercantile sector initially, many of these became redundant as still more such structures were added to the city. All too often, little imagination or innovation was used in determining which projects would best serve over the years to preserve the endower's glory. Khans had proved to be a safe bet in the sixteenth century, and so they were still popular a century later even though the utility of more such structures seems to have been, in retrospect, questionable. Such was the case of the *khān al-wazīr.*

The *khān al-wazīr* was constructed by Grand Vizier Kara Mustafa Paşa in the year 1681. It is an undeniably magnificent structure with delicately carved stone windows and an elegant facade, leading some to say that it is the crowning achievement of Ottoman commercial architecture in Aleppo. Yet at the time it was constructed, the structure was already destined to become a useless bauble in a city that had passed its zenith as a caravan center.

In 1736, the daughter of Kara Mustafa and the administrator of the *waqf* of the khan, Abide Hanım, petitioned the Porte outlining her father's ambitions in constructing the khan. She wrote that he had intended the building to serve as a hostel for merchants traveling with the caravans from Basra, Baghdad, and Iran. To promote that end, he had secured government decrees granting the khan a monopoly in that service. But the khan's fortunes had fallen on hard times, and Abide Hanım was seeking redress from the government. She complained there and elsewhere, that others, most notably the administrator of the *waqf* of the Adlīya Mosque, had been interfering with her business by diverting merchants to their establishments.[51] Her appeal was supported, in principle, by all the authorities concerned, but the fact that Abide Hanım had to claim her rights repeatedly is an indication little could be done.

Simply put, competition had intensified among the various executors of the city's khans, as the number of merchants for whom the khans were built was dwindling. This decline in demand for accommodations by traveling merchants, which reflected the changing fortunes of the caravan trade in the eighteenth century, may account for the greatly reduced number of khans mentioned by Russell. By the middle of the eighteenth century, the process of converting these hostels into more routine commercial properties, often for warehouses and workshops and other such purposes for which they are generally used today, had already begun.

The financial administration of the khans, as we have just seen in the case of the *khān al-wazīr,* was in the hands of the executor of the pious endowment *(mutawallī),* who was usually a descendant of the endower. The endower had the right to stipulate who would be eligible to administer the trust. Usually, it was the eldest son of the eldest son and so on, down the line, but not always. The courts themselves were responsible for the implementation of the bequest, which, after all, was a contract written with the community of the faithful for eternity. As upholder of the community's moral vigor, the chief judge of the city would usually appoint an overseer *(nāẓir)* to insure that the terms of the endowment were indeed carried out to the letter of the will by the heirs.

In addition, many of the khans had a caretaker known as the *odabaşı,* who was hired by the executor of the endowment and paid out of the khan's revenue. His responsibilities were to insure that the operation of the khan ran smoothly and to collect dues and rent from the merchants. Russell reported that in his time the persons fulfilling this function were most often Armenian, which seems reasonable given their general knowledge of foreign languages and the large number of Armenians who would most probably be staying in the khans.[52] But in a list of khans registered a century earlier only three of the thirty-one men listed as performing that task citywide were identified as being Christian.[53] The apparent shift in the ethnic makeup of the persons serving in even such a mundane occupation as hoteliers seems to be yet a further indication of the growing importance of the Levantine Christians in various levels of the empire's internal trade by the second half of the eighteenth century.

Once the merchants were established in the khans, they would conduct their business in the city's extensive covered markets, its bazaars, or as they were known locally, its *sūq*s. These were the city's pride and its cause for fame. In physical area, the covered bazaar of Aleppo exceeded the markets of any city in the Arab Levant and rivaled in its grandeur the famous covered bazaar of Istanbul itself. In the Ottoman period, as today, it overwhelmed the first-time visitor with its sights, smells, and sounds. It was described by Evliya Çelebi, as follows:

This city of Aleppo cannot be traversed from top to bottom, street by street, without encountering market after market. The *sūq al-Sulṭānī* [imperial market] consists of five thousand, seven hundred shops in all with two *bedestan* like khans. A goodly number of merchants possessing over 100,000 *ghurūsh* are there. Except for the elixir of life all other sorts of rare and precious merchandise can be found in the city. . . . Most of the khans and markets are covered with lead roofing so that severe heat does not affect them; even in July, the market is cool like the cellars of Baghdad. On most of the streets, watersellers pass by dispensing coolness while the shopowners and their companions pass the time in comfort. . . . All the main thoroughfares are lined with Frankish sidewalks [i.e., paved]. Night and day, trash collectors are busy tidying up the streets with their baskets. The waste is then burned in the bath houses and the streets remain quite clean. . . .[54]

and by Russell:

The Bazars, or markets, are lofty stone edifices, in the form of a long gallery, for the most part very narrow, arched above, or else roofed with wood. . . . In many of the old bazars these shops are so confined as barely to leave room for the shopkeeper to display his wares, and for himself and one guest to sit conveniently. The buyers are obliged to remain standing on the outside; and, when opposite shops happen to be in full employment it is not easy for a passenger to make his way through the crowds. Some of the modern bazars are indeed wider, and the shops much more commodious, but all are gloomy; the sun being excluded as much as possible to keep them cool: for a like reason, they are watered two or three times a day in the summer. . . .[55]

In general, the city's commercial life was conducted in the extensive covered markets at the foot of the citadel, which constituted what the locals referred to simply as *al-madīna* ("the city"). This area included the prestigious imperial market and the city's two *bedestan*s. A *bedestan* was an enclosed market area that could be easily secured and defended. It usually was located in the center of an Ottoman market complex and was used by the merchants dealing in costly commodities as it could be locked at night against all intruders. The fact that Aleppo had two such institutions is an indication of the importance of the trade that was conducted in the city.[56] But in addition to the central market area, the Ottoman period also witnessed the growth of suburban market complexes in Aleppo, most especially in the eastern Bānqūsā quarter and in the northern suburb of Judayda. For the most part, however, these were employed by merchants selling items for local consumption and usually did not attract the attention of the long-distance merchants.

Except for matters of taxation, the market organization was not tightly regulated by the state. An individual market might consist of dozens or even hundreds of individual shops, and while many, if not all, of these might be *waqf* property, it was extremely rare for one individual executor to be in charge of an entire market. Rather, most of the shops were subdivided into separate *waqf*s designated to benefit various causes, and each of these would have an independent executor. The overall administration of a market was obviously at best a difficult and often a seemingly nebulous operation.

As mentioned before, there was no guild of long-distance merchants; rather, merchants were organized according to the market in which they conducted their business. These, in turn, were linked almost invariably to the product being sold. The responsibilities of the market organization included the general maintenance of cleanliness and order in the marketplace. Each such organization had its own chief, the *shaykh,* whose function was largely administrative rather than that of a policymaker. An entry dated October 16, 1662, in the Aleppo court records gives us an idea of how the head of the merchants in one of the city's *bedestan*s was chosen. It reads as follows:

The judge appointed the holder of this document, Shaykh Ḥasan b. Ḥājj Muṣṭafā, as *shaykh* of the *bedestan* in the city of Aleppo, also known as the *sūq al-sibāhīya,* in place of the deceased Qāsim Basha. The judge gave him [Shaykh Ḥasan] authority over whatever affairs have been traditionally the prerogative of the office, and this was accepted completely by him. This was done at the request of the "Pride of the Merchants" Ḥājj Yūsuf Çelebi b. Shaykh ᶜAbd al-Qādir al-Ḥalāwānī, the "Pride of the Merchants" Sayyid Abū Bakr Çelebi b. al-Sayyid Sharaf al-Dīn al-Ṭablah, ᶜAlī Çelebi b. al-Qassām, Ḥājj Murād B. Muḥammad, Hüseyin Bey b. Ahmed [head of the guild of the makers of *darāᶜī* cloth], Ibrahim Bey b. Abdullah, Ḥājj Aḥmad b. Alījā Sīdī ᶜAṭa Allah b. Muhammad, Ḥājj Aḥmad b. ᶜArab, Muḥammad b. Qāsim, Shaykh Ibrāhīm b. Aḥmad *[shaykh* of the silk *sūq],* ᶜUmar b. Aḥmad, Jamāl al-Dīn b. ᶜAbd al-Laṭīf Çelebi and his brother Bākir and others beside them from the afore mentioned *sūq* and from outside it, who have given their consent that the one so appointed speaks for them in the place of the deceased *shaykh.*[57]

This document is of interest as it helps to underline the difference between the responsibilities and authority of a *shaykh* of a market and one of a trade guild. First, those who gave their consent to the market *shaykh*'s appointment, in the above case, included persons who were not merchants: the *shaykh* of the guild of the *darāᶜī* makers and the *shaykh* of the silk market, for example. Nonetheless, these were spokesmen for people who had interests in the maintenance of order in the *bedestan.* Guild *shaykhs*, on the other hand, were chosen only by their own membership.

Second, although the *shaykh* of the *bedestan* was authorized to act as a spokesman for the merchants who operated there, he was not given authority to determine the policies of the marketplace, but only to enforce those established by the consensus of the merchants involved.[58] This differed from the guilds, where once a *shaykh* was selected, he could determine policies for the membership at large, as long as they did not interfere with the established practice of the guild. Furthermore, when a dispute arose involving the merchants of a particular market and outsiders, official or not, they would send a collective delegation to present their case before the court rather than rely, as would a guild, on the representation of their *shaykh.* An internal dispute between two merchants in a particular market would also be settled by them through litigation in court rather than outside it by the *shaykh.*

Two examples help to illustrate the ways in which this collective organization worked in practice. In the first, registered on March 16, 1645, a delegation of Muslim merchants from the Timūr Tāsh market and that of the *waqf* of the Vizier, Mehmed Paşa, both located at the foot of the citadel, charged that some Christian merchants were standing outside the two markets, directing potential customers away, presumably to their own shops. The judge affirmed that such actions were indeed contrary to practice and the law, and he fixed a fine of fifty *ghurūsh* on anyone who attempted to divert customers away from either market in the future, with the fine itself going as a donation to the *waqf* of the Umayyad mosque in the city.[59]

In the second case, dated February 25, 1663, certain Christian merchants selling *khām* were asked by the other merchants in the market where they were conducting their trade to help contribute to a special tax levied on the market as a whole. The Christian merchants declined, saying that they were not regulars of the market *(min ahālī al-sūq)*. Upon hearing this reply, the judge warned them that if they were not ready to contribute to the taxes collected from the market, they would be issued an injunction from selling their wares there.[60]

Within each individual market, there were a score of persons who, while not engaged in trade directly, made their livelihood from commerce, as the process of buying and selling in a Middle Eastern city required the services of a large group of agents, brokers, and middlemen who connected buyers to sellers for a commission made off the sale. In Aleppo, these functions were filled by the *simsār*s and *dallāl*s. Although the two terms are never used interchangeably in the sources, and thus involved presumably different functions, the practical differences are not so easily determined.

The *simsār*s divided up the commerce of the city among themselves, receiving as their area of operation a particular khan or market, but all owed their allegiance to a chief who was the officially recognized head of their guild and entrusted to look out for the interests of the *simsār*s citywide.[61] Typically, a *simsār* of a particular market would be approached by a potential buyer for help in finding an item, and if a sale was completed, the *simsār* would then receive a finder's fee from the purchaser. This remuneration, in most cases, was fairly small. The finder's fee in the silk market was set in 1661, for example, as one *akçe* for every piece sold.[62]

The *dallāl*s were for all practical purposes commercial brokers. They could possess as their area of jurisdiction a particular khan like the *sim-*

*sar*s, but more typically they specialized in a particular product. Such was the case of a certain Ṣāliḥ b. Ibrāhīm, who held the brokerage, in the form of a monopoly, over all the *khām* that was brought to Aleppo from Gaziantep in 1687.[63] Therein lay a crucial distinction between the *simsār*s and the *dallāl*s. Individual *dallāl*s seem to have won virtual monopolies over the control of the trade in certain items, if not a monopoly over the item itself, procuring the right that all such sales pass through their hands and hence untold opportunities for kickbacks from merchants competing for sales. This was especially true in the eighteenth century, when it seems that most of the *dallāl*ships in the city were converted to *malikane*s (life-tenured tax farms).

With such authority, the position of *dallāl* offered the holder the chance for a very lucrative livelihood and the competition was correspondingly great. The *dallāl*s were organized into guilds according to the commodity they brokered, and as in the case of other guilds, membership was usually passed down from father to son.[64] But as with other trades, a great deal of pressure was exerted on the integrity of the guilds as janissaries sought to gain a foothold in the business. Despite various orders from the central government forbidding them from engaging as commercial brokers,[65] the janissaries were firmly entrenched among the ranks of the brokers in Aleppo by the middle of the seventeenth century. Unlike the *simsār*s, who were often non-Muslim (in a list of *simsār*s in the city in 1631, for example, 23 were Christian, 11 Jews, and 8 Muslim),[66] the *dallāl*s were almost exclusively Muslim. This is a probable indication that the position was seen more as a sinecure than a functioning service as the janissaries were never noted for their personal industry. Supporting this contention is the case of a Muslim woman living in Damascus in 1700 who held the post of *dallāl* of the *khān al-ḥarīr* in Aleppo.[67] One can hardly imagine her actually fulfilling the role of broker from that distance.

Even as a sinecure, the position of *dallāl* could tempt the holder to use his or her position as a stepping-stone to greater wealth. How such opportunities might present themselves is brought to light by litigation registered on June 6, 1725, when representatives of several guilds involved in the production of cotton cloth complained that certain *dallāl*s were hiring women to spin cotton thread for them, circumventing the guild of male cotton-thread spinners and undercutting their prices. The *dallāl*s were then turning around and selling the thread to the artisans at an inflated price. The guilds asserted that it was their collective opinion that the *dallāl*s should not weave cloth or sell it; neither were they to enter into the marketing of cotton thread, either as buyers or sellers. In this, they were supported by the judge, who chastised the *dallāl*s for their presumptions and threatened severe, although unnamed, punishments if they persisted.[68]

Despite the *dallāl*s' often questionable value to the merchants, over the course of the seventeenth century they engaged in persistent, and often successful, attempts at raising their fees. They claimed this was necessary, as many of the merchants were, not unreasonably it would seem, trying to conduct their trade without the *dallāl*s' mediation.[69] As the position of *dallāl* came with an imperial order conferring on the holder the right to collect his or her fees, it had to be purchased from the central treasury, following Ottoman practice, with a lump-sum payment supposedly equivalent to future revenues. Larger fees were, therefore, needed constantly by the holders of the office just to retain their positions from year to year. The posts were obviously perceived as being a good investment, and others were continually seeking to buy the right of *dallāl*ship out from under the current holders by bidding that they could collect more for the central treasury. In this way, the *dallāl*s were institutionalized to a degree not equalled by the *simsār*s. With the codification of their vocations came ensuing opportunities, and even a need, for corruption, which, coupled with their political clout, would seem to negate any positive benefit they had ever performed for commerce.

In addition to the brokers, each market in the city of Aleppo also had attached to it a number of persons serving as guards and security men, supplementing the guard attached to the governor's retinue. By the middle of the seventeenth century, this function was fulfilled by a group of men known collectively as the *maghāriba*. As their name would indicate, some of these were originally from North Africa. It is not clear, however, whether they all, in fact, were entirely North African or whether they simply took their name as a unit from the ethnic origin of some of their membership.

North Africans were prominent in Syria during the Ottoman centuries as auxiliary military forces. They do not seem to have had any such function in Aleppo during the period of this study, although they are known to have constituted a military unit in the city in the second half of the eighteenth century.[70] North Africans were, however, a part of the ethnic mix in the city. In addition to the individuals encountered in the sources, there was at least one Sufi hostel in the city, the Zāwīyat Ḥaḍrat Sīdī Ghūth, which was administered by the local North African community.[71]

The *maghāriba,* whatever their actual ethnicity, constituted a guild with a citywide membership. Their *shaykh* held a tax farm for life, *(malikane),* issued to him in the form of an imperial decree *(berat).* Each time a new chief's investiture was registered with the court, the functions of the guild were listed. These included protecting stores and markets, providing security in the government customs station, and acting as messengers to carry merchants' letters of credit from one city to another.[72] The wages of the guards, who were expected to stay overnight in the market to which they assigned, were paid by the merchants whose shops they protected, with each individual merchant assessed a fee by the market organization to be collected monthly. From time to time, however, the merchants needed protection from their own protectors, as there were frequent charges of misconduct, including public drunkeness, brought against the *maghāriba* by the merchant community.[73] Luckily perhaps for the merchants, the incidence of urban crime was fairly low,[74] and the *maghāriba* were not required to be sober that often.

As with problems with the *maghāriba,* general cases of public nuisance in the markets were taken to the courts for restraining orders to be issued against the offending parties. From such cases, we can get some idea of the sense of propriety that permeated the marketplaces of Aleppo. In one case, an injunction was issued to a group of Christians who had been frying fish and selling them in the street, thereby offending their neighbors' sense of smell, to cease and desist.[75] In another, other Christians were ordered to close their tavern, as they were contributing to public drunkeness and the misconduct of ne'er-do-wells toward proper Muslim women.[76] Still other cases indicate that shop owners could not dump their garbage in public places and that people deemed rowdy could be evicted from khans or *qaysārīya*s if their neighbors objected to their continued residence.[77] Thus, far from being disordered and chaotic, Aleppo's markets possessed an internal code of behavior that reflected the general sense of public order and decency.

The one public arena where commercial transactions were often conducted in a slightly less than decorous atmosphere were the city's coffee shops. It is not certain when coffee was introduced to Aleppo, but it was mentioned in the account written by Leonhard Rauwolff in 1586.[78] It would seem reasonable to assume, therefore, that it became popular in the city at roughly the same time that it was introduced throughout the cities of the empire, that is, by the middle of the sixteenth century. By 1600, coffee shops were already an integral part of the city's social and commercial life, as noted by William Biddulph:

Their coffa houses are more common than Ale-houses in England; but they use not so much to sit in the houses, as on Benches on both sides the streets, neere unto a coffa house, every man with his Fin-ion full; which being smoaking hot, they use to put it to their Noses and Eares, and then sup it off by leisure, being full of idle and Ale-house talk, while they are amongst themselves drinking of it; if there be any newes, it is talked of there.[79]

A century and a half later, the city's coffeehouses had become more substantial, as described by Biddulph's compatriot Russell:

The coffee-houses naturally attract the notice of a stranger, more than any of the objects he meets with in ramblings over the city. They are found in all quarters of the town, and some of them are spacious and handsome. They are gaudily painted, and furnished with matted platforms and benches: those of the better sort have a fountain in the middle, with a gallery for musicians. A row of large windows discovers to a passenger all that is gong on within, and the company, being supplied with small, low, wicker stools, often choose in the summer to sit before the door, in the open air.[80]

Not only were the coffeehouses numerous, some could reach almost mythic proportions. Evliya Çelebi, a travel writer not noted for his use of understatement, reported that the coffee shop of Arslan Dede (a part of a *waqf* dedicated to the memory of a local Sufi saint of the same name) in Aleppo could hold two thousand customers at a time. But before we dismiss this figure out of hand as just another of the author's infamous prevarications, we should note that Aigen stated that some of the coffeehouses of the city could seat several hundred guests and that the coffeehouse constructed as a part of the *waqf* of Ibşir Paşa in 1653 was one of the largest public structures in the city, with an area rivaling that of some of the city's's mosques.[81]

In addition to supplying coffee to their customers, these establishments were places of entertainment. We have already noted that coffee shops were the usual places where the people of the city gathered to hear the storytellers, and such shops also hosted singers, dancers, and shadow puppeteers *(kara göz)*. Evliya rhapsodized in his description of the city that an evening in Arslan Dede's coffee shop, watching the dancers, was about as close to heaven as any mere mortal could ever get.[82]

It was the show-business side of the trade, as well as their perceived invitation to indolence, that worried the religious guardians of public morality. In his important ruling outlawing coffeehouses, the chief legal counsel of the Ottoman Empire, the Şeyhülislam Ebussuûd Efendi (1545–74), cited that they were places where the unemployed and lazy would gather to play chess and backgammon, smoke opium, and engage in general lewd and disorderly conduct.[83] In this characterization, he was supported two centuries later by Russell, who said that the establishments in Aleppo were generally frequented only by the city's lower classes and that the entertainment provided in them could often be not only lascivious but seditious as well.[84]

Nonetheless, Ebussuûd's ban was lifted by a successor, Bostanzade Mehmed Efendi, in 1591. Although after this date there were periodic attempts to close the coffee shops down in the capital, there seems to have been little concentrated effort to spread the ban to Aleppo.[85] One might suppose that this reluctance may have been due in part to the lucrative role coffee had in the city's economy and the influential individuals, including judges and governors, who engaged in its marketing.[86]

GOVERNMENTAL INSTITUTIONS OF TRADE

In addition to the unofficial institutions of the caravan trade, there were others that were maintained as a part of the Ottoman provincial administration. Ottoman government in Aleppo was self-consciously Islamic, as were its institutions. As such, while these might be refined by the Ottomans, they were rarely altered in any significant way. In areas where there were no precedents, the Ottomans had a certain amount of leeway for innovation, but in general, they acted conservatively and rarely sought to introduce anything totally new.

The most fundamental commercial institution was the Muslim court system, with the office of the chief judge *(qāḍī)* and the supplemental office of the interpreter of the law *(muftī)* standing at the top. The city of Aleppo had five courts: a *shafāᶜī* court that was a holdover from the former Mamluk administration; courts in the quarters of Bānqūsā and Salāhiya; a court named after the region of Jabal Samᶜān, to the northwest of the city, which handled principally but not exclusively the cases arising from that area; and the central court *(maḥkama kubrā)*.

Of these five, the central court was obviously the most important. All judges were, in fact, appointed by Istanbul, but the post of the central court was one of the more prestigious ones in the realm, and the judge there held a position almost on a par with that of the governor in terms of the provincial hierarchy. Thanks to a system of independent judiciary accountable to a different governmental bureaucracy than that of the provincial administration, the *qādī* of the *maḥkama kubrā* served as a conduit through which the central government made its regulations known to the populace and through which the people could approach Istanbul to complain of abuse by the governor and his subordinates.

The services provided to merchants by the Muslim court system were manifold. Among these was the role of notary public through the court's authentification of contracts and loan agreements. It also served as a public records office, to which a claimant had access to support his or her case in a commercial dispute. The court was the enforcer of contracts, whether they were guild agreements or involved commercial ventures. As such, a party who was ruled to be in violation of contract had to face the moral and political authority of the *qāḍī*, who, if necessary, could also rely on the city's garrison to back up his decisions.

Besides underwriting all contractual agreements, the courts served in the disposition of the wealth of a deceased person and in the assignment of shares to the rightful heirs. This function was filled by two officials appointed by the chief judge of Anatolia: the *qassām al-ᶜaskarī*, who was responsible for the valuation of the estates of deceased members of the *askeri* (i.e., the Ottoman official class),and the *qassām al-baladī*, whose responsibilities included everyone else.

According to Muslim law, the property of a deceased person had to be divided up according to established formulas among all his or her legal heirs. In order to ensure equitable distribution, all the property of the deceased was inventoried by the court, under the supervision of the judge and the *qassām*s, and a cash value was placed on every item based on the current market rate. The total value of the estate, minus various service fees and taxes, as well as outstanding debts owed by the deceased, would then be divided up by the *qassām* according to the formulas of the law.

Examples of these listings are given in chapter 5 in the discussion of wealth and investment in Aleppo.

As the power inherent in the office of *qassām al-ʿaskarī* was particularly great, the holders of the office were prominent members of the local religious establishment *(ʿulamā)*. The office was held by the influential head *(naqīb)* of the *ashrāf* throughout most of the seventeenth century. These individuals were almost exclusively drawn from the Ṭahazādah family, one of the wealthiest in the city (see below in chapter 5).[87] As the appointments to the office were made directly by the chief judge of Anatolia, the office was freed from the direct control of the local judiciary. Thus the office provided a preserve of influence to local notable religious families, in the same way that the office of *shāhbandar* served local mercantile interests.

Additionally, the court was responsible for the safekeeping of valuables left by merchants. This practice, referred to as *amāna,* filled at least in part the void in a Muslim economy left by the absence of banks. The court could not, however, lend out any wealth so left while the merchant was away. Finally, as seen above, the courts supervised the administration of the *waqf* foundations. Serving all these multiple functions, it is easy to understand why the courts are considered the primary institution of trade in Aleppo. This had been the case for Muslim societies in pre-Ottoman times, and it remained largely unchanged in the Ottoman period.

After the courts, the governmental institution to have the greatest import for trade in Aleppo was that of the office of the tax farmer of the imperial customs, the *emin-i gümrük*. The collection of customs duties was one of the many areas of civil administration the regulations of which were not clearly articulated in the traditions of Muslim law, so it was left to the central government's discretion with the presumption, at least in Sunni legal theory, that the state acted for the common good of the community of believers as a whole.

In the somewhat secular theory of imperial government as it developed within the context of the Islamic, and especially Iranian, political tradition, customs duties were considered of vital importance to the overall health of the state revenues, and it was felt that to safeguard them they should be kept at fair, therefore presumably low, levels, so that trade would flourish, enriching the state. The fragility of a prosperity based on the transience of the caravan routes was thereby recognized. The routes could change if a state sought to kill the proverbial goose by raising transit taxes, leaving it impoverished and off the beaten track of trade and progress. It had happened before in the history of the Muslim peoples, and the theoreticians of state power in Istanbul were painfully aware of that point.

Within the Ottoman Empire, as a self-acknowledged heir to this tradition, the customs regulations were established by imperial decree, but much was left to the initiative of the person holding the post of customs collector for actual implementation. Like most Ottoman civil government positions and all those involved with the collection of revenues, the holder of the Aleppo customs office farmed the taxes—that is, he bought from the central treasury the right to collect the taxes. According to the patent issued him, the customs officer agreed to supply the treasury with a stipulated amount of money each year from the customs revenues he collected. He was bound by the province's civil code *(kanun-name)* as to the amount of tax he could charge as customs duties on any particular item. Within those limits, all monies he collected above the stipulated amount were his to keep. The amounts registered in Istanbul for the Aleppo customs office over the course of the seventeenth and eighteenth centuries, therefore, do not reflect the actuality of the amounts collected. Rather, we will assume that in every case the customs officer actually collected more, otherwise there would be no incentive to bid for the office year after year.

There are many copies of the *berat*s issued to the various *emin-i gümük*s of Aleppo preserved in the records of the financial department of the central government in Istanbul. These are all remarkably similar, all the more so given the fact they span a century and a half in the date of their issue, in that they stress the customs officer's responsibility to follow the guidelines set down in the province's *kanun-name* as to the rate of taxation charged and to obey Muslim law and imperial decrees in all other matters. But as Aleppo was one of the wealthiest cities in the Ottoman Empire, with a steady stream of valuable merchandise brought in by the caravans from the east and by ship from the west, the temptation to share in that wealth was undeniably great, causing the *emin-i gümrūk*s to overstep the boundaries of the authority granted to them. Perhaps this was to be expected, as no other post offered such opportunities for the accumulation of easy wealth.

Throughout the period under study, there were numerous complaints from the merchants that the customs officers were abusing their authority. These complaints usually fell into two generalized categories: those in which the *emin-i gümrük* was said to be trying to alter the procedure for taxation on items stipulated as taxable and those that claimed he was attempting to tax items that had been traditionally exempt from taxation in the first place.

In the *berat*s confirming the customs office upon a particular individual, the rate of taxation was invariably given at 2.5 *gurūsh* for every 100 *ghurūsh* value of merchandise brought in by Muslim merchants either from within the empire or from outside it, and 5 *ghurūsh* for every 100 *ghurūsh* value if the merchant were a non-Muslim. The rate for European merchants, as we have seen, varied by nationality and time period and was subject to the treaties negotiated between the European powers and the Porte. In addition, both Muslims and non-Muslims, but not Europeans, had to pay an extra one-percent tax called the *muzayaka,* an extraordinary tax that once levied became institutionalized.[88] By the eighteenth century, the same rate of excise taxation continued but was apparently renamed the *kasabiye* and was designated to help subsidize the supply of meat to the capital.[89]

Because it was a more convenient way of assessing taxation and most probably offered a higher rate at that, the customs officers often tried to tax the merchants not by a percentage of the assessed value of the goods they imported but rather by their volume and type. The merchants' usual response to such actions was to appeal to Istanbul to outlaw the innovation. Sometimes in an apparent contradiction to what would seem their own best interests, merchants would assert that the customs officer should return to the age-old practice of charging a set tax per load, regardless of value or commodity, in a variation on the practice they so often protested themselves.

The apparent contradiction is explained in a complaint from the *emin-i gümrük* in 1702 in which he outlined the merchants' own strategem vis-à-vis customs, which was to overload their animals before they entered the city. The usual load for a camel was 180 *okka*s while that of a mule was 120. It seems the merchants were routinely overloading the pack animals to 350–380 *okka*s for a camel and 200 for a mule, thereby reducing their taxes by a half should they be levied by load rather than by value.[90] It was clear from the complaint that the customs officer himself was still trying to tax the merchants by the load in violation of the imperial regulations, but was bested by the merchants at his own game. In all such cases, however, the central government maintained that the customs agents were to follow the precedents that had been set—that is, taxation at a rate based on the cash value of the merchandise, and not on its volume or on the nature of the commodity.[91]

In the second generalized category of abuse of office, the *emin-i gümrüks* sometimes extended their authority to items not legally taxable. This practice was most frequent in attempts to tax the lucrative soap industry of northern Syria, or more precisely its raw ingredients, olive oil and potash *(qilā)*. These two items were produced locally—the olive oil in the regions of Idlib and Sarmin, while the potash was supplied by the beduin—and the soap itself was actually produced in workshops, either in Idlib or Aleppo.

In one instance, in 1640, Mūsā w. Ishāq sent his agents to Idlib to collect taxes on the olive oil and potash before it could be made into soap. This action was protested by both the chief judge of Aleppo and the town notables of Idlib, who resented an intrusion into the town's chief industry. The town notables produced an injunction and an imperial order interdicting Mūsā from taxing the two raw ingredients in Idlib. The judge issued a restraining order that may have temporarily halted the intrusion by the customs bureaucracy, at least for the time being, but we know that attempts to gain the right to tax soap in its production as well as its final form, the latter permitted by the *kanun-name*, continued over the century with no apparent resolution.[92]

Occasionally, an enterprising *emin-i gümrük* might exceed the bounds of his authority to the point that he was faced with a virtual tax revolt by the merchants, as a case in 1640, which also involved Mūsā w. Ishāq, illustrates. In his first year of office, probably to recoup the cost of buying his post, Mūsā raised the transit tax on sugar, safflowers, ammonia, and cloth coming from Egypt and Damascus and bound for the other towns of Aleppo's hinterlands: Sarmīn, Idlib, ʿAzāz, and Kilis. In response, merchants traveling to those towns avoided Aleppo altogether. This was illegal but apparently difficult to interdict, and revenue collected at the Aleppo customs station started to drop off precipitously. To counteract this, Mūsā was forced to agree to compromise rates set at 10 *ghurūsh* per load of cloth; 5 *ghurūsh* per *kile* of fine indigo; 3 *ghurūsh* per *kile* of lower-quality indigo; 5 *ghūrūsh* per load of gum lac; and 7½ *ghurūsh* per load of pepper. What is interesting about this compromise is that although Mūsā said the merchants were in agreement, the rates were in fact set along illegal lines, as we have seen, in that they were established according to commodity and volume and not by value. Still the case illustrates the merchants' most successful method of dealing with corrupt customs agents—boycott.[93]

In figure 5 the names of some of the men who held the post of *emin-i gümrük* for Aleppo during the seventeenth and early eighteenth centuries are listed, as far as can be reconstructed from various references in the court records of the city, the financial records in Istanbul, and the Levant Company archives. Although the list is incomplete, it presents a clear picture of trends experienced by the office as well as insights into crucial junctures in the process of transformation of the office over the century.

One of the most notable features is the domination of the post by non-Muslim minorities, either Armenians or Jews, until 1660. Of the men who held the post in that period, the two most important were Sanos

Figure 5. *Emin-i Gümrük*s of Aleppo

1596	Ṣafar w. Manṣūr (C)
1612	Bedik (C)
1614	Mūsā w. Ishāq (J)
1616	Bedik
1627	Bedik executed; Sanos replaces him
1635	Sanos (C)
1636	Iskender w. Sanos (C)
1640	Sanos loses his post to Mūsā w. Ishāq al-Khākhām (J)
1649	Mūsā w. Ishāq (J)
1654	Dawūd (J)
1660	Hac Ibrahim Ağa (M) from Dawūd
1664	Hasan (M)
1672	Şaban Ağa (M)
1687	"
1687–90	Hac Yusuf (M), former *defterdar*
1690	Mustafa b. Ahmed Paşa (M)
1696–1707	Abdürrahman Paşa (M)
1715	Abdürrahman Paşa (M)
1721	Osman Ağa (M)
1731	Halil Ağa (M)
	(C) Christian; (J) Jew; (M) Muslim

Karagözoğlu and Mūsū w. Ishāq al-Khākhām. The two shared an intense rivalry, exacerbated as each sought to unseat the other.

Mūsā held the office of customs agent for Iskenderun at the end of the sixteenth century. He was apparently one of the individuals who had worked to get Iskenderun recognized as a customs port by the central government and to have it attached to Aleppo's rather than Tripoli's jurisdiction.[94] Following the revolt of Ali Canpulatoğlu, however, Sanos and his brother Bedik had managed to take over the post. Bedik was able to buy a nine-year lease on the post in 1612, but he was apparently soon afterwards replaced by Mūsā, as Sanos tried to unseat him again in 1614. By 1616, Bedik was back in the position as he was negotiating directly with the Dutch consul over the amount of tariffs to be paid by the Netherlands in Aleppo, in direct violation of his mandate from the Porte.[95]

Sanos and Bedik were among the Julfa Armenians who settled in Aleppo during the first half of the seventeenth century. Between them, the two were able to amass a considerable fortune through commerce and government service. As an example of the wealth this post could generate for them, in his last year in office, 1639, Sanos collected 5,406 *ghurūsh* from the caravans and 7,934 from the Europeans, with an additional 4,086 *ghurūsh* from the stamp *(damgha)* tax. Furthermore, he was accused of extorting several thousand *ghurūsh* from the English merchants.[96] In addition, the brothers had a network of commercial agents who traveled as far as Holland. As good citizens of the Armenian diaspora, they also contributed heavily to the support of the Armenian community in Aleppo, adding extensively to the church of Surp Karsunk, which was to become the seat of the Cilician Catholicos (Sis).[97]

Their success, and perhaps their greed, eventually caught up with them, however. Bedik was executed at government orders in 1627, partly due to the complaints sent to the Porte by the European consuls about his rapacious behavior, and Sanos was removed from his office in 1640, for reasons that are not clear but were obviously serious, as he was executed shortly thereafter. Members of his family remained in government service after his death, however, as we know that his son Iskender held the customs office of Baghdad in 1646.[98]

Like Sanos, Mūsā accumulated wealth during his tenure as *emin-i gümrük,* and he acquired additional important tax farms in the city, which he in turn subcontracted to others. It is not certain what Mūsā's fate was, but we can tell that after 1660, all the persons who held the post were Muslim and apparently from the military ranks.

This reflected a trend throughout the whole of the Ottoman Empire, in which the local Jewish community witnessed an eclipse of its position in the Ottoman financial administration as Jews were replaced by Muslim bureaucrats. Despite this, Jews remained prominent in the ranks of the scribes and secretaries of the customs house of Aleppo and even claimed in at least one deposition to the central treasury that it was their hereditary right to do so.[99]

The change to domination by the military bureaucracy did not improve the moral rectitude of those holding the post of *emin-i gümrük,* however. The English, in particular, seemed to have complained constantly about the men serving in that post and were not above paying bribes to the central government to have particular individuals whom they disliked removed from office, as was the case of Abdürrahman Paşa in 1707.[100]

The courts and the customs house, then, seem to stand on the two extreme ends of the spectrum of governmental institutions in Aleppo. Despite some individuals who were corrupt, the courts were generally viewed as being the guardians of the Muslim concepts of justice and equity, while the customs officers seem to have been universally regarded as corrupt and venal with few, if any, saving graces. To say, as do critics of the Ottoman system, such as Steensgaard, that the entire framework of internal Middle Eastern trade rested on principles of venality seems unfair in the light of what we know about the court system in Aleppo. But at the same time, it has to be realized that the reality of the system for Muslims fell far short of the golden age promised either by the age of the Rāshidūn (the "Rightly-Guided Caliphs" who served as a model of Sunni propriety) or the wisdom of Anushirvan (the Iranian ideal of good government).

The institutions of trade in Aleppo, like the caravan routes, were themselves tried and tested. Despite the radical shifts that were occurring in the region's trading patterns, they seem to have been little affected in the Ottoman period. True, the Ottomans, as was their custom, instituted a greater bureaucratization over some of the offices, such as that of the *shāhbandar* or the *qassām al-ʿaskarī,* than the Islamic world had known before, but at the same time little was really innovative in their policies. Just as trade continued to follow the caravan routes up until the end of the eighteenth century, so too did Middle Eastern merchants, on the whole, continue to rely on the same institutions they always had. Indeed, there was no reason to change. The effectiveness of those institutions for regulating trade as it had been practiced made it seem unnecessary to alter them as long as the caravans continued to arrive in the city.

NOTES

1. Jean Sauvaget, *Alep: Essai sur le developpement d'une grande ville syrienne des origines au milieu du* XIXe *siécle* (Paris, 1941), pp. 228–30.
2. Tavernier 1:158.
3. Sahillioğlu, "Bir tüccar kervanı," *Belgelerle Türk Tarihi Dergisi,* 2, no. 9, pp. 63–69.
4. Douglas Carruthers, ed., *The Desert Road to India: Being the Journals of Four Travellers by the Great Desert Caravan Route between Aleppo and Basra, 1745–1751* (London, 1929), p. xxxiii.
5. Aleppo 36:10.
6. Carruthers, pp. 62–63.
7. Carruthers, p. xxxiv.
8. Aleppo 19:172; 45:194.
9. Carruthers, p. 127.
10. Aleppo 20:122; 36:10.
11. Aleppo 21:212; SP 110/20:101, 6 Aug. 1696.
12. Tavernier 1:179, 192.
13. Carruthers, pp 93, 98.
14. SP 110/22:111, 8 Sept. 1701.
15. Aleppo 21:225; 28:132; 51:268.
16. MD 81:28, 10 Müharrem 1025/29 Jan. 1616.
17. P. Green, *A Journey from Aleppo to Damascus* (London, 1736), pp. 24–25.
18. MM 9841:195, 17 Cemaziyelahır 1065/25 April 1655; MM 9871:66, 9 Rebiyülevvel 110/1 Jan. 1689.
19. Barbir, *Ottoman Rule in Damascus, 1708–1758* (Princeton, 1980), p. 98.
20. Longrigg, p. 39.
21. Aleppo 45:71.
22. SP 110/17:150, 21 March 1686; Russell 2:16–17.
23. Teixeira, pp. 84, 88; al-Ṭabbākh 3:216.
24. Naima 4:104–10.
25. Aleppo 105:115. There were, however, breakdowns in the agreement, as in 1726 when the Mawālī beduin raided in the vicinity of Aleppo (al-Ghazzī 3:296).
26. Aleppo 78:19.
27. For a listing of years in which the hajj caravan was attacked, see Barbir, *Ottoman Rule in Damascus,* pp. 196–197.
28. Pococke 10:537, 541.
29. SP 105/118:186, 25 Jan. 1750.
30. Aleppo 45:101; AS 1:73; MD 102:623, Evail Cemaziyelahır 1103/Feb. 1692.
31. AS 1:99; Suraiya Faroghi, "Rural Society in Anatolia and the Balkans during the Sixteenth Century, II," *Turcica* 11:113.

32. Ahmet Refik, *Anadolu'da Türk Aşiretleri (966–1200)* (Istanbul, 1930), p. 108.
33. Refik, pp. 171–73.
34. Refik, pp. 106–08; MM 3473:264–265, 2 Recep 1109/14 Jan. 1698; AS 3:123.
35. Rafeq, *The Province of Damascus.*
36. Teixeira, p. 121; SP 105/118:366, n.d.
37. SP 110/27:195–99, 20 Dec. 1737.
38. SP 110/27:201, 22 Dec. 1737.
39. Charles-Roux, pp. 70–72.
40. Aleppo 42:45; MM 2777:212, 8 Zilkade 1124/7 Dec. 1712; AS 1:38, 60.
41. Aleppo 32:170.
42. Aleppo 28:545.
43. Aleppo 42:45.
44. Russell 1:18–19.
45. Ibid.
46. Tavernier 1:151; d'Arvieux 6:377; Polonyalı Simeon p. 124; Evliya Çelebi, *Evliya Çelebi Seyahatnamesi* (Istanbul, 1896–1938), 9:376.
47. Aleppo 15:717; Russell 1:18; Aleppo 85:4.
48. Aleppo 28:200; Russell 1:36.
49. Aleppo 19:384, 390; Aleppo 35:34.
50. Aleppo 20:15, 88; AS 1:102.
51. AS 1:200, 201, 210.
52. Russell 1:19.
53. Aleppo 15:717.
54. Elviya Çelebi 9:337.
55. Russell 1:20–21.
56. Inalcik, "The Hub of the City: The Bedestan of Istanbul," *International Journal of Turkish Studies* 1:1–17.
57. Aleppo 52:508.
58. Aleppo 52:56.
59. Aleppo 24:115.
60. Aleppo 28:627.
61. Aleppo 17:352.
62. Aleppo 28:347.
63. Aleppo 36:177.
64. Aleppo 45:193.
65. Aleppo 43:138; MD 79:276, n.d.; 467, n.d.
66. Aleppo 15:717.
67. Aleppo 41:325.
68. Aleppo 52:631.
69. Aleppo 25:59, 308; Aleppo 34:263; SP 110/27:236, 1 Nov. 1739.
70. Rafeq, "The Local Forces in Syria in the Seventeenth and Eighteenth century," in *War, Technology, and Society in the Middle East,* ed. V. J. Parry and M. E. Yapp (London, 1975), pp. 286–87; Herbert Bodman, *Political Factions in Aleppo 1760–1826* (Chapel Hill, 1963), p. 24.
71. Aleppo 45:432.
72. MM 9874:295, 25 Zilkade 1140/3 June 1728; Aleppo 45:10.
73. Aleppo 52:56.
74. Russell 1:22.
75. Aleppo 45:178.

76. Aleppo 3:668.

77. Aleppo 18:433, 45:120; See also Marcus, "Privacy in Eighteenth-Century Aleppo: The Limits of Cultural Ideals" *IJMES* 18:165–84.

78. Leonhart Rauwolf, *Aigentliche Beschreibung der Raiss inn die Morgenländer* (Graz, 1971).

79. *Purchas His Pilgrimes* 8, extra series, p. 266.

80. Russell 1:23.

81. David, pp. 32–36; Evliya Çelebi 9:377; MM 9871:100, 2 Zilhicce 110/17 Sept. 1689; Aigen, p. 32.

82. Evliya Celebi 9:377.

83. Ertuğrul Düzdağ, *Şeyhülislam Ebussuûd Efendi Fetvaları Işığında 16. Asır Türk Hayati* (Istanbul, 1983), p. 149. See also Ralph Hattox, *Coffee and Coffeehouses: The Origins of a Social Beverage in the Medieval Near East* (Seattle, 1985).

84. Russell 1:147–48.

85. *Anthology of Islamic Literature,* ed. James Kritzeck (New York, 1966), p. 335.

86. Aleppo 3:947; 35:176.

87. Aleppo 33:7, 49, 159.

88. MM 3595:26, 27 Şevval 113/27 March 1702; MM 7326:43, 1 Cemaziyelevvel 1070/13 Feb. 1660.

89. Faroghi, *Towns and Townsmen in Ottoman Anatolia* (Cambridge, 1984), p. 233; MM 3462:292, 18 Ramazan 1108/10 April 1697.

90. MM 7326:46, 3 Cemaziyelevvel 1070/15 Feb. 1660.

91. It seems to have been Ottoman policy to tax valuable imported goods on a rate based on their retail value, while locally produced, bulky items were taxed by the load. MM 3462:281–82, 5 Ramazan 1108/10 April 1697.

92. Aleppo 21:211; MM 9838:160, 29 Zilkade 1064/11 Oct. 1654.

93. Aleppo 23:304; 22:364.

94. Sahillioğlu, "Taghayyur al-ṭurūq, al-tijāra wa'l-tanaffus bayna mina'ay Ṭarablūs al-shām wa'l-Iskandarun fi al-qarn al-sābiʿa ashr." p. 11.

95. A. H. de Groot, *The Ottoman Empire and the Dutch Republic, A History of the Earliest Diplomatic Relations, 1610–1630* (Leiden, 1978), p. 118; MD 80:1339, n.d.

96. Aleppo 26:269; MM 9829:36, 15 Safer 1044/10 Aug. 1634.

97. Polonyalı Simeon, p. 153.

98. MM 2765:40, 18 Safer 1055/15 April 1645.

99. de Groot, p. 177; MM 2777:5, 3 Recep 1124/6 Aug. 1712.

100. SP 105/115:446, 23 May 1707.

CHAPTER V

Money, Credit, and Investment

Upon examination, it seems obvious that except for a creeping bureaucratization of the tax structure, there was little significant evolution in the practice of the caravan trade in the Muslim Middle East from the thirteenth through the eighteenth centuries. Yet during the same period, remarkable transformations were occurring in the commercial life on the other side of the Mediterranean. These included the development of banking systems and the joint-venture-capital trading companies, which facilitated the extension of credit and the financing of trade. At the same time, excess capital generated by commercial ventures was often reinvested in trade, either in the form of direct credit relationships, in stock, or, increasingly, in production. All of these elements of change are familiar components of the process that saw mercantilism merge into a nascent capitalism in northwestern Europe.

The comparison of the two economic demiworlds, the Ottoman Empire and western Europe, which were frequently in contact, and often in competition, with one another, raises the question of whether the absence of a parallel transformation in the commercial life of the Muslim lands necessarily indicates a decline in their competitive edge vis-à-vis the West. The lack of any cross-fertilization from the West in the ways in which the Levant conducted its business might seem at first puzzling, as some of the mainstays of mercantile practice in Europe, such as the commenda agreements and letters of credit, seemed to have had their origins in the Middle East. There were also definite similarities between the economic position of merchants in Ottoman society and that of merchants in the states of early modern Europe, linked to the central role of trade in their respective economies, and these lead us to expect a similar evolution in their commercial activities and organizations.

It is apparent, however, that the same movement toward capitalism did not occur in the Levant. The underlying reasons why it did not are complex. In chapter 3, the process by which trade with the West was marginalized to the non-Muslim minorities was examined, and in the following chapter we shall discuss some institutional and philosophical barriers that prevented investors from establishing the ties to production that were becoming increasingly an option to their competitors in Europe. In this chapter, however, we will turn our attention to credit as it functioned in Aleppo, as an underpinning of the caravan trade and as an investment opportunity, as well as to the general patterns of investment that were chosen by the wealthy of the city, as a way of delineating the available options for investment that might have been more attractive than commerce and more accessible than crafts production. In short, it seems one of the prime reasons that money made from trade was not reinvested in protoindustry, as it was in England, Holland, or western Germany, was the availability of a host of other, more attractive options for returning profits to investors.

MONEY, TRADE, AND CREDIT

Although trade implies the exchange of commodities, there can be little doubt that it was specie, and especially silver, that oiled the mainsprings of the caravan trade in the Ottoman Empire. The regions of the Levant suffered a chronic deficit in their balance of trade with Asia, for although the spices, dyes, and cotton cloth of India all enjoyed high demand in the markets of the Middle East, the region produced little that could be offered in exchange. The shortfall had to be made good with the export of bullion. As an English merchant wrote in 1621:

> The Persians, Moores, and Indians, who trade with the Turkes at Aleppo, Mocha, and Alexandria, for Raw Silkes, Drugs, Spices, Indico, and Callicoes; have alwaies made, and still doe make, their returnes in readie money: for other wares, there are but few which they desire from forraine partes; some Chamblets, Corrall, wrought Silke, woolen-Cloth, with some trifles, they do yearely vent in all, not for above 40. or 50. thousand pounds sterling.[1]

The same author went on to estimate that the value of specie exported from the Levant to Iran, Yemen, and India to pay for imports from those places was twenty times that amount.

In fairness, it should be noted that the Aleppines consumed little of the Persian silk imported, as it was in large part reexported to Europe, underlying another aspect of the patterns of trade of the period. Just as the Middle East exported specie to Asia to meet its trade deficit, so the European merchants during the early seventeenth century had to import coins in large quantities to the Levant to finance their purchases there. It seems the Venetians alone were able to maintain a balance in their trade by exporting high-quality consumer goods, while England, the Netherlands, and France all had to import coins.[2]

The Europeans, and especially the English merchants with their mercantilist philosophy of trade, were well aware of this outflow of specie and were troubled by it. One of the frequent charges leveled against their competitors, the East India Company, after all, by the burghers and politicians of London was that it drained coinage away from England. This was countered by the company's argument that as England had forbidden the export of the coin of the realm, the specie used in the Asia trade was of European provenance earned on the continent through the sale of English goods.[3] To its credit in the eyes of all good mercantilists, the Levant Company did not suffer to the same extent as did its rivals from such nativist concerns, as by the middle of the seventeenth century the bulk of its purchases in the Middle East were financed through the sale, or barter, of broadcloth.

Nonetheless, the export of tin and broadcloth from England did not meet all the company's needs for silk, and bullion was necessary to make good the difference in the trade balance. Troubled by this reliance, the Levant Company issued an order in 1718 restraining the import of specie into the Ottoman Empire. But this order seems not to have been effective, as one factor wrote in 1725: "By reasons of the various ways of valuing the goods, the terms of a bargain are often doubtful, but what is bought for ready money will admit no dispute."[4]

Evidence that this attitude was fairly prevalent can be found through a casual perusal of the transactions in Aleppo registered by company factors in the first quarter of the eighteenth century. Those so preserved reveal that about a third involved cash. But despite the factors' willingness to use silver, the Levant Company's board of directors was not to be deterred from its policy, and it made subsequent attempts to enforce the ban in 1744.[5] By 1750, it seems to have been largely successful, although the victory may have been pyrrhic as the English refusal to pay with coin was often cited as one reason behind the decline of British commercial interests in Syria, and France's gain.[6]

While the Levant Company stockholders may have been troubled by the export of money to the Middle East, the Ottoman authorities clearly welcomed it. This is demonstrated by their early reduction of the duties assessed on coins: 1% to be taken at Iskenderun and 2% at Aleppo, as opposed to the 3% charged on all other goods at both stations.[7] Even this small impost was totally eliminated by the capitulatory agreement signed between England and the Porte in 1675.

But whatever the reason why bullion entered Syria, there is no doubt that substantial amounts of European currency entered the country, as it was the major medium of exchange in Aleppo's markets. Almost all transactions listed in the court records of Aleppo for the seventeenth century were given in values of either *ghurūsh riyālī* or *ghurūsh asadī*, the Spanish *réal* and the Netherlands *leuventhaler* respectively, and the basic Ottoman unit of currency, the *akçe*, locally called the *ʿuthmānī*, made its appearance only occasionally and then primarily in governmental decrees.

A vivid example of both the multiplicity of currencies in use in Aleppo and its predominantly European origin was the hoard of coins left in the estate of the merchant al-Sayyid Aḥmad al-Ghazzāl, discussed above in chapter 2. At his death al-Sayyid Aḥmad possessed 59,771 *ghurūsh* in coins, of which 2,326 were *ghurūsh riyālī;* 18,461 were *ghurūsh asadī,* the two given as being equivalent in value at that time; 5,113 gold Ottoman *şerifi* worth 11,078 *ghurūsh;* 6,205 gold Venetian ducats worth 15,512 *ghurūsh;* and 5,464 gold English coins worth 15,512.[8] The identification of some of the coins as English seems dubious at best, given the ban on the export of minted coins from England, but it is, of course, possible.

One of the problems arising for Aleppo's merchants out of this reliance on foreign coins was quality control. There were frequent complaints by the Ottomans that the Europeans were importing debased coinage, a charge admitted, to the chagrin of Levant Company consuls, who issued orders in 1664 and 1675 that all coins brought in on British ships be carefully checked lest the English reputation as fair traders in the Levant be ruined.[9] Ottoman coins were equally subject to counterfeiting and debasement techniques. But, in general, this practice was not as potentially profitable in their case as the coins of the realm were less in demand. This was due to the fact that their silver content was lower per weight of the coin, confirmed in an order to the mint in Aleppo in 1656, by which the standard of pure silver in the coinage to be minted was set at 80%.[10]

Interestingly, a similar lower standard was attempted in seventeenth-century England as a means to discourage the export of coins. The English experiment was not a whopping success, and it led eventually to the establishment of the gold standard for the pound sterling.[11] But in the Ottoman case, the state, hampered by the lack of the central control the English authorities had at their disposal, could neither effectively outlaw the use of foreign coins nor ban the export of its own money. Correspondingly, they suffered more from the attempt. In the end, all that was accomplished from their efforts was that no one trusted Ottoman currency.

This was shown aptly by a crisis that struck Aleppo in 1696, during which coins almost completely disappeared from the market for over six months as everyone waited to see what new coins rumored to be planned by the Ottoman mint would be like. It was hoped by the government that the establishment of a new monetary standard, albeit with a lower silver content, would help reduce the flow of silver to Iran by requiring a mandatory conversion of all foreign coins into Ottoman currency. What in fact happened was that the few European coins in circulation disappeared completely as they were hoarded by merchants fearful of losing their liquidity. Hoarding brought trade to a virtual standstill, with credit based on speculation on the new coins, now already devalued in the minds of the merchants, serving as the only medium of exchange. Prices fell in terms of Western currency, and the Levant Company factors wrote home urging the shipping out of large quantities of coins to take advantage of the situation, thereby ending the dearth of coins.[12]

Despite the failure, the Ottomans did not halt their efforts to establish a uniform coinage. In 1725, they issued a new coin called in the Aleppo sources either, aptly enough, the *ghurūsh jadīd* (the new *ghurūsh*), or the *ghurūsh zalāṭa,* an Arabic rendering of the official Ottoman name, *zolota,* which was reduced by the English to "zelotes." This time the government had more success in getting their coin accepted. The acceptance was due, in part, to the new coin's increased silver content per weight, but more to the stringent orders sent out from Istanbul that the money changers should collect all other silver coins and send them to the mints to be melted down.[13] Old ways die hard, however, and thirty years after the issuance of the new coin, the old ones still circulated in the marketplace, even if prices were routinely given in terms of the new *ghurūsh*.

The actual shortage of coins, coupled with the imbalance of internal trade within the Ottoman Empire, necessitated the wide-scale use of letters of credit for capital transfers between various cities. As noted earlier, these had been an intrinsic part of Muslim commercial life for centuries. Known as *ḥawāla* in Arabic and *poliça* in Ottoman Turkish, the system was fairly simple. Merchant X in Aleppo would swear in court that he was transferring a debt owed him by merchant Y in some distant city to merchant Z, also present in the Aleppo court, in return for either merchandise or payment of an outstanding debt. Merchant Z would then be issued a *ḥujja* by the court, listing the agreed-upon conditions, which he could present to Merchant Y when he arrived in that distant city. Upon payment of the terms of the letter, Merchant Y would be issued a second *ḥujja* (a notarized account of the transaction) from his neighborhood court to the effect that he was free from any outstanding debts owed Merchant X. The letter of credit, although representing a somewhat convoluted process, allowed merchants to carry a minimum of cash while traveling great distances and thus supplied the Middle Eastern version of the traveler's check.[14]

One significant application of the letters of credit was its use by English merchants resident in Aleppo. Throughout most of the Ottoman period, the English ran up a chronic deficit in the markets of Aleppo, purchasing far more silk than they sold broadcloth. In part, this was made up with the import of specie, but it was also financed by letters of credit drawn up in Istanbul, where the English sold more than they bought.[15] Presumably, the Aleppo merchants would, in turn, use the credit accumulated in Istanbul to pay taxes, purchase influence, or to buy Bursa silks and Salonica woolen cloths, both products listed as being imported from the north. An example of a letter of credit written by an English factor in Aleppo addressed to another in Istanbul on March 23, 1726, went as follows:

Sir,
This accompanys our sole bill of exchange for $500. say the summ of Dollars five hundred courant money of your Place payable at 31 days light unto Abdurahim Effendi brother to the Caddi of Aleppo for like

value here received by Hagi Nahan [sic] which pray accept and discharge as usual noting it so before your own account with premio of 1½ pct. not to be refused tho' we drew on you $2000 yesterday.[16]

Many similar examples could be drawn from the Aleppo records, with the exception that interest charges, mentioned in all such cases registered by the Levant Company, were absent. As with the case with loans to be discussed shortly, we are left to wonder if there were hidden service fees, or some other way to finance the risk of the transaction, in the letters of credit registered with Muslim courts. In at least one instance, the English factors noted in their dispatches that the local merchants were hesitant to accept letters of credit, as a new judge had just been appointed to Aleppo and they were waiting to see whether or not he would allow interest to be assessed on the letters.[17] This would seem to indicate that provisions for the taking of interest were, in fact, usually included in these arrangements.

Another possible attraction for entering into such agreements, besides hidden interest payments, lay in the fact that European coins differed in their real value from one Ottoman city to another, with their value being greater on the whole in Aleppo than in Istanbul, and greater still in Baghdad.[18] A letter of credit written in Istanbul for Aleppo in *ghurūsh asadī* would, therefore, have an implicit profit already written into it, as the coin was worth more in Aleppo than in Istanbul in absolute terms. The reverse would hold true for one written in Aleppo and carried the other way.

Human nature being then what it is now, the system sometimes broke down. An example of the potential for failure can be seen in a summary of an actual case. Merchant Z tried to collect from Merchant Y only to find him broke. When he pressed his case, Merchant Y fled the city leaving Merchant Z no other recourse but to return to the city wherein Merchant X dwelled and call him to court. There the judge ruled that as the letter was entered into in good faith on the part of Merchant Z, Merchant X remained in debt to him for the original amount as if the *ḥawāla* had not been established. Furthermore, it was up to X to collect from Merchant Y whatever he was owed by him originally. In another case, a Jew from Aleppo was only able to collect payment on a letter of credit, issued to him by an English merchant resident in Aleppo, from an English merchant in Istanbul after England's ambassador at the Porte intervened and forced the second English merchant to honor the letter of credit of the first.[19]

Even with disappointments such as found in the two preceding examples, the letters of credit found widespread application within the Ottoman Empire and even between the empire and Iran. But as Braudel has noted in his distinction of the European world system from that of Islam, letters of credit did not pass back and forth between the two geographical regions.[20] This should not surprise us, however, as we have seen it was extremely rare for Levantine merchants to operate in western Europe. Furthermore, as the Europeans had an overall trade deficit with the Middle East, such letters would seem to have little applicability in financing the import of European goods into the region. On the other hand, the absence of any letters in Aleppo relating to the Indian trade seems conspicuous, as we know from European sources such letters existed. The puzzling lack of any such letters registered in Aleppo may reflect the intermediary role of merchants in Basra and Baghdad who, being much more directly involved with the eastern trade, may have absorbed letters of credit from both directions. Lacking an examination of the court records of Baghdad, however, this can only remain a matter of speculation.

LOANS AND CREDIT

Despite Islam's well-known ban on usury, a dependence on credit in various forms permeated the entire fabric of Aleppo's commercial life. As we have seen above, credit was often necessary to finance long-distance trade in a region where coinage was in short supply and where there were chronic deficits in the balance of payments. But in addition to commerce, credit was also applied to the purchase of real estate, the payment of taxes, and the cost of craft production. Not surprisingly, then, we find that cases involving credit arrangements make up a substantial portion of the entries registered in the court records of Aleppo during the seventeenth century.

Interestingly, no one particular ethnic or social group emerges from these cases as the dominant creditors to the exclusion of all others. Muslims were the overwhelming majority of those registered as creditors, but they were also the vast majority of borrowers as well. Not all creditors were registered, however, as we shall see in the next section, and this raises the question as to the degree any sample taken from the court records might be skewed by the categories of persons who would use the courts. There are very few cases involving Europeans, for example, yet the letter books of the Levant Company are filled with accounts of loans either given to or taken from local people.

Additionally, there is a clear trend in the eighteenth century away from registering any loan agreements except those to villagers. But taking these cautions under advisement, the Muslim courts remained the only legal force a creditor had to collect an outstanding debt, and as such we will assume the cases so registered represent the patterns of credit as they existed in the seventeenth century, with the exception of credit relationships involving Europeans.

Figures 6 through 8 summarize data collected from 1,196 individual cases involving loans, extracted from the court records of Aleppo from the seventeenth and eighteenth centuries. To provide a representative sample, volumes were selected at random, and all cases involving loans from within were included in the total. In setting up these tables, the

Figure 6. Summary of Court Cases Involving Loans, Aleppo Court Registers, Volumes 17 (1630–33) and 20 (1635–37)

	Number of Cases	*% of Total*	*Average Amount* (ghurūsh)	*No. With Multiple Borrowers*
Military to villagers	239	34	318	123
Muslims to villagers	164	23	113	65
Military to Muslims	62	9	90	13
Muslims to Muslims	122	17	50	11
Women borrowers	9	1	75	—
Women lenders	19	3	56	6
Military to *dhimmīs*	11	2	145	1
Muslims to *dhimmīs*	31	4	64	3
Dhimmīs to Muslims	9	1	134	—
Dhimmīs to *dhimmīs*	13	2	63	—
Guardian as lender	8	1	45	1
Waqf as lender	11	2	145	—
Muslims to military	2	—	—	—
Military to military	7	1	77	—
Total	707			

designation *Muslim* has been used to indicate those persons identified in the court records as being Muslim males, but without any further indication as to their either having *askeri* status or being from a village. Similarly, *dhimmī* identifies the participants as either Christian or Jewish males. The category of women lenders was not broken down by religion, as almost all were Muslim. In categories where there were five or fewer cases obtainable, no average was given, as the sample was deemed too small to be meaningful.

Although these cases supply many insights into the economic life of Ottoman Aleppo, perhaps the most outstanding feature they reveal is the credit relationship that existed between wealthy urbanites and the villages of the surrounding countryside. Loans to the villagers were significant not only for the percentage of the total credit transactions they represented but for their actual volume. As these cases involved such large sums of money, we will presume that they were registered more conscientiously than were smaller day-to-day intraurban transactions. Therefore their overall share of the total number of cases may be exaggerated, but there can be little doubt as to the importance of the relationship they highlight. Their very numbers provide us with a painfully

Figure 7. Summary of Court Cases Involving Loans, Aleppo Court Registers, Volumes 31 (1665–67) and 35 (1683–86)

	Number of Cases	*% of Total*	*Average Amount* (ghurūsh)	*No. With Multiple Borrowers*
Military to villagers	109	33	524	64
Muslims to villagers	86	26	265	38
Military to Muslims	11	3	145	6
Muslims to Muslims	51	16	104	18
Women lenders	12	4	118	5
Muslims to *dhimmīs*	29	9	163	12
Dhimmīs to Muslims	8	2	69	2
Dhimmīs to *dhimmīs*	9	3	41	2
Muslims to military	3	1	—	—
Military to military	4	1	—	—
Waqf as lender	6	2	43	—
Total	328			

Figure 8. Summary of Court Cases Involving Loans, Aleppo Court Registers, Volumes 50–52 (1722–27)

	Number of Cases	*% of Total*	*Average Amount* (ghurūsh)	*No. With Multiple Borrowers*
Military to villagers	108	67	3,328	101
Muslims to villagers	21	13	2,481	17
Military to Muslims	3	2	—	1
Muslims to Muslims	14	9	379	3
Women lenders	4	3	—	—
Muslims to *dhimmīs*	3	2	—	—
Dhimmīs to *dhimmīs*	4	3	—	—
Waqf as lender	2	1	—	—
Muslims to military	1	—	—	—
Military to military	1	—	—	—
Total	161			

clear vision of the cycle of debt that linked the rural areas to various wealthy and influential individuals in the city.

The belt of villages dependent on Aleppo stretched out dozens of miles in all directions in a radius that encompassed Idlib, Ḥarīm, Jabal Samʿān, ʿAfrīn, Akhtārīn, and al-Bāb, thereby including within the perimeter of this rough circle the limits of the agricultural hinterlands of Aleppo in the Ottoman period.

The reasons why the villagers needed the loans were usually given in the registers. This feature is atypical of most urban loan cases, which simply registered that money was borrowed without a reason being elaborated for its need. We know, therefore, that the bulk of the money so borrowed by the villagers was needed to pay the taxes that had been levied collectively on their villages. The agricultural economy of Syria at this time does not seem to have been monied, as the peasants survived on a subsistence level with a barter economy. As a result, the peasants could only raise the cash that was demanded by the central government's tax collectors through borrowing. This need for cash, in turn, created burdens of dependence for the villagers that soon led to all spheres of their livelihoods.

Having turned their crops over to moneylenders to repay the loans, the peasants often needed to borrow more money to buy food to survive, creating interminable cycles of debt. In a typical scenario, the peasants would borrow money in one year only to find themselves having to borrow again to buy seed grain and food a few months later. It was not at all unusual for delegations to come to Aleppo from the various villages, year after year, to renegotiate their loans from the moneylenders. Each time this was done, the loan was increased, and the likelihoood that the peasants would ever be free from their burden of debt became ever slimmer.[21]

The usual pattern in such arrangements was for the villagers to borrow these sums collectively, with each adult male in the village responsible for a share. The combined pressure of debt and increasing taxation forced many to flee their responsibility by going to the mountains or to Aleppo. An indication of this was a petition sent to Istanbul in 1693: the judge of Maʿarrat al-Miṣrīn asked that the number of *avarız hanes* ("taxable households") assessed in his village be reduced from thirty-two to twenty as so many people had moved away.[22]

There was not much the village collectively could do in such cases. If the runaways had fled to Aleppo, the village elders could petition that the offenders be forced to contribute to the village's taxes for fifteen years. But in almost every single case brought before a judge in Aleppo to get a recalcitrant ex-villager to contribute to help his former neighbors, the case was dismissed, as the ex-peasant was able to find witnesses from his new urban neighborhood who were willing to testify that he had lived there longer than the statutory fifteen years.[23]

The actual registration of the loans to the villagers was usually affirmed by a large delegation who would swear they represented the village collectively. The villagers in turn would have a prominent urban personality, usually a member of the *ʿulamā*, the military or the merchants, who would act as the village's guarantor *(kafīl)*. In addition, the villagers would often offer as a mortgage agricultural lands in their villages. While we might expect that these would include houses, orchards, and olive groves, all classified by Muslim law as private property *(mulk)*, these tracts, oddly, might sometimes include fields *(filāḥa, mazraʿa)*, which according to Muslim law belonged to the community as a whole, represented by the state *(miri)* and could not be sold.[24] Through the villagers' subsequent default on such loans, we can trace the process by which village land passed into the possession of urbanites, well documented for the eighteenth century, as having been in full swing by the middle of the seventeenth century.[25]

The peasants' creditors represented the various wealthy elements in Aleppo's upper echelons. Although members of the *askeri* class were by far the majority of those engaged in such activities, civilians were also prominently involved, among them the famous seventeenth-century Shafaʿī *muftī* Shaykh Abū al-Wafā al-ʿUrdī, the *shāhbandar* Muṣṭafā Çelebi, and a Greek Orthodox bishop who lent money to Muslim villagers. The extension of credit, therefore, was clearly not solely a prerogative of the military, although by the end of the century they had emerged as the peasants' leading creditors. This assertion is supported by Figure 8, where the military constituted a full eighty percent of those lending money to the peasantry. This movement toward a monopolization of credit by the military was most probably traceable to several factors: the military's frequent contact with the villages in the roles of administrators, tax collectors, and policemen; its increasing domination of most spheres of Syria's economic and political life in the eighteenth century; and the simple fact that as a group it had access to a large amount of surplus cash in the form of taxes and bribes, as well as the only armed force available to collect the taxes in the first place.

In his study of credit in Anatolia in the early seventeenth century, Ronald Jennings made a convincing case for his characterization of moneylending in that region as having been atomistic, with no discernible class of moneylenders.[26] In Aleppo, however, this was not always the case. The incidence of both multiple creditors—that is, those who were registered as having extended credit in more than one case—and partnership borrowings is relatively low in the urban examples. This would support a characterization of credit as being atomistic. On the other hand, the occurrence of such cases involving villagers is striking. In figure 6, 138 of the 239 total cases in the category "military to villagers" involved multiple creditors, as did 69 of the 164 cases listed under "Muslim to villagers." In sharp contrast, only 5 of the 62 cases listed under "military to Muslims" and only 11 of the 122 "Muslim to Muslim" category did so.

A similar ratio can be found in figure 8, where Osman Efendi, the tax collector of Aleppo, was the lender in 44 out of the total 108 cases in the category of "military to villager," and a certain Yeğen Hasan Ağa b.

Ahmed Ağa was involved in another 20. With two individuals accounting for over half the total number of loans in that category, there can be little doubt that there were wealthy individuals in Aleppo who acted as major moneylenders. This premise is given further validity below with the abstracts from the *mukhallafāt* register (the inventory of the estates of deceased Aleppines kept by the *qassām al-ᶜaskarī* discussed above in chapter 4). Contrary to stereotypes, these large-scale moneylenders were not from the non-Muslim minorities, but were members of the city's military and religious elites.

The use of credit in Aleppo itself departs somewhat from that which we have seen in the countryside. The first important divergence was that the number of multiple creditors, and, therefore, of potentially large-scale moneylenders, was a much smaller percentage of the total than existed in the rural areas. These patterns of credit are therefore much more in line with Jennings's findings for Anatolia. Most of these urban loans were small, and the majority of creditors' names only occurred once in the registers. There were, of course, exceptions to this generalization, however, and some of the persons who occurred as frequent lenders to the villagers, Shaykh Abū al-Wafā al-ᶜUrdī, for example, also registered multiple loans within Aleppo.

Another pattern of credit in the city that is disclosed by these cases is the relationship between the various guilds and wealthy individuals, a parallel to conditions in the countryside. In these, the usual pattern was for the creditor to supply the craftsmen with the necessary capital to buy the materials of the trade. The loan in turn would be repaid by installments taken from the craftsmen's earnings.

An example of this type of arrangement was registered on March 24, 1634. In a deposition given before the court, the Christian Yaghūb W. Baghrāṣ and his son Luṭfī attested that they owed Ḥusayn Çelebi b. Ḥājj ᶜUthmān eighty *ghurūsh*, which was the price of raw silk they had obtained from him. In return, they promised to repay the loan in monthly installments and offered as a mortgage a half share in a shop with a silk loom located in the Judayda quarter.[27] Such cases underlie the relatively low economic status of skilled craftsmen in Ottoman Aleppo, as there are many such cases of craftsmen having to borrow from wealthy merchants to stay in business. Another indication of their less-than-favored position is the frequent occurrence of multiple ownership of workshops by the wealthy of Aleppo (see figures 9–11 below). Thus many of the city's craftsmen were dependent on the wealthy not only for capital but for their workplaces as well.

With this extensive support of both the peasantry and the craftsmen through the use of loans, we are left wondering what the profit motive was in these relationships for the creditors. The court records of Aleppo, in contrast with those of central Anatolia studied by Jennings, are silent as regards interest, with the exception of two narrowly defined categories: loans made from the inheritance of orphans and cash *waqf*s. This omission raises the question of why the courts in different parts of the empire took widely diverging attitudes toward the question of interest.

Jennings found that in most cases he studied interest charges were registered with the loans, with the permissible interest charged being set at twenty percent. This is in seeming contradiction to Muslim law and the practice of the courts in Syria. The traditional Muslim interpretation held that the lending of money at interest constituted usury *(ribā)*, which was disallowed under most circumstances. Legal tricks were developed over the centuries to contravene the ban, but it nonetheless remained in force de jure, even if not totally de facto, in Ottoman Syria.[28]

There can be no question as to the Aleppo courts' attitudes toward loans that charged interest, as there was a uniformity in the rulings on its illegality that, following the letter of Muslim law, they handed down. Typical of their response is a case registered on January 22, 1641, in which Ṣafā bnt. ʿAbdullah charged that a man named Mustafa Çavuş b. Derviş Mehmed Efendi owed her 120 *ghurūsh*, remaining from the principal of 200 *ghurūsh* she had lent him. Mustafa replied in his deposition that he had already paid Ṣafā 140 *ghurūsh*. She acknowledged the receipt of the money but said that only 80 *ghurūsh* had gone to repay the principla, as the other 60 *ghurūsh* were due as interest. Hearing this, the judge reminded her that *ribḥ* (literally "profit," but in this context more broadly interpreted to mean "usury") was unlawful. He stated that Mustafa was only responsible for the remaining amount of the principal, 60 *ghurūsh*, he had borrowed.[29]

This case clearly disallowed interest at any percentage, and not just interest deemed usurious, as the judge stated that any gain constituted usury. Nonetheless, we know from the Levant Company papers that the English merchants frequently made loans to local people charging rates of around twenty percent, and they speak of this as being a universally practiced custom in the city. This assertion is, in turn, supported by Volney:

> But nothing is more destructive to Syria, than the shameful and excessive usury customary in that country. When the peasants are in want of money to purchase grain cattle, &c. they can find none but by mortgaging the whole, or part, of their future crop, greatly under its value. . . . the most moderate interest is twelve per cent. the usual rate is twenty, and it frequently rises as high as even thirty.[30]

Volney was writing at the end of the eighteenth century, but there seems little reason to suspect that the moneylenders of his day were any less altruistic than were those of a century before.

In further support of this assumption were the activities of the money changers' guild (*ṣarrāf*s) in the city. As seen above, theirs was a necessary occupation in a city where so many different currencies were in circulation at the same time. This guild, which had a largely although not exclusively Jewish membership, exchanged the various coins, charging a commission for the service. As they had large amounts of coins on hand, it would seem that they often lent money out at interest as well. The seventeenth-century German visitor Aigen reported that they did so regularly, charging as much as twenty-four percent annually on their loans.[31] Besides this definitely unfriendly account, there is additional evidence of this guild's moneylending activity in the court records, including a case where a Muslim established a *muḍāraba* agreement with a Jewish money changer that netted a handsome profit. But even in these cases, no mention of interest is made,[32] although as those involved were making a profit, we must suspect that there was.

The religious ban on interest was not universal, however. Cash *waqf*s and the estates of orphans were allowed to charge interest under the theory that the interest supported charitable causes. The cash *waqf* is an interesting Ottoman legal innovation, having been disallowed by legal scholars in the pre-Ottoman periods. A recent study by Jon Mandaville has shown that even among the Ottoman legists themselves, an often bitter controversy raged over whether Muslim law allowed for the establishment of cash *waqf*s, the principals of which could be loaned out at interest. Despite the debate, such pious endowments were a prominent feature in Ottoman Anatolian life, although Mandaville's study raised the question of whether they were ever established in the presumably more conservative Arab provinces of the empire.[33]

The court records of Aleppo answer the question for at least that part of the Arab world, as they contain numerous references to cash *waqf*s whose principals were lent out at interest. It is not clear when the custom was introduced in Aleppo, but al-Ṭabbākh refers to a *waqf* established by the governor Ahmed Mataf in 1597, consisting of ten thousand gold dinars. The terms of the endowment set the chargeable *ribḥ* (the use of the term here denotes permissible profit as opposed to illegal *ribā*) at ten percent and stipulated that the money could not be lent to an amir, or anyone who held wealth or office.[34] As in the case of the Ahmed Mataf's *waqf*, most other cash *waqf*s in the city were designed to help the poor, and the interest earned was often designated to pay the extraordinary taxes levied on a particular city quarter.

An illustration of how this worked is found in a case registered on October 11, 1660, in which the administrator of the *waqf* established by a certain Mehmed Ağa for the poor of the quarter of al-Farāfira presented an accounting of the *waqf*'s activities for the year 1659–60. From this we learn the principal of the endowment was 500 *ghurūsh*, from which he collected 100.5 *ghurūsh* as interest during the year in question. Of that money, he spent 95 *ghurūsh* to help the quarter pay its taxes. The remainder of the money, as well as 4 *ghurūsh* left over from the year before, was spent on unnamed projects that he affirmed, benefited the quarter. The rate charged seems to have been 20%, and not the 10% set by the *waqf* deed of Ahmed Mataf. It was, however, the higher rate that was most often registered in such cases.[35]

While *waqfs* established for quarters list interest rates, those established to assist older, more established pre-Ottoman institutions, such as those of the Umayyad Mosque and Sulṭān al-Ghawrī, never mentioned the word *ribḥ*. These *waqf*s made extensive loans, especially to villagers, but, apparently following older practice, shied away from declaring whether or not they were charging interest.[36] This would indicate that as far as the *waqf*s in Aleppo were concerned, two separate traditions coexisted at this time. On the one hand, there was the continuation of a pre-Ottoman *waqf* institution, represented by such venerable institutions as the Umayyad Mosque, which may have considered lending money without interest as a part of their charitable function, and the distinctly Ottoman practice of the cash *waqf.*

In addition to the cash *waqf,* the other general exception to the ban on interest was the case of loans made from the estates of orphaned minors. This exception mirrors a traditional concern in Muslim law for the plight of orphans. In those situations, the orphans' guardians were allowed to charge interest on loans they contracted from their charges' principal, if they swore that all profits so earned would go solely for the material support of the orphans. This practice engendered none of the controversy in Ottoman legal circles that the cash *waqf* did, and it appears to have been a common practice throughout the empire. The interest charged in these cases, like those of the cash *waqf,* fell into the ten- to twenty-percent range. But as the amount represented by the orphans' estates was generally small, this interesting example of the flexibility of Muslim law in allowing interest must be recognized as being fairly insignificant as far as Aleppo's overall economy was concerned.[37]

If we have trouble finding mention of interest, there are also few references to actual default, given the large number of loans registered. This is of interest in itself, but also because a study conducted on Aleppo in the second half of the eighteenth century found defaults to be commonplace.[38] We cannot be certain of the reasons for the discrepancy for the reporting of defaults from one century to the next, whether they actually increased or were only reported more conscientiously. But we would suspect that the rate of loan repayments was in fact high due to the nature of Muslim society, in which families constituted corporate bodies, responsible for the actions of individual members.

Most loan agreements established the responsibility of a guarantor *(kafīl)* for the debt, if the borrower defaulted, family members could be held responsible for repayment of a relative's debt for up to fifteen years after the loan was contracted.[39] Should the debtor be present in the city but unable to repay the loan on schedule, two options were possible. The first involved rescheduling the loan into installments *(taqsīṭ),* a set amount per month until the total was repaid. The repayment schedule itself often resulted in disputes over the terms. In response to one such dispute, the judge admonished both parties and set forth the principle that installment payments were only legal if they had been stipulated at the time the loan was contracted, or if both parties had agreed in court later on to a rescheduling of payments. Failing either of these conditions, the loan had to be repaid in toto at the time stipulated by the original loan contract.[40]

The second alternative involved delaying the payment until a later specified date *(ta'jīl)*. This action also required the agreement of both borrower and lender in court before it was legally binding.[41]

If either of these compromises failed to refinance a debt and if there were no family members to assume it, the debtor would be put into prison in the city's citadel. In most cases, however, the term of imprisonment was not long before a delegation from the quarter in which the debtor lived would present itself before the court and assume the responsibility of the debt's repayment.

Typical of such actions was a case registered on July 31, 1718, in which a delegation from the quarter of Shaykh Yabrāq, all Muslims, testified that a certain Christian, Naṣir w. Khabūr, who had been imprisoned for debt should be released from the citadel as he possessed neither money nor property, other than the clothes he wore, with which he could repay his debt. As such, by the terms of Muslim law he should be released, as the imprisonment of people without the means to pay was deemed unjust. The people of the quarter in turn swore that they would collectively bear the responsibility of Nāṣir's debt, and he was released into their custody.[42]

CAPITAL INVESTMENT

One of the problems facing the wealthy in any preindustrial society was finding a secure haven to invest their money once they had gotten hold of it. We have seen that both commerce and moneylending offered opportunities for generating wealth to enterprising Aleppines, and in this there was a close parallel between Ottoman Syria and mercantilist Europe. The important difference between the two societies, however, came in the options that were available in each for securing that wealth and the patterns of investment that evolved from them. Once raised, however, capital was almost always reinvested in both economies. In the Middle East, this was largely due to the scarcity of specie that we have already noted, but perhaps a residual fear of robbery or confiscation had a part in determining the societal attitude toward investment as well.[43]

The tracing of the patterns of investment is not easy, but some insight is provided for seventeenth-century Aleppo through the existence of one remaining *mukhallafāt* register (Aleppo Court Records, volume 33, 1676–80). Despite its richness of detail, the estates register has some important limitations as a source for social history.[44] The first is the absence of non-Muslims from the register, which prevents us from making comparisons as to the relative wealth of various ethnic groups in the city as well as from discovering preferred patterns of investment among the various communities. It is also obvious that the volume does not give a complete listing of even all those with *askeri* status who died between the years 1676 and 1680, as the wealthy and males are clearly over represented.

Of the 93 individuals listed in volume 33, only 29 were women, and of the total of both genders, 26 individuals fell into the category of possessing over 1,000 *ghurūsh* in wealth at the time of their death, the criterion for being listed in figures 9–11; 45 possessed property valued between 100 and 999 *ghurūsh;* and only 22 held property valued at less than 100 *ghurūsh*. This apparent imbalance prevents any kind of general statement on the makeup of economic classes in the city, either to their proportionate numbers, or to their composition, either by occupation or ethnicity. What this material does reveal are the identities and occupations of what were certainly some of Aleppo's wealthiest Muslims and the ways in which they invested their wealth.

But even within the boundaries of this reduced parameter, there is an important lacuna: the actual percentage, in terms of monetary value, that real-estate holdings constituted of a deceased individual's total financial worth. As real estate was divided by Muslim legal practice into twenty-four portions *(qiraṭ)*, it was divisible among the heirs as it was, without having to be sold. The heirs would simply get the number of shares of every piece of real estate owned by the deceased corresponding to the share of the total estate to which they were entitled. There was no need, therefore, for the court to assign a value to the property unless it were needed to meet an outstanding claim against an estate that had no other assests. As a result, while property is listed by name in many of the estates, we do not know its commercial value, causing real estate to be underrepresented as a percentage of the monetary value of the investments presented in figures 9–11.

Despite these shortcomings, it must be acknowledged that the estate registers provide a unique glimpse into how wealth was invested. Admittedly, the examples provided by only one such register can not begin to

Figure 9. Composition of Wealth Held by Members of Aleppo's Military/Bureaucratic Elite, Aleppo Court Registers, Volume 33 (1676–80)

Individual's Name	*Total Wealth* (ghurūsh)	*Cash*	*Real Estate*	*Commercial Goods*	*Debts Owed Deceased*	*Animals & Slaves*	*Household*	*Debts Deceased Owed* (*% of Wealth*)
Hac Ebü Bekir Çorbacı b. Hac Yusuf	8,189	—	19%	49% (soap)	23%	5%	4%	−5%
Mehmed Ağa b. Abdallah	32,616.75	—	26%	2%	61%	1%	10%	—
Canpulatzade Ali Paşa	8,284.25	42%	—	—	4%	—	54%	—
Hac Mehmed Ağa b. Mahmud Ağa, *dizdar* of citadel	19,760.75	—	14%	—	80%	3%	2%	—
Hac Murad Çorbacı b. Hasan	2,102	84%	—	3%	6%	4%	3%	—
Mehmed Paşa b. Kasım	3,008	1%	NA	—	92%	5%	3%	—
Ahmed Paşa b. Mehmed Maarezli	1,786.5	—	11%	—	68%	15%	6%	—
Hüseyin Paşa b. Ibrahim	2,273	—	4%	33% (soap)	51%	7%	4%	—
Mehmed Paşa b. Hüseyin	7,260.25	7%	NA	28% (rice)	58%	—	7%	—
Salim Bey b. Hac Yusuf, ibn al-Balaṭ	8,901	11%	NA	2%	76%	3%	8%	−21%

Figure 10. Composition of Wealth Held by Members of Aleppo's Civilian Elite, Aleppo Court Registers, Volume 33 (1676–80)

Individual's Name	*Total Wealth* (ghurūsh)	*Cash*	*Real Estate*	*Commercial Goods*	*Debts Owed Deceased*	*Animals & Slaves*	*Household*	*Debts Deceased Owed (% of Wealth)*
Sayyid ʿAṭā Allah Efendi	2,002.25	—	44%	—	—	20%	35%	—
Sayyid Aḥmad b. Sayyid Muḥammad al-Ghazzāl	87,947.25	68%	—	15% (tin, cloth, dyes)	17%	—	—	−20%
Sayyid Muṣṭafā Efendi Tahazādah, *Naqīb al-ashrāf*	27,915.5	—	NA	51% (lye, soap, grain)	16%	6%	27%	—
Bektaş Çelebi b. Ahmed Efendi	1,871.5	—	75%	—	—	—	25%	—
Ḥājj Ibrāhīm b. Ḥājj Yasīn Kethüda of gardeners' guild	3,284	18%	78%	—	—	—	3%	—
Sayyid Mūsā Efendi b. Sayyid al-Rām Ḥamdānī	7,055.5	8%	14%	10% (grain)	61%	—	2%	−5%
ʿAlī Efendi b. Muḥammad Qudwat al-Mudarrisīn	1,529	—	NA	—	92%	—	8%	—

Figure 11. Composition of Wealth Held by Aleppo Women, Aleppo Court Records, Volume 33 (1676–80)

Individual's Name	*Total Wealth* (ghurūsh)	*Cash*	*Real Estate*	*Commercial Goods*	*Debts Owed Deceased*	*Animals & Slaves*	*Household*
Melike Hanım bnt. Yusuf Paşa, wife of Mustafa Ağa	15,066.5	—	19%	—	52% (*mahr* 7%)	11%	17%
Ṣāliḥa bnt. Kurd Ağa, wife of Siray al-Din Çelebi	7,011	—	2%	—	14% (*mahr*)	1%	82%
Ḥājja Ṣāliḥa bnt. Ḥājj Yasīn, married to Safer Paşa	4,355	21%	9%	—	44% (*mahr* 18%)	—	26%
Qarhābū bnt. Abdullah, wife of Seyyid Mehmed Bey	3,944	—	—	—	13% (*mahr*)	4%	22%
Āmina bnt. Ilyās	2,704	—	27%	—	—	—	73%
Emine Hanım bnt. Müselli Ağa, wife of Ahmed Ağa	1,830.5	—	52%	—	22% (*mahr*)	4%	22%
Ḥājja Amina Khatūn bnt. Shaykh Abū Bakr al-ʿUmarī	1,720	—	81%	—	7%	—	12%
Fāṭima Khatūn bnt. Halil Paşa, wife of Sayyid ʿAbd al-Qādir Efendi	1,240	—	57%	—	8%	—	35%

supply a comprehensive survey of wealth in Aleppo in the seventeenth century. They can, however, tell us a great deal that is useful when supplemented by the materials contained in the day-to-day recordings of the court registers.

Based on these two sources, we can safely say that the areas of investment favored by the Aleppines were real estate, tax farming, *waqf*s, trade, and moneylending. Real estate was typically the most common investment choice in various premodern Muslim societies, as it was in most preindustrial societies everywhere. Under Muslim law, however, there were certain limits on what could be privately owned. While fields were legally the property of the state (*miri* lands) in its role as guardian of the interests of the Muslim community as a whole, and were, therefore, inalienable, buildings, gardens, and orchards were designated as belonging to the sphere of private ownership *(mulk)*. Although Aleppines were technically barred from buying *miri* lands, obtainment of real estate within the *mulk* category was clearly a high priority for them, and almost all those listed in the estates register owned at least some property.

It is difficult to ascertain any clear trends from these cases, but it would seem that the civilian elite typically held a greater percentage of their total wealth in the form of real estate than did members of the *askeri* group. A possible explanation for this might lie in the more transient nature of the military, the upper ranks of which were often transferred from one end of the empire to the other within the space of a few years. Another factor to be considered was the more intrinsically conservative character of the established civilian elites, which may have inhibited them from engaging in alternative enterprises such as moneylending and tax farming. Neither explanation is entirely satisfactory, however, as there were *askeri* individuals who invested in real estate at a rate seemingly equivalent to that of the local notables. Additionally, there were examples of local notables pursuing what were more typically military investment patterns.

The types of real estate chosen for investment again offers no discernible pattern. Rather, it would seem diversity was the key feature in real-estate acquisition, with most individuals in the register owning both commercial and agricultural properties. Nonetheless, there was sometimes a certain degree of specialization. The administrator *(kethüda)* of the gardeners' guild, Ḥājj Ibrāhīm b. Ḥājj Yasīn, for example, while owning one shop, had, appropriately enough, most of his real-estate holdings in gardens and vineyards.

More typical were the holdings of the *naqīb al-ashrāf,* Sayyid Mūsā Efendi Ṭahazādah. His real-estate holdings including 10 houses, 13 shops, a coffeehouse, 6 bakeries, a dye house, a *qaysārīya,* as well as gardens and vineyards. Similarly, a representative of the *askeri,* Mehmed Ağa b. Abdullah, possessed gardens worth the considerable sum of 3,000 *ghurūsh,* 2 houses worth 2,000 *ghurūsh,* a *qaysārīya* worth 1,000 *ghurūsh,* a coffee shop worth 300 *ghurūsh,* a dye house worth 400, 2 gold shops worth 200 total, 4 other shops worth 200 total, and a half share in a soap factory in Idlib worth 1,000 *ghurūsh.* These two examples are drawn from representatives of the city's *askeri* and the religious elites, but we find a similar pattern of diversity for a merchant's estate from an earlier register, that of the *fakhr al-tujjār* Sīdī Muḥammad Çelebi ibn al-ʿArīf, who owned 2 shops, 2 cloth-weaving establishments (one with 5 looms, the other with 2), and orchards and fields outside the city's walls.[45]

Loans were also considered to be an appropriate investment for the wealthy, and the patterns presented by the estates register are interesting in what they confirm about the trends presented in the abstracts on loan cases already discussed above. In the first place, they show that moneylending was ubiquitous in Aleppo. Of the 93 persons whose estates were registered, 33 had loans outstanding to them at the time of their death, 26 owed outstanding debts to creditors, and 13 of the 33 creditors also owed outstanding debts to others.

In the protracted cases settling the estates that are also contained in the register, our suspicions that not all debts were registered is confirmed, for as we have seen the loans registered at court were usually large and to villagers. By contrast, the loans we learn about through postmortem legal wranglings were usually both to persons living within the city and of small amounts. The vast majority of loans registered in the estates were under fifty *ghurūsh* in value, although the truly wealthy made sizable loans to both peasants and members of the various craft guilds. This information complements the trends contained in the abstracts, confirming the supposition that moneylending was, in fact, one of the prime areas of capital investment for wealthy Aleppines.

From these examples, it becomes obvious that real-estate investments and moneylending in Ottoman Aleppo, like capital investments in general, were extremely diversified. In fact, the most outstanding general feature in the economic life of the city in this period was an apparent lack of specialization in either commercial activities or investments on the part of the wealthy members of the society. This diversity in investment behavior seems to be in sharp contrast to the patterns developing in contemporary England, if not Europe as a whole. There were, of course, exceptions. Sayyid Aḥmad b. Sayyid Muḥammad al-Ghazzāl, discussed above, seems to have had strictly merchant interests. But nonetheless, it seems safe to venture that most wealthy Aleppines maintained an interest in a number of economic endeavors.

Another problem in assessing patterns of investment is presented by the tax farms (*mukata'a*, or, if held for a life tenure, *malikane*). In the seventeenth century, these tax farms were not, strictly speaking, personal wealth, and so were not registered as possessions at the time of a person's demise. Yet this institution, which was becoming a fixture of Ottoman fiscal operations in the seventeenth century, was an important opportunity for investment. An individual, by paying a set fee to the government, was entitled to collect the taxes in a a given agricultural region or village, from a specific trade, or some other tax-producing activity, such as the customs office, keeping all the extra taxes collected for him- or herself. We have already seen that this institution generated considerable wealth for the city's customs officers, but a multiplicity of other tax farms provided others with an equal opportunities to return profits on their investments.

We are told by al-Ghazzī that in 1693, Aleppo received an imperial order declaring that the tax farms, in effect, constituted private property for the holder in that they could be sold for cash, were the holder's to keep for life, and could be inherited by the holder's children upon his death.[46] This provided the legal acknowledgment of an unofficial process that was already under way. Doubtless, its introduction as state policy encouraged the wealthy to consider tax farming as not only a profitable but a secure investment.

Register 33 was composed at a time when this fiscal transformation was occurring, although only one individual, Mehmed Bey Çorbacı b. Halil, is listed as holding a tax farm, that of the *dār al-ghanam,* the taxes collected on sheep brought into the city. After the order of 1693, the process shifted into high gear, and numerous cases of the registration of tax farms occur. Two independent studies of Aleppo in the second half of the eighteenth century amply demonstrate that by then the holding of tax farms was the most lucrative investment Aleppines could make, insuring not only wealth but political power and status.[47] This was understood by the Levant Company factors, as well, and they often rated potential debtors' ability to repay loans based on the tax farms they held.[48]

The pattern in Aleppo that showed an evolution toward the privatization of tax farms closely followed developments in the Ottoman Empire as a whole. By the middle of the seventeenth century, the classical Ottoman *timar* system, which gave land to a soldier in return for military service to the state, had become moribund and anachronistic. It no longer served its original purpose of providing a cavalry force for the empire, which, finding itself with a need for an infantry equipped with modern firearms, could no longer afford to maintain its system of *timar*-holding cavalry.[49] In the place of the *timars*, the central treasury began to sell the rights to collect taxes from the villages, formerly held by the cavalry as *timars*, to various wealthy individuals. This arrangement supplied the government with the cash to equip and hire infantry troops and provided the tax farmers with an unprecedented opportunity for acquiring wealth.

In the Aleppo region, there was a very close parallel between the individuals who lent money to the villages and those who emerged as those same villages' tax farmers. Significantly, both the overwhelming majority of moneylenders in that category and of those who were tax farmers *(mukata'acı, malikaneci)* were from the *askeri* class, and in the registers from the early eighteenth century, many of the moneylenders to the various villages are identified as being the tax farmers of the same villages, confirming the link between the two activities.

Like the tax farm, *waqf* endowments could form another category of hidden investments that would not appear in a deceased person's estate listing. In theory, *waqfs* were properties that were turned over by the endower to the Muslim community as a whole to provide income for some charitable cause. In this form, known as the *waqf khayrī*, family members could be designated as the administrators of the endowment and therefore entitled to an income, but the bulk of the endowments were designated for some religious or humanitarian purpose. Falling into this category were all the magnificent Ottoman structures—mosques, khans, and bazaars—built in Aleppo in the sixteenth and seventeenth centuries by prominent government officials.

There was, however, another type of *waqf,* whose legality was often in question, favored by the less prominent members of Aleppo's society.

This was the *waqf ahlī,* which in effect established the charitable cause to be supported by the *waqf* as being the endower's own family. In this form, the *waqf* must be seen as having constituted a capital investment for the endower. The advantages of such an arrangement were manifold. The property was tax-exempt, it could not be confiscated, and it was not subjected to the Islamic laws of inheritance. The last characteristic was probably one of the most important incentives, as it allowed the property to remain intact, not only in the family's possession but in the hands of only one designee, the executor *(mutawallī),* in effect establishing a Muslim equivalent of primogeniture.

An example of such a *waqf ahlī* is found registered on July 12, 1633. A widow from the village of Darkūsh declared on that date that she had rented lands left to her and her descendants as a *waqf* by her husband. The *waqf* was extensive, consisting of olive groves and mulberry orchards in several villages in the vicinity of Darkūsh, as well as implements for silk spinning. Correspondingly, the rent was also high, 2,520 *ghurūsh* for the period of seven years. As no other chartible cause was listed as the beneficiary of the endowment, we must assume that the cause so favored was none other than the woman and her family.[50] Such family *waqf*s became increasingly popular in the late Ottoman period and represent a significant proportion in many individual family's investment portfolios. This assumption is supported by a recent study that puts the number of *waqf*s established in Aleppo between 1718 and 1800 as being 687, of which 50.7% were *khayrī,* 39.3% were *ahlī,* and 10% were mixed.[51]

The non-Muslims also established *khayrī waqf*s in the city, although on a scale far below that of their Muslim neighbors. They were administered similarly to those established by the Muslim community, and sometimes even had Muslim executors.[52] Unlike Muslim *waqf*s, however, Christian *waqf* property could be sold for cash, but in other respects, the rules governing them seem to have been drawn from the Muslim tradition.[53] Christian *waqf*s were for the most part designated to help the poor of the various Christian communities, the Greek Orthodox and Suryanis being the groups most frequently benefited. But before we jump to the conclusion that this is yet a further sign of assimilation of those two communities into mainstream Muslim society, there is the question of whether the Maronites and Armenians, generally more prosperous than the other two communities, might simply have chosen not to register their charitable foundations with the Muslim courts. A similar problem arises with the Jewish community, as although al-Ghazzī lists one Jewish *waqf* as having been established in the eighteenth century, cases involving *waqf*s administered by that community are absent from the Muslim court records.[54]

In summary, we can say that property in its various forms, and investments based on property, such as tax farms were clearly the major form of capital investment for Muslim Aleppines, and even loans, which were the second most popular arena of investment, were largely tied to the agricultural rather than the commercial sector. In addition, another form of property, *waqf,* formed a secure haven for wealth. But the estates register also reveals the possibility of commerce as an investment option to individuals whom we might not normally consider to have been merchants.

This confirms the earlier supposition that trade in Aleppo was not confined to a specialized group; rather, like real estate or moneylending, it was perceived as having been a viable investment option for those who had excess capital and wanted to broaden the scope of their seventeenth-century "portfolios." This is not to say that no one specialized in trade almost to the exclusion of all other activities, but that in addition to these, individuals who might not be properly be considered as merchants were occasionally active in mercantile projects as well. Similarly, we have seen that merchants such as the Arīḥāwīzādahs often secured their wealth in other forms of investments, a trend further confirmed by one of the most extensive *waqf*s established in eighteenth-century Aleppo, that of the merchant Ḥājj Mūsā al-Amīrī.[55]

Examples of such "part-time" merchants in the *mukhallafāt* register were the *naqīb al-ashrāf* Muṣṭafā Ṭahazādah, who held a vast quantity of agricultural products at the time of his death, underlining his creditor relationship with the peasants as well, and two representatives of the *askeri* group, Hac Ebü Bekir Çorbacı and Mehmed Paşa b. Hüseyin, who were trading in soap and rice, respectively. These examples point to another interesting characteristic of those individuals whom we might term Aleppo's commercial elite: the bulk of the trade items in which they had invested were not transit goods, either Persian silk or Western broadcloths, but local products. While this evidence is only anecdotal, it helps to support the contention that the transit trade lay outside the realm of large-scale Aleppine participation, at least as far as the Muslim community was concerned. For them and the city at large, the real profits lay in the local production of foodstuffs, soap, and cloth (both cotton and silk), which were consumed largely within the boundaries of the Ottoman demiworld system.

This is where the absence of any comparable information on the estates of the non-Muslim communities becomes critical. We will assume that given the difficulties they faced in investing in either tax farming or moneylending, the bulk of their profits were reinvested in trade, much of it long-distance, in contrast to Muslim investors. This is supported in part by their increased activity in commercial ventures in the eighteenth century, as already discussed, and by the evidence that they did not invest in real estate in Aleppo to any degree comparable to that of their Muslim compatriots.[56] On the other hand, the rich *ḥawājas*, like the ʿĀʾidas and Yūsuf Dīb, invested heavily in real estate and even were known to sublet village *malikanes* from the Muslims who held them legally,[57] giving rise to the possibility that wealthy Christians mirrored the investments of wealthy Muslims, wherever possible.

WOMEN AS INVESTORS

While we know very little about the ways in which the non-Muslims of Aleppo invested their wealth, we are fortunate to know more about yet another of the unsung segments of Aleppo's population, the Muslim women. The place of women in Muslim history has long seemed at best enigmatic, at worst, practically nonexistent. This ambivalence has been accentuated by the virtual absence of information on women in the chronicles and biographical dictionaries that constitute the bulk of traditional Muslim historical writings.

History in most premodern cultures was typically a male-dominated genre in which the contributions made by women to a given society were lost amidst the recounting of the glories of battle and the heroic deeds of kings. In the Islamic tradition this bias was strengthened by the social barriers, symbolized by the veil and the harem, that prevented Muslim women from fully participating in the public forums of their societies. As a result of this segregation, Muslim women could only rarely enter into the political or the mainstream religious lives of their world.

Nonetheless, on one area, that of the economy, Islam guaranteed women certain rights of participation, even if not on an equal footing with that of the males, in the ownership of property and the right to enter into contract. Yet it must be recognized that while these fundamental rights allowed women to become actors in Aleppo's economic life, the social barriers of custom forced that participation into patterns that differed from those of their male coreligionists. The most important difference lay in the opportunities to create wealth in the first place. While class differences may not have created insurmountable barriers to Aleppo's male population in the Ottoman period, the same could not be safely said for Aleppo's women, as they were not allowed by custom to set off on the road as agents in *muḍāraba* agreements, nor could they enter the two most profitable career lines, the military and the clergy.

It was only on the level of craft production that women could, and did, work outside the home, and these options could not produce wealth for women any more than they could for male craft workers. In what was already the economic lower class of the crafts, women were clearly on the bottom rung of the ladder, working in occupations that men did not want. They were especially to be found in carpet making and in jobs auxiliary to Aleppo's textile production: carding, spinning, and so on. In general, these activities were carried out by women working at home or in small workshops, without men present.[58]

In at least one marketplace, the *sūq al-ghazl,* however, women spinners worked and sold their thread directly to male customers. Significantly, the women in the market were not allowed into the spinners' guild, yet their activity outside the guild created competition that their male counterparts felt to be unfair. The guild members would not, however, deal with that competition by admitting women into their guilds, as such a step would have been unthinkable and deemed immoral by the male guild members.[59] Although the craftswomen failed in this case to gain parity with the men, the barriers were not always so formidable.

In a case registered on March 18, 1762, a Muslim woman was listed as being a member of the guild of edible-starch makers *(nashshāwwūn).*[60] We will assume that the woman in question inherited her place in the guild, but nevertheless her testimony was accepted by the judge along with that of her Muslim and Christian male colleagues as to what the practices of the guild were. Unlike her male coworkers, however, she needed two male witnesses to establish her identity, in conformity to Muslim law. Whether this case is unique or not, it raises the possibility that women were not completely barred from membership in the guilds, although the exceptions were undoubtedly few and far between and the guild in question was definitely one with very low status.

As they were effectively prohibited from earning wealth through their own initiative, social mobility was much more limited for women than for men. In fact, it would seem that the only plausible way for a woman to ascend the social ladder was through marriage. It has been noted elsewhere that marriage provided the means through which a female slave could advance to the highest levels of Ottoman society, in much the same way that the janissary corps furnished a vehicle for advancement to males of slave origin.[61] This would seem especially true in the imperial urban centers of the realm, and indeed we have the historic example of the famed Hürrem Sultan, wife of Süleyman the Magnificent, to confirm this.

But in Aleppo during the seventeenth century, this option seems to have been far more limited. By and large, the wives of the members of the *askeri* and civilian elite classes came from the same group as did their husbands, or as sometimes happened, males with *askeri* status married daughters of the local notables, especially if they were from the *ashrāf* (see figure 11). This trend is, perhaps, to be expected given the Arab, if not Muslim, preference for cousin marriage, but it also shows a tendency to use marriage as a means to create political and economical alliances. In figure 11, only one individual, Qarhābū bnt. ʿAbdullah, was a former slave. All the others are identified as being the daughters of locally prominent men. Furthermore, only a handful of the seventy-six men listed in the *mukhallafāt* register were married to women of slave origins. So while marriage was perhaps the only vehicle of class mobility available to Ottoman women, it would seem that in provincial Aleppo it was much less frequently employed than in the capital.

If the women of Aleppo had little opportunity to enter into career lines that would create wealth and rarely married above their own class, the question might be posed, how then did women acquire wealth? The answer is relatively simple: they inherited it. The Qurʾan clearly states that daughters are to inherit half the shares of their parents' wealth designated for their brothers. While women were clearly discriminated against in this division, it is important to note that they were nonetheless guaranteed a share.

Women's improved status under Muslim law in respect to their inheritance rights over women's status in pre-Islamic Middle Eastern societies is demonstrated by the practice of Aleppo's Christian population. Canon law (as practiced by Aleppo's Christians) made no stipulation that daughters were entitled to a share of their fathers' wealth, and among the Christian community we find none of the protracted legal wranglings over disposition of estates so characteristic of Muslim families in the Ottoman period. In some cases, the Christian practice was to establish a dowry for their daughters, which often included property, rather than to designate them as legal heirs.[62]

But in addition to this holdover of a pre-Islamic practice, there are cases of local Christians following Muslim custom, with women receiving a share of a legacy, even when there were surviving male relatives.[63] There is no way to be certain which law, canon or *sharīʿa* took precedence in most Christian families, but in any dispute taken outside the community, Muslim law would prevail. It would therefore seem likely that Christian women who felt they were being overlooked in the settlements of their parents' estates might appeal to Muslim justice for redress. But the fact that Christians often took such cases willingly to Muslim courts for solution testifies to the powerful normative effect the *sharīʿa* had on the non-Muslim communities.

In addition to inheriting from their fathers, Muslim women were also entitled to a share of their husbands' estates. Marriage in Islam was legally a type of commercial contract. So while custom clearly expected all women to marry, a Muslim woman's status did not derive from that of her husband. Rather, a Muslim woman entered into the marriage contract, in theory, as a full partner with certain rights guaranteed, and throughout, her identity lay with her father's family rather than her husband's. In part, the appearance of a Muslim woman's financial independence as a partner in a contract was guaranteed by the practice of dividing the bride price *(mahr)* paid by the groom in two parts. The first portion would typically be paid to the father of the bride at the time the marriage contract was signed, while the second part, called the delayed *mahr (maḥr muta'akhkhar)*, would be held in keeping to be given to the wife should the marriage be dissolved, providing her with a means of support. Should the husband die before his wife, the *mahr al-muta'akhkhar* would be included among his debts to be settled by the court from his estate.

The extent of the *mahr* in the composition of most women's overall wealth is illustrated by the cases summarized in figure 11, where it constituted from seven to twenty-two percent of the totals. In cases where the wife's death preceded that of her husband, the *mahr* would pass to her legal heirs, as an outstanding debt owed by a partner.

As a further indication of a married woman's separate economic identity, her property, whether acquired before or after the marriage contract was signed, was strictly her own. Upon her husband's death, his creditors could not attach her personal property if his wealth could not cover his debts, and her claim to the *mahr* was given equal validity to any of theirs. Although women were not responsible for their husbands' debts, they often entered into loan agreements with their husbands as partners, with the wife guaranteeing the loan with their personal wealth, just as any other credit partner would.[64]

In addition to receiving wealth directly through inheritance, women could inherit the position of *waqf* administrator or even tax farmer. While women were clearly a tiny minority of the *waqf* executors, individual women could at times manage considerable endowments, carrying with their responsibilities prestige and power. Earlier we encountered the example of Abide Hanım, who managed the *waqf* of the *khān al-wazīr* in the early eighteenth century, and she was not alone in obtaining such a position of influence. From other court cases, we learn that in the years 1687 and 1706, the executors of the *khān al-burghul* (or *khān al-Shaybānī*, as it was also known) were women; the granddaughter and great-granddaughter, respectively, of the *waqf*'s founder, ʿAlī al-Shaybānī.[65]

Having seen that Muslim society established differences in the ways in which men and women obtained their wealth, we would assume that the same social restrictions would condition the ways in which women invested it. While women could appear in court to present their cases directly, more frequently they were represented by a male agent, usually a relative. This was no doubt partly due to the tenet of Muslim law that required a woman appearing before the court to present two males who would verify her identity before she was allowed to speak. But such a reluctance, no doubt, also arose out of Muslim male society's demand for a demure behavior from its women relatives. This obviously colored the ways in which women invested their wealth, as a valid contract usually required court registration.

This difference is demonstrated by a comparison of figure 11 to figures 9 and 10. While Aleppo's males invested heavily in moneylending and real estate, most women held the greatest percentage of their wealth in household effects, a category that includes jewelry. A similar situation would probably be found in any society where women were prevented from participation in active commercial activity, but in Muslim societies where there was no such ban, jewelry contained an implicit attraction to women investors in that in case of divorce, it represented highly mobile capital. While such investments were understandable, women who so invested their wealth were only marginal to Aleppo's economic life.

Nonetheless, it is apparent that there were individual women who transcended the barriers of a patriarchal society and actively participated in the city's economy in the areas of moneylending and real-estate manipulation, although on a scale much more circumspect than that of males. Of the loan cases presented in abstract above, for example, only thirty-five involved women lenders, and while all the women in figure 11 had outstanding debts owed them, these for the most part consisted of the *mahr* owed them by their husbands. Both Melike Hanım and Ḥājja Ṣāliḥa were exceptions to this pattern, however, although there was a difference in their lending activities. In a pattern parallel to that of their male counterparts in the *askeri* and civilian elites respectively, most of Melike Hanım's outstanding loans were to peasants in villages where she owned property, while those of Ḥājja Ṣāliḥa were all proffered to city folk.

The reluctance on the part of most women to avoid moneylending was mirrored in the types of real-estate investments they made as well. Thus while men would invest in workshops, shops, and orchards, all revenue-producing and involving contact with renters from outside the family circle, women typically invested almost exclusively in houses. From the external evidence of the actual number of real-estate cases registered in the court records, it would seem that women were almost as active as men in the real-estate market. This ratio is misleading, however, as it reflects the peculiarity of Muslim inheritance law regarding property rather than any parity of women to men in the ownership of real estate. As a result of the inheritance laws, property was divided up into almost infinitesimal fractions, and most real-estate transactions registered seem to have been attempts to consolidate these fragments of property as much as possible rather than to acquire new property.[66]

If we discount these intrafamily dealings, the number of women active in the real-estate market shrinks considerably, although again there are notable exceptions. Two such exceptional women are found in figure 11, Āmina bnt. Ilyās and Ḥājja Āmina Khaṭūn. Interestingly, both women were from local notable families, while the women moneylenders mentioned above were from the *askeri* group. But before we leap to the conclusion that these cases are indicative of their respective social groups' investment patterns, we should note the purchase by an *askeri* woman of a package of real estate that included fourteen stores, a bakery, a vineyard, a mill, and various gardens from a woman from a local family, for the huge sum of five thousand *ghurūsh.* Significantly both buyer and seller had recently inherited their wealth. So while these cases do not unravel the secrets of social class in Ottoman Aleppo, they nevertheless demonstrate that although the amount of real estate held by women in general may have been small, individual women could, and did, have substantial holdings.[67]

Finally, in discussing women's investment opportunities, it is significant that none of the women in figure 11 held any of their wealth in commercial goods, in contrast to the men. For the most part, as we have seen, social custom restricted women from being involved directly in business, and it further forbade them from traveling except to make the pilgrimage to Mecca.[68] Any woman's ability to engage in the caravan trade was limited, therefore, to being an investor in *muḍāraba* agreements. We are left, however, with at least one tantalizing case in which a woman brought charges against another for the recovery of raw silk left with her for spinning. The amount of silk was significant and raises the question of whether the first woman was a silk merchant, a possible confirmation of the contention, supported by fragmentary evidence from elsewhere in the Empire, that women did in fact engage in commerce.[69]

In summary, we can say that women in Aleppo, like those in most other premodern Islamic societies, lived an existence separate from, but rarely equal to, that of the male population. Muslim women maintained a social culture that paralleled but rarely infringed upon that of their fathers, husbands, and brothers. This feminine subculture was due partly to Islam, which guaranteed men a superior status over their women, and partly to antifeminist traditions of the Middle East that the Muslims inherited. There was, however, another undercurrent to the Muslim legal position on women based on their Qurʾanic rights to own property and to enter into contracts.

Nonetheless, the number of women who were able to take advantage of these rights was undoubtedly small. Their societally imposed seclusion obviously prevented Aleppo's Muslim women from full participation in the economic life of their city. Women were rarely allowed to work outside their homes, and those who did so would have doubts cast on their respectability and honor. Consequently, there were few opportunities for women to create an independent supply of capital, in contrast to the male population. Indeed, the major difference in the economic status of women in Ottoman Aleppo from that of men was their lack of opportunity for social mobility. Thus while all women were guaranteed the right of participation in the city's economic life, it was in fact only the women of the city's political and economic elites who benefited from it, employing the wealth they had inherited from males.

Returning to patterns of investment in Aleppo in general, it would seem that there was no tradition of specialization in investment, either by the city's men or women, or by any particular social group. The importance of this phenomenon seems to lie in its inhibition of the emergence of a true mercantile economic class that would promote its interests with the policymakers in the capital.

On the contrary, changes in government policy toward taxfarming, coupled with a laxer interpretation of what constituted a legal *waqf*, led many wealthy Aleppines to move their wealth into those two areas of investment, supplementing the already most favored profit-making venue, moneylending. This pattern stands in contrast to that of contemporary northwestern Europe, where for a number of reasons merchant capital could not find an outlet in land accumulation. One of the most important of these was the clear-cut social distinction between the established landed gentry and the upstart entrepreneurial capitalists, which resulted in limitations being placed on the latter group's liberty to acquire land.[70]

In Aleppo, the upward mobility of merchant dynasties such as the Arīḥāwīzādahs and the Amīrīzādahs amply demonstrates that such barriers were practically nonexistent. The simple fact that their family names carried the honorific *zādah* ending reserved for the elite few is a clear indication of their acceptance into the ranks of the city's notables. In contrast to the developments in England, in particular, it would seem that at the very time when long-range commercial ventures to the East were becoming less feasible in Aleppo, new investment sectors were opening up. It could be argued, therefore, that the death of the caravan trade had a relatively small impact on limiting the investment opportunities for wealthy Aleppines, as it was accompanied by increased investment opportunities in other sectors of the economy. It was, therefore, not an issue of apparent concern for the city's economically powerful.

NOTES

1. McCulloch, p. 13.
2. Ibid.; Berchet, pp. 158–59; Sella, "Crisis and Transformation in Venetian Trade."
3. Chaudhuri, *The Trading World of Asia;* pp. 160–74.
4. SP 105/116:335, 19 Dec. 1718; SP 110/25:169, 20 Jan. 1726.
5. SP 105/118:147, 27 April 1750.
6. SP 110/29:212, 30 July 1765.
7. MM 9830:116, 18 Şevval 1058/6 Nov. 1648; MM 7326:43, 1 Cemaziyelevvel 1070/14 Jan. 1660; MM 9850:73, 6 Şevval 1083/25 Jan. 1673; Kurdakul, pp. 107–21.
8. Aleppo 33:129.
9. SP 105/113:85, Aug. 1664; SP 105/114:10, 16 Sept. 1695.
10. Aleppo 22:372; see also Haim Gerber, "The Monetary System of the Ottoman Empire," *JESHO* 25:308–24.
11. Chaudhuri, *The Trading World of Asia,* pp. 164–65; Braudel, *The Perspective of the World,* pp. 356–61.
12. SP 110/20:196–98, 15 Feb. 1696; SP 110/19:46, 20 July 1696; SP 110/19:63, 24 Feb. 1696.
13. AS 2:268; SP 110/25:20, 26 July 1725.
14. Sahillioğlu, "Bursa kadı sicillerinde iç ve diş ödemeler aracı olarak 'Kitabü'l-Kadi' ve süfteceler," in *Türkiye İktisat Tarihi Semineri,* ed. Osman Okyar (Ankara, 1975).
15. Davis, *Aleppo and Devonshire Square,* pp. 196–99.
16. SP 110/25:232, 23 March 1726.
17. SP 110/20:121, 28 Aug. 1696.
18. AS 2:262; Carruthers, p. 128.
19. Aleppo 28:147; 3:741.
20. Braudel, *The Perspective of the World,* pp. 67–68.
21. Aleppo 35:111, 382, 388.
22. AS 1:75–76; for the central government's response to such pleas, see Inalcik, "Adaletnameler," *Belgeler* 2, nos. 3–4, pp. 49–145.
23. Aleppo 3:287; Aleppo 21:171; Aleppo 45:159; Aleppo 51:167; AS 1:100; AS 2:141.
24. Aleppo 17:377; 18:89.
25. A similar process was occurring in Damascus; see Jean-Paul Pascual, "The Janissaries and the Damascus Countryside at the Beginning of the Seventeenth Century According to the Archives of the City's Military Tribunal," in *Land Tenure and Social Transformation in the Middle East,* ed. Tarif Khalidi (Beirut, 1984), pp. 357–70.
26. Jennings, "Loans and Credit in Early 17th Century Ottoman Judicial Records," *JESHO* 16:168–216.
27. Aleppo 19:218.
28. Inalcik, "Osmanlı idare, sosyal ve ekonomik tarihiyle ilgili belgeleri: Bursa kadı sicillerinden seçmeler," *Belgeler* 10:1–91; Rafeq, "Economic Relations between Damascus and the Dependent Countryside, 1743–71." *The Islamic Middle East 700–1900: Studies in Economic and Social History,* ed. A. L. Udovitch (Princeton, 1981) pp. 653–85. Raymond,

however, has discovered interest charges for loans made in Cairo during the eighteenth century (*Artisans et commerçants au Caire*, pp. 280–82).

29. Aleppo 22:131.

30. Volney 2:411–12.

31. Aigen, p. 73.

32. Aleppo 35:260; Aleppo 95:71.

33. Jon E. Mandaville, "Usurious Piety: The Cash-Waqf Controversy in the Middle East," *IJMES* 10:289–308.

34. al-Ṭabbākh 3:218.

35. Aleppo 28:59.

36. Aleppo 50:50, 53.

37. Aleppo 22:395; Aleppo 36:12.

38. Marcus, "People and Property in Eighteenth Century Aleppo," p. 116.

39. Aleppo 28:729.

40. Aleppo 35:140.

41. Aleppo 35:464.

42. Aleppo 45:70.

43. Inalcik, "Capital Formation in the Ottoman Empire," p. 107.

44. Inalcik, "15. asır Türkiye iktisadi ve içtimai tarihi kaynaklar," *İktisat Facültesi Mecmuası* 15:51–75; Barkan, "Edirne askeri kassamına ait tereke defterleri," p. 8.

45. Aleppo 17:78.

46. al-Ghazzī 3:292.

47. Meriwether; Jean-Pierre Thieck, "Décentralisation ottomane et affirmation urbain à Alep à la fin du XVIIIème siècle," in *Mouvements communautaires et espaces urbains au Machreq,* ed. Guy Leonard (Beirut, 1985), p. 36.

48. SP110/22:93–94, 14 Aug. 1701.

49. Inalcik, "Centralization and Decentralization in Ottoman Administration," in *Studies in Eighteenth Century Islamic History,* ed. Thomas Naff and Roger Owen (Carbondale, 1977), pp. 27–52.

50. Aleppo 19:121.

51. Marcus, "People and Property in Eighteenth Century Aleppo," p. 157.

52. Aleppo 47:115–16.

53. Aleppo 34:27; Aleppo 47:23.

54. al-Ghazzī 2:541.

55. Gaube and Wirth, p. 226.

56. Marcus, "People and Property in Eighteenth Century Aleppo," pp. 82–83.

57. Aleppo 78:106, 108, 121, 151.

58. Russell 1:161; John Barker, *Syria and Egypt under the Last Five Sultans of Turkey* (London, 1876), 1:75.

59. Aleppo 52:631.

60. Aleppo 94:88.

61. Ian Dengler, "Turkish Women in the Ottoman Empire: The Classical Age," in *Women in the Muslim World,* ed. Lois Beck and Nikki Keddie (Cambridge, 1978), p. 234.

62. Aleppo 22:216; Aleppo 42:120.

63. Aleppo 17:41.

64. Aleppo 17:224; Aleppo 19:269; Aleppo 35:617.

65. Aleppo 35:26, 33; Aleppo 43:120.

66. See also Marcus, "Men, Women, and Property: Dealers in Real Estate in 18th Century Aleppo," *JESHO* 26:138–63.

67. Aleppo 19:144.

68. There are numerous cases of single women arranging for their own transportation to Mecca. It must be presumed that these women were elderly, or they would not have been allowed by the standards of public decency to travel alone with the cameleers they hired to escort them.

69. Aleppo 3:733. Dengler also reports an example of a woman capitalist in sixteenth-century Bursa with her own factory and female slave workers (Dengler, p. 235). In another case from the Aleppo Court Records, 34:91, we learn that two Christian women hired a man in *muḍāraba* to make cloth for them with silk thread they had supplied.

70. On the limits of investment opportunities for English merchants, see, for example, Peter Kriedte, *Peasants, Landlords, and Merchant Capitalists: Europe and the World Economy, 1500–1800* (Cambridge, 1983), pp. 99–100.

CHAPTER VI

An "Islamic Economy" in an Age of Mercantilism

Amidst the changing commercial alignments of the eighteenth century, two very distinct economic systems, mercantilist western Europe epitomized by Great Britain and an Islamic imperial state structure headed by the house of Osman, were locked in competition for control of the Levant trade. The trans-Asian caravans arriving in Aleppo had managed to hold on to a significant share of Asia's trade with the West for almost a century and a half after their premature death knell had sounded with the attempts to divert Iran's trade through the Persian Gulf. Nonetheless, the motor force of the Levant trade had shifted westward. Even if its mainstay, the silk trade of Iran, had not gone into recession by 1730, it is doubtful whether the monopoly the long distance caravans enjoyed over it would have survived the century, succumbing at last to better Western technology and organization. The handwriting was on the wall. But the Ottomans remained blissfully unaware of the high stakes that were involved in the commercial battle being waged in the Levant, or even that they were in competition with the West.

This lack of awareness was no doubt due to a host of other far more pressing problems the Ottomans faced: the very real military and political challenges to the empire in the Balkans, the fiscal crisis that was destroying its ability to govern, and the fact that its political control over the provinces was slipping away. But the Ottoman leadership was also plagued by a fatal lethargy that had emerged from a sense of security bred by centuries of success and a contempt for the West. Ironically, Ottoman overconfidence was coupled with a seemingly contradictory fatalism, which held that if the empire's demise was forewarned, then so it was written. The acceptance of a self-fulfilling prophecy of decline among the Ottoman political elite was echoed by the growth in the popularity of ibn Khaldun's theory of the inevitable organic cycle of growth and decay of all dynastic states. For a time the malaise was cast aside, and from 1718 to 1730 the empire, or at least its capital, went through the euphoria of the Tulip Period *(Lale Devri)*. This brief interlude ended, however, in the ugly urban riots that brought down the reign of Sultan Ahmet III in 1730, providing a graphic reminder that real change would only come painfully.[1]

Nonetheless, neither that brief flirtation with Westernization at the court nor the violent reaction that followed fundamentally changed the economic philosophy of those who governed. And yet, with its peaceful commercial invasion of the Levant, the West had set into motion a challenge that would undermine an Islamic economy that had functioned in the Levant for centuries.

FOUNDATIONS OF THE ISLAMIC ECONOMY

The debate over what constitutes an Islamic economy has become an intense intellectual issue for Muslim theologians and scholars in the twentieth century. The appeal of an economy to be anchored in the principles of Muslim law, which would both provide social justice and guarantee the rights of private ownership, is compelling to peoples who have recently freed themselves from colonial domination yet who see flaws in the economic systems of both the Western and the Eastern blocs. For scholars promoting an Islamic solution, the formulation of a Muslim economic system has the obvious advantage of being rooted in the traditions of the people it would serve. It is an ideology that would not have to be imported and grafted onto a resistant culture; rather, it would allow Muslims to be Muslims and still face the twenty-first century.

While the nostalgia for such a system is almost universal among Muslims, there is a great deal of controversy over what exactly an Islamic economy should entail. The only historical model on which all could agree as being a truly Islamic state was the Prophet Muhammad's *umma* in Madina, and that, unfortunately, provides few clues on how the complexities of the twentieth century should be handled. The problem, however, is not unique to our own century. Throughout most of its existence the Ottoman Empire, which was history's most successful Muslim state in terms of its longevity, grappled with many of the same questions that are now perplexing modern Muslims. The most crucial of these was how to apply the standards of God's law to a complex and multidimensional state.

It might seem strange to some that the Ottoman Empire, which has come to be associated with corruption and oppression (the *ẓulm al-turk* of Arab folk memory) in the modern nationalist versions of history of many of the Balkan and Middle Eastern peoples, including the Turks themselves, could be labeled as an Islamic government. But whatever its reputation today, there can be little question that the Ottoman imperial house perceived itself as the protector and defender of the faith. The law of the realm it ruled was consciously proclaimed as Muslim. Furthermore, it was in the language of a Muslim state that the Ottoman Empire viewed its historical confrontation with the Europeans, whose generic name "Frank" in Ottoman documents evoked the perception that they were the heirs of the Crusaders.

This self-proclaimed Muslim state's economic policy was based on traditions of government that had evolved over the centuries in the world of Islam. Yet critics of the regime are right to point out that there were other, non-Islamic currents present in the Ottoman state ideology. The most important of these were the ancient Iranian ideas of statecraft, which glorified the ruler as the shadow of God on earth, even while stressing the need for justice on all levels of society if the state were to continue to function smoothly.[2]

The classical Iranian system was hierarchical to the extreme, insisting on the separation of the ruled into social classes that individuals should never endeavor to leave. The Iranian ideal of state contrasted markedly with the idea of social equality implicit in the notion of the Islamic *umma,* creating a tension that was never resolved. Likewise, the two traditions differed in their approach to the economy: The Iranian model advanced the notion of a tightly controlled, state-managed economy, designed largely to produce revenues for the ruler. In it, justice was indeed important, but it was a justice whose implementation was necessary, not for any higher ethical goal of bringing about the city of God on earth, rather to preserve the monarch's throne. The Islamic ideal, on the other hand, took the higher moral ground, emphasizing the sanctity of property and of contract, as a way of attaining salvation in the hereafter. It stressed an ethical system of the marketplace, which maintained the golden mean of ancient Greece, disallowing unfair profits and the abuse of the poor, while demanding fair pricing and honest advertising. Profits and trade were legitimate, but not to be abused. The persistence of the two sometimes disparate traditions meant that there were often contradictory impulses in the implementation of economic policy within the empire, coming from the twin religious and civil bureaucracies.

The distinction between the two philosophies was symbolized in the Ottoman Empire by the existence of two separate codes of law: Muslim law, as interpreted by the judges and legal scholars of the empire, and imperial fiat *(kanun)*, made binding on all Ottoman subjects by pronouncement from the Porte. It was understood, however, by even the most powerful of Ottoman sultans that the proper arena of *kanun* encompassed only those matters not covered by Muslim law and that *kanun* could not contradict *sharīʿa*. There was doubtlessly some blurring of the distinction, as Uriel Heyd's study of the Ottoman penal law code suggests,[3] and both were administered by the same religious judges. But on the whole, *kanun* rendered unto Caesar the fiscal affairs of the state, while the *sharīʿa* rendered unto God the morality and ethics of the marketplace.

Added to this duality in its economic philosophy, which often led the Ottoman state to act in ways inscrutable to contemporary Western observers, was the fundamental reality that the empire in 1750 teetered on the edge of financial ruin and political fragmentation. Its response to external stimuli, such as changes in the trade patterns, could, therefore, only be conservative. For it was a conservatism bred out of the necessity of survival, not tradition alone. In retrospect, however, such a holding action to preserve the empire may have been all that was possible, given the marked decline in the quality of the men who served the far-flung empire as its bureaucrats.

The decay in the quality of the Ottoman governing class is a historical development that has long been recognized, if not totally explained. While the empire in the sixteenth and early seventeenth centuries had boasted men of integrity and caliber to match any in the known world, a century later those serving the state seem to have been as venal and unimaginative as were ever produced anywhere. This decline has been ascribed to the end of the *devşirme* system, which, while brutal, produced men of outstanding quality; to the decay of the leadership at the top with the incarceration of the sultans-to-be in the harem; but most convincingly to the changes in the Ottoman fiscal system, which witnessed the heightened buying and selling of government posts throughout the realm, opening the floodgates to influence peddling and fiscal corruption.[4]

As we have already seen in the case of the positions of the *shāhbandar* and the customs inspector in Aleppo, this practice of selling offices led to an observable decline in the interests of those who had purchased their office to enforce the law. Rather, they usually sought a quick infusion of cash to recoup what they had expended to obtain their offices in the first place or to bid for yet more influential and therefore more lucrative posts. Merchants were often perceived by such officials, strapped for cash, as being a natural mark, described by one European observer as follows:

The merchants are considered as more immediately under the protection of the mohassil, and therefore not so subject to the Avanias made by the Bashaw. Nevertheless, they have sometimes, when the city was afflicted with famine, been obliged to contribute to a fund for the specious purpose of purchasing corn; the imposition however was loudly complained of as usual. But merchant strangers have too often reason to complain of the Mohassil himself, who, by vexatious exactions, turns away the trade to Damascus, and, for the sake of a temporary triffling advantage, does lasting injury to the town.[5]

Whatever the causes, the system had ceased to produce administrators who had an interest in upholding either the *sharīʿa* or *kanun*, even if they were not themselves personally corrupt. It just did not pay them to do so, and there was little chance that the imperial government, divided as it was, would take any notice anyway, no matter what they did. This produced an indifference and lethargy that the European observers were quick to assign to the "Oriental mentality" without troubling themselves to ask how such "Orientals" had nearly managed to conquer Vienna a century before.

The following story, recounted by Volney, serves as a classic example of how Ottoman officialdom was viewed by the Europeans in the eighteenth century:

A few years ago, the merchants of Aleppo, disgusted with the numerous inconveniences of Alexandretta, wished to abandon that port and carry the trade to Latakia. They proposed to the Pacha of Tripoli to repair the harbour at their own expence, provided he would grant them an exemption from all duties for ten years. To induce him to comply with their request, the agent they employed talked much of the advantage which would in time result to the whole country: "But, what signifies to me what may happen in time," replied the Pacha? "I was yesterday at Marach; to-morrow, perhaps, I shall be at Djedda; why should I deprive myself of present advantages, which are certain, for future benefits I cannot hope to partake?"[6]

It doesn't matter that the account is most probably apocryphal, as the details are not as important as the attitude the narrator sought to portray. Although the tale is undoubtedly exaggerated, it must be admitted that there were Ottoman officials to whom the story was applicable. The Levant Company records provide at least one historical example that such men existed. In 1722, the factors offered to build a bridge over the Euphrates, at company expense, in an attempt to lure the caravans to Aleppo. Despite the obvious benefit of a bridge, this early example of foreign aid was rejected by Aleppo's governor, for a reason similar to the one given by the official in Volney's story.[7]

Without doubt, much of the Ottoman Empire's failure to perceive the danger the West posed and to take adequate steps to remedy direct economic challenges as they occurred can be attributed to the corruption of Ottoman officials at the highest levels, but not all. The Ottoman Empire in the eighteenth century was under siege, but it had not collapsed, and it still possessed a free will to deal with many of the economic problems it faced. In part, its failure to react effectively was conditioned not by an inability to act but rather by an interpretation of the problems and their possible solutions based not on a mercantilist worldview but an Islamic one, culled from the inherited traditions of centuries gone by.

In this chapter two basic issues, recognized as fundamental to a healthy economy by the ideologues of mercantilism—the use of tariffs to promote industry and exports while discouraging imports, and the breakup of the guilds—will be examined from an Ottoman perspective. These examples, although culled from a case study of Aleppo, help to demonstrate how a state policy emerged in the empire as a whole that was diametrically opposed to those of contemporary Europe. To preserve the empire's economic health, the Ottomans would have had, necessarily, to understand the rules of the game the Europeans were playing. But these two cases illustrate that they did not. Instead, rather than exhibit any movement toward a change in policy, Ottoman policymakers did not waver significantly from their inherited traditions throughout the period in question.

The two case studies serve also as a useful device to gain an understanding of the duality of the Ottoman state ideology. In the first case, we find represented a response conditioned by the secular traditions of Iranian philosophies of sound government, while in the second, the government's action can only be termed Muslim.

THE OTTOMAN RESPONSE TO SHIFTS IN INTERNATIONAL TRADING PATTERNS

The classical tradition of Islamic statecraft recognized the value of international trade, not only for the luxuries that it produced for the court but also for the transit taxes it generated. Muslim rulers schooled in the genre of "Mirror for Princes" literature considered the transit trade to be something with which a wise ruler did not tamper. Revenue was the oil that greased the mechanism that caused the circle of justice to turn. In this system, no revenue was seen as being more easily obtainable than import duties.[8] The contrast between this attitude and that of the mercantilists, who saw the encouragement of exports and the discouragement of imports as a primary objective, could not have been more dramatic. Although the desired end result, the accumulation of wealth for the state, was the same in both ideologies, there were clearly diametrically opposed approaches to that end in these differing worldviews.

The attitude of the traditionalists was not, however, universally held by all Ottomans, as the following discussion given in Naima's history, but attributed to Fakhr al-Dīn Maʿnī, demonstrates:

> In the books of the sages of old it is said that it is not wise for a ruler to become particularly fond of luxury goods and deluxe wares that originate in enemy lands, or even fond of those which are obtained from regions belonging to other states, lest through the ruler's fondness for them those goods become the mode so that because of them the money and wealth of the state go to other lands. Instead of this, rulers ought for the most part to show a fondness for those rare goods that are produced in their own lands so that wealth will not be scattered from their kingdoms to other places.
>
> To those who object that the money received from customs duties is of benefit to the state, we answer as follows: If those who import goods from other kingdoms and sell them to us spend the money that they thus receive on goods produced in the Muslim lands, on goods that they need,

then the currency remains in the [Ottoman] kingdom. In this case, customs duties collected time after time are to be considered a benefit. An example of this is the Frankish crew [European merchants] who bring woolens and other cloth and who buy from the Muslim lands mohair and galls and alum and potash and lye and similar permissible wares. It is not only [the cargoes of] ships which are disembarked at Smyrna, Payas, Sayda, and Alexandria, but also *esedi altin* (gold coin). Even the regions of Ankara and Sayda and Tripoli [in Syria] and the whole of the Jebel Druze are full of this wealth.

But as for the money spent by us on sables and other sorts of expensive furs that come from the regions of Moscow, those accursed ones spend nothing for goods produced in Muslim lands. In the same way, how much wealth goes for goods from India while the people of India buy nothing the Ottoman provinces! Indeed, what we have to sell is not what they need. They are in the position of having incomes so large that the supposed utility of customs collections is not even a moral deterrent to them, while they spend nothing in other lands because they have no needs. Hence the wealth of the world gathers in India, just as it does in the Yemen because of its coffee, and wealthy men there are like Croesus.[9]

Such a clear articulation of mercantilist principles could not have been better stated by one of the good burghers at the Amsterdam or London commodities market in the eighteenth century. Nonetheless, those sentiments are a clear departure from the received wisdom on trade that circulated among the Ottoman elite. Significantly, this view of trade is ascribed to one of the Maʿnīs, a family who in their capacity as paramount amirs in Mount Lebanon had promoted the production and export of silk to Europe, a process that brought that region into a world economy before any other in the empire.

The traditionalists, on the other hand, left few accounts of their philosophy to rival the tracts being printed in contemporary London or Amsterdam, or even the dissenting view preserved in Naima, on the benefits of commerce. But we can re-create their understanding of their economy, to some extent, through the measures that the Ottoman government took to deal with trade crises that emerged to confront it. One of the most troubling of these was the decline of the Iranian silk trade in the early eighteenth century.

The continuation of the caravan trade with Iran had been tentative throughout the seventeenth century. The English factors in Aleppo, dependent on the arrival of Iranian silk in the Levant for their profits, periodically voiced their fears that the trade would dry up, due to competition offered by their rivals in the East India Company, or by a diversion of the caravans to Izmir. While both options at times threatened, Aleppo managed to retain its position as the principal outlet for Iranian silk. In stark contrast to the gloom over the trade's future manifested in the letters written to London by the Levant Company factors, however, the possibility that the trade would suddenly end was not an obvious matter of concern for the Ottoman authorities. Yet once signs that all was not well in Iran began to manifest themselves at the beginning of the eighteenth century, the Ottomans could not help but take notice as customs revenues began to fall.

In 1705, the customs inspector at Erzurum (the major entry point for Iranian silk into the empire) reported that the volume of silk passing through his station bound for Europe *(Firenkistan)* was diminishing. The central government, in response, instructed its agents to be vigilant lest the decline be due to an abuse of the silk merchants by Ottoman authorities, which might have soured them on using the Ottoman trade routes. The imperial orders further instructed the customs inspectors to file a full report on the trade conditions along the border.[10] Unfortunately, we don't have the inspectors' responses, but other dismal reports on the decline of the silk trade continued to arrive in the capital.

Reading these reports, the officials of the central government urged the various customs inspectors to be on the lookout against smugglers, lest the decline only be on paper. Another remedy that the tradition offered was the use of lower tariffs to attract trade. The rate of customs duties exacted on the transit trade was purposely set low with that objective in mind and had remained constant throughout the early centuries of the Ottoman period. As discussed in chapter 4, the official Ottoman import duties were established at a flat 2.5% of the value of the goods for Muslim merchants, and 5% on non-Muslims.[11] This rate was augmented in the early seventeenth century by an additional 1%, called the *muzayaka,* charged indiscriminately on Muslims and non-Muslims alike. Although meant as only a temporary expediency, this tax, renamed the *kasabiye,* became a permanent institution by the latter part of the century, but not without protest from the merchants who charged it was innovation *(bidʿa),* the worst possible offense from a theological point of view.[12] Despite their sudden burst of religiosity, the merchants were unsuccessful in getting the tax removed. *Kanun* had taken precedence over *sharīʿa* for the good of the community.

Nonetheless, with a very real decline of revenues being reported, the Ottomans, who unlike the English seem not to have realized that the depression in the silk production in Iran was the key to the crisis, decided that perhaps it would be helpful to lower the customs duties at Erzurum and to eliminate some of the internal customs stations along the silk route in Anatolia.[13] Such responses were drawn directly from the "Mirror for Princes" literature and were largely ineffectual. But then, that tradition offered few suggestions on how to deal with the changing world in which the Ottomans found themselves. Individual Ottoman strategists had sagely predicted that the European conquest of the New World and the Indian Ocean would pose grave threats to the House of Islam.[14] Unfortunately, their advice seems to have been largely ignored. This Ottoman myopia was not unique for the time, however, as various Mediterranean Christian states seemed equally ill at ease with the new face of the economic world of the eighteenth century.[15]

The Ottomans were clearly willing to make concessions in the short run, in the hopes of encouraging the wayward trade to return to their realm, but with the conditions in Iran, these could make little difference. Given the hindsight of two hundred years, it would seem the only practical option for the Ottomans to replace their declining tax revenues would have been to encourage local silk production to meet the demand in Europe. While it is clear that a decline in the quantity of Iranian silk reaching the Ottoman Empire did, in fact, lead to an increased output from the silk-growing regions of Syria and Anatolia, the impetus for this seems to have come from local producers, who realized that the Europeans were willing to buy their silk in the absence of what the Europeans deemed to be the superior raw silk of Iran.[16]

The dynamics of this increased output is unfortunately not completely understood, nor is the increasing commercialization of Syria's cotton production at roughly the same time. The end of the caravan trade was accompanied by the rise of exports of raw fibers, cotton and silk, which were produced in Syria itself, or, at the most distant, in northern Iraq and southeastern Turkey. The process by which peasants shifted from subsistence crops to export ones is most probably linked to the transformation of the land-tax system to *mukataʾa* holdings, but we cannot be sure. A few clues to the transformation are to be found in Aleppo's court records, but these do not extend much beyond establishing the credit relations that existed between town and country and references to the advance of cotton seed for planting to peasants by wealthy Aleppines who were their creditors.

But what is clear is that the increased production of cotton and silk in northern Syria was not due to the monopolization of production in the hands of a military strongman, as was the case of Ahmed Cezzar Paşa in eighteenth-century Palestine, Tepedelenli Ali Paşa in Greece, and the most famous of all the Levantine warlords, Mehmed Ali of Egypt, the last two both in the early nineteenth century. As opposed to these examples, it would seem that in northern Syria the inability of any political faction or individual to emerge as the dominant political force left the transition to commercial agriculture in the hands of a more diverse group of individuals, whom, for lack of any better identifying label, we will call the *aʿyān* (usually translated as "local notables"). This characterization must remain tentative, however, until further study of the transformation of Syria's agricultural life can be done. Such a development, however, is suggested by a parallel transformation of the rural economy that occurred at roughly the same time in the Menderes valley, linked to the commercial rise of the fortunes of the port city of Izmir.[17]

Key to a Syrian rural transformation was the increasing exportation of local silk to Europe in the early eighteenth century. Although cotton came to be king in the Levant, before 1750 Syria's silk was of greater interest to the Europeans. Syria had long produced silk, but before the drastic drop in Iranian production it was largely consumed by local weavers, with only the product of Mount Lebanon being exported to Europe. The Europeans considered the quality of northern Syrian silk, divided locally into four categories—*shaṭṭī, ablāq, andārī,* and *baladī,* depending on the thickness of the thread[18]—inferior to the Iranian product. The *baladī* silk produced by beduin in the Euphrates valley was especially ill-regarded.[19] But even the other types were criticized for the dirt and debris that were routinely left in the bundles prepared by the producers.[20]

Despite these reservations about Syrian silk, the Europeans started to buy up the local stuff when it became clear that Iranian imports would no longer be available. Forced to reconsider their options, Levant Company factors wrote that the silk of Antioch was the equal of that of Lebanon. Nonetheless, the resistance to any but Lebanese silk remained strong in London, causing the factors to employ false advertising by labeling Antioch or Payas silk as being from Tripoli (i.e., Lebanon).[21] Such creative marketing techniques provided dividends. By 1730, it was estimated that the bulk of Syria's silk production, whether from northern Syria or Mount Lebanon, was being exported to Europe. Conversely, despite the virtual halt to Iranian exports, the overall European import of Middle Eastern silk did not decline precipitously.[22]

While Syrian silk began to be exported to Europe in great quantity, its price remained relatively constant in Aleppo's markets, at least for the first three decades of the eighteenth century.[23] This was partly the result of some increased local production, but also, more important, of a redirection of Anatolian silk from its traditional market centers to Aleppo. Even before the crisis in Iranian silk, the silk of Bursa and Tokat had been preferred by Aleppo's textile industry over all others. This was a preference the factors of the Levant Company were happy to see, as it reduced competition for Iranian silk and later Syrian stuff, but they never fully understood it.[24]

It is not at all clear what volume of Anatolian silk was arriving in Aleppo during the years of the early eighteenth century. British reports state, however, that it commanded prices that were double those of Syrian silk, due to the preference for it held by the local weavers. There was, then, clearly an economic incentive for merchants to bring it south. In turn, the demand for Bursa silk in Aleppo had a negative impact, on the silk workers in Istanbul.

On August 25, 1724, the imperial government issued a decree directed to the governors of the provinces of Hüdavendigar, Adana, and Konya that prohibited the export of silk from Bursa to Aleppo. It stated that while the artisans of Aleppo had enough locally produced silk to meet their demands, the draining away of Anatolian silk southward created immeasurable harm for craftsmen in the capital. To prevent this, Bursa silk could no longer be transported to Aleppo. Anyone caught contravening the order would be summarily punished by having all his merchandise confiscated for the state treasury.[25] It is doubtful whether the law was completely effective, as four years later a caravan of fifteen mules arrived in Aleppo loaded with Bursa silk, and the English merchants reported its continued availability in the city after the date of the imperial order.[26] But the fact that prices for silk began to rise steeply in Aleppo after 1730 suggests that there was at least a partial interdiction of the shipment of Anatolian silk southward.

Ottoman policy, in the case of Anatolian silk, was designed to preserve tax revenues as they existed. This fiscal conservatism contrasts again with that of the mercantilists, who were willing to sacrifice current revenues for a long-term greater good, namely, the accumulation of specie. To be fair to the Ottomans, their policy was not entirely based on greed for immediate gain alone, as it was also tinged with a concern for justice for the Istanbul silk workers. The order had noted that the Syrian craftsmen had enough silk to maintain their industry, with the important qualification being on maintenance and not expansion, while the Istanbul workers were suffering. The policy was also, no doubt, a product of an immediate practical political concern, created by the fear of what discontented craftsmen in the capital might do, balanced against the interests of those in a far-off provincial center.

This discouragement of expansion to save uncompetitive older crafts is a characteristic feature of Ottoman state economic planning. Furthermore, it underlines one of the sharpest contrasts between the mercantilism and Ottoman systems: that of their differing attitudes toward craft production. In adherence to the mercantilist philosophy, local European industries were given indirect subsidies through their government's imposition of high tariffs on imports. As a result, Middle Eastern and Indian cloth were slapped with high customs duties in England and the Netherlands, which resulted in the loss of their competitiveness while London's nascent silk industry was given a boost.[27] The Ottomans, on the other hand, discouraged any new industry that would reduce revenues from import duties or that threatened the livelihood of workers already employed. In other words, a proved source of revenue was to be maintained at the expense of potential new sources even when the revenue base of the older sources was declining.

A case illustrative of the Ottoman economic conservatism was a clause in the order governing the customs duties in Aleppo registered in 1665 and 1673, which stated that due to an increase in the manufacture of *aṭlāṣ* cloth in Aleppo, imports of cloth from Europe had fallen off, adversely affecting the customs revenues in the city. To make up for the difference in lost revenues, the customs officials were empowered to collect an internal tariff of three percent on Muslim weavers and five percent on non-Muslims from all such cloth produced in the city.[28] A comparable decision had come earlier with regard to a type of cloth produced in Diyarbakır in imitation of imported Persian stuffs, with similar results.[29] In both instances, the official policy put a nascent local industry at a severe disadvantage. The principle of preserving revenues was again at work, even if it meant a reliance on imports. Imports, after all, were not seen as bad, as a transit tax could always be levied on them to enrich the coffers of the state.

The government policy of maintaining an established tax source, even if it had become antiquated, could also be detrimental to the development of internal Ottoman trade. Such was the case in the controversy that emerged between the customs officials of Tripoli and those of Aleppo over where *hak-i belis* (literally "the dirt of Balīs," a town to the east of Aleppo in the desert) could be sold. *Hak-i belis* was a kind of alkali ash produced by burning saltwort. It was marketed largely by the beduin and was used in making soap and glass. Great quantities of the material were exported to Venice in the sixteenth and seventeenth centuries. Aigen reported that as late as 1656, twenty thousand *qinṭar*s of the alkali ash were being exported yearly from Tripoli,[30] and in 1681, the tax on the ash's export earned ten thousand *ghurūsh* for the provincial treasury in Tripoli.[31] It seems natural, therefore, that the customs officials of the province became alarmed when, during the seventeenth century, the beduin started to take the ash to Aleppo to sell rather than to Tripoli.

The reasons why the beduin altered their traditional trading pattern seem fairly obvious. Aleppo provided a much larger market for their product than did Tripoli, because of both the presence of the Europeans there and the need for the ash in northern Syria's soap industry.[32] Additionally, Aleppo was much closer to the source than was Tripoli.

This shift in markets was bitterly resisted, however, by the governors of Tripoli, who perceived it as a diversion to another province of tax revenues that were properly theirs. The central government consistently sided with Tripoli in this dispute, with the justification that the tax revenues generated by the sale of the alkali ash had always belonged to Tripoli and so there they should remain.[33] Furthermore, the government ordered the authorities in Aleppo to turn the beduin away from the city and not allow them to sell their product there. Despite the orders, it is clear that they were unsuccessful in this, as complaints continued to filter in from Tripoli that the beduin were taking the ash to sell in Aleppo.[34]

In maintaining this policy, the Porte displayed a degree of rigidity that ultimately produced negative results for the treasury. The beduin seeking the best market possible for their product continued to go to Aleppo, where, as it was illegal for them to sell the ash in the first place, they simply paid no taxes at all. As the government officials in Aleppo had nothing to gain by turning the beduin away, they also did nothing. This case underlies one of the persistent, and ultimately tragic, flaws in the Ottoman state system in that it provided no incentive for its bureaucrats to obey the imperial directives, or any effective checks should they disobey, other than threats.

Once the officials in Aleppo realized that the government's reach had shrunk noticeably, they felt no need to expend efforts forcing the beduin, not always the most tractable of people, to do something that would only result in the enrichment of their rivals in Tripoli. In response, the provincial government in Tripoli could only raise the taxes it collected elsewhere to equal what it was losing through the beduin's defection, leaving the beduin the only real winners in the affair.

THE GOVERNMENT AND THE GUILDS

Muslim political theorists divided their economy into three sectors: commerce, agriculture, and the crafts. Of the three, commerce was not only the most prestigious but, as we have seen, the one deemed the most worthy of preservation by the Ottoman state. Agriculture, on the other hand, never elicited the same sort of concern in Muslim books on good government. In Abū Yūsuf's *Kitāb al-Kharāj* and later political tracts, peasants were treated as a producing class that was largely taken for granted. Although Muslim philosophers never fully agreed with the pre-Islamic Persian view of peasants as being serfs bound to the land they worked, there was a discernible ambivalence toward them. They were to be treated justly, but their position on the land remained ill-defined.

While commercial taxes were not mentioned in the Qur'an at all and were, even with the rise of the Islamic states, deliberately kept low, the agricultural sector was perceived as the rightful inheritance of the Muslim community, to be exploited as was necessary. Muslim peasants may not have suffered to quite the same degree as peasants in other premodern agrarian states, as they were never equated to chattel, but no one could argue that their legal rights resembled those of their coreligionists in the cities or towns of the Muslim world. An example of this is the tax *(çift bozan)* that Ottoman peasants were required to pay should they leave their villages.

Within what may be termed a traditional Islamic state, the urban craftsmen fell somewhere in between the peasants and the merchants, in terms of both economic opportunities and the legal control exercised by the state over their livelihood. The exact boundaries of either those opportunities or the extent of outside control, however, is not entirely clear. The question of the role of the guilds in the Ottoman economy has generated controversy among scholars studying them, to the point that even the question of whether the term "guild" is truly applicable to the Ottoman craft corporations has been raised. In general, the scholarship so far suggests that the guilds as they existed in the seventeenth-century Levant were an Ottoman innovation designed to enhance government control over the urban economy, by creating a hierarchy of craftsmen who could be easily taxed and whose prices and production could be controlled to meet state needs.[35] This view, in the extreme, is summarized coherently as follows:

In the Ottoman social formation, urban craft production was undertaken by guilds under strict regulations *(hisba)*. The state controlled the production process, that is, allocation of raw materials; quantity and quality of the goods produced: and it also fixed prices. The supervision of urban production was in part achieved through the mechanism of the state's control over trade.[36]

In Aleppo, however, one has the suspicion that although the guilds may have been formed at government instigation, it was not the government but the guilds that exerted pressure for their continued maintenance. Such a policy was, after all, in the guild membership's own best interests, as the institution of the guild provided for the monopolization of a particular craft in their hands, protected by Holy Writ and preserved from competition. Furthermore, the underlying legitimization of the guild's authority lay not with imperial decree but with Muslim law. Under its interpretation in the Aleppo courts, the guilds were considered to be legally binding partnerships, entered into willingly by the guild's membership.

The internal organization of a guild reflected its voluntary character and brings into the question the assertion of government coercion. Each guild was headed by a *shaykh* who was chosen by the general membership. After his election, the candidate was presented by a delegation of prominent guild members to a judge. Once these representatives had sworn before the judge that they were accepting the authority of the *shaykh*, the court issued the head of the guild a written document confirming him in his post.[37] The verbal affirmation before the judge, however, rather than the document, formed the basis of the contractual agreement between the membership and its leader. The terms of that verbal contract would govern the ways in which all ensuing conflicts within the guild would be settled.

This process seems to have run into trouble by the second half of the eighteenth century, however. We have already seen that, in an attempt to bolster revenues, the Ottoman government was increasingly forced to sell off to private individuals the right to collect various taxes. By the middle of the eighteenth century, this included the right to collect the by then institutionalized extraordinary taxes that were levied on the various guilds, as well as villages, city quarters, and religious minorities. In the case of the villages, the process of establishing *mukata'a*s, to be replaced by *malikane*s, led to the unofficial alienation of what was legally crown land to the next best thing to private holdings for the tax farmers. The same process was also apparently applied to the guilds, with confusing and often disruptive results.

A case in point was the complaint of the guild of the makers of *alājā* (a silk and cotton cloth mixture), *ṣandal* (a silk taffeta), and *darāʿī* (silk and cotton taffeta) cloth in 1752, that contrary to the established practice, an unnamed individual had purchased from the central treasury the right to be the *shaykh* of the *ṣandal* makers. The collective membership asserted that all three cloths were made by one guild and that a certain Ḥājj Yaḥya b. Fatḥ Allah was their *shaykh*, as were his father and grandfather before him. They were supported in this assertion by documents from the court and an imperial *berat*. Although the judge made no ruling other than to register the principles stated, the purpose of the collective representation was to serve to establish a precedent in future cases.[38] What had apparently happened was that the *malikaneci* had overstepped his authority by attempting to have his own man named *shaykh* of a breakaway guild. This particular case provides, then, a graphic illustration of the ways in which *shaykh*s had been chosen, as well as an example of the process by which that tradition was being challenged.

Once chosen, a *shaykh* could exercise varying degrees of authority, but his role was properly one of spokesman for his guild in all its affairs with the outside world, an arbiter of internal disputes, and an enforcer of the guild's regulations. Sometimes that power might verge on autocracy and exploitation, as in the case of the *shaykh* of the gallnut sellers who in 1662, acting on an insider's tip, bought up all the stock held by the guild and then resold the nuts a few days later to European merchants at a higher price.[39] The judge who handled the dispute ruled that the action was not illegal, as the guild members had freely sold their stock. But as the *shaykh*'s authority had resulted from the collective agreement of the guild itself, that same collective will could remove the *shaykh* from office if the gallnut sellers felt he had broken the contract he had made with the membership.

Just as the leader of the guild was elected by mutual agreement, the guild's internal rules were also enacted by the membership. Once those rules were assented to by the membership, however, they formed a verbal contract that was binding on the individual members who had given their consensus to the agreement. Typical of such guild rules were those mentioned by the fullers of *khām* on December 30, 1718. In their deposition, the fullers declared that all the *khām* to be bleached was to be divided up among them according to a schedule registered with the court under the supervision of the *shaykh*. Furthermore, it was agreed that the guild members would rinse their cloth in only one place, a spring outside the city, and not in the River Quwayq itself, and that no fuller would go individually to meet the caravans in order to conclude a business agreement of his own with the merchants.[40] Through these self-imposed regulations, individual initiative was discouraged, while a means of supervision—the rule that all work was to be done in one central place, thoughtfully positioned away from the city's water supply—was included.

Things became more complicated, however, when the guild's activities extended beyond the boundaries of the corporation and simple contractual relationships. One responsibility of good government inherited by the Ottomans as a part of the Islamic tradition was the maintenance of justice in the marketplace. This was interpreted to include the establishment of fair prices and uniform standards in production. Historically, the supervision of the market was administered by the official known as the *muḥtasib,* who was empowered to enforce market standards and prices. In the Ottoman Empire, the state, at least in the capital, took the tradition one step further and established prices for most commodities sold in the marketplace, periodically issuing revised price listings, called *narh defterleri* ("registers of official prices").[41] While the Ottomans hoped this system would bring order to the marketplace, it often had the opposite results. As goods brought in by the merchants from outside a city were largely free to command whatever price the market would bear, they often undermined an orderly system of price controls, producing a shortage of local goods whose prices had been set too low.

In Aleppo, however, the process seems to have been less formalized than it was in the capital. There are very few references to the *narh* registers in the court records, and there is the counterfactual evidence of the wildly fluctuating prices for imported commodities, such as coffee and indigo. Nonetheless, representatives of the various guilds would come periodically before the judge of the city's central court to register the prices the guilds had decided collectively to charge for their products.[42] This process was a benefit to the guilds, as it provided a legal leverage to be used against members who were underpricing goods. Even given that it was the guilds themselves that set the prices, any further registration of those prices by an authority outside the guild itself was seen by the membership as an infringement of guild authority and was resisted.

The attempt to have the guilds register their standards of production with the court raised even more resistance. In 1655, representatives of the guilds representing various cloth makers said that the *muḥtasib* wanted them to register the standards of their cloth in his register. The guilds felt that this was an unwarranted intrusion into their affairs, as it would give the official information about the crafts that they did not want to go outside their own closed circle. They cited as their defense that this had never been done before, and the judge, seemingly eager to prevent innovation, ruled in their favor.[43] As a result of their intransigence, the *muḥtasib* would have no way of knowing whether the cloth makers were maintaining their standards, in any complaint registered by a consumer, other than through the testimony of the guilds themselves. A part of his job's responsibility had been effectively sabotaged. Rather than being an independent ombudsman for the market place, as his post was conceived by his architects of Muslim statecraft, the *muḥtasib* had been reduced to being an enforcer of guild policies.

In what seems to be a further erosion of the *muḥtasib*'s authority, in any case where two separate guilds' pricing policies came into conflict, the arbiter of compromise was the judge and not the *muḥtasib*. When, for example, the makers of dyed soft leather *(ḥūr)* requested permission to raise the price of their product, as the price of gallnuts had risen in the open market in 1665, their request was denied by the city's chief judge, who said that such an action would in turn have an adverse affect on the city's saddle makers. In an earlier case, however, registered in 1648, the Suryani makers of *ʿirāqī* cloth had been allowed to raise their prices, as the cost of their raw materials had risen.[44]

The reason for the different rulings in these two cases was that a price increase in the first would affect other crafts in a ripple effect, causing prices to rise across the market, as the leather was used by several other craft guilds. It was to forestall this that the request was turned down. On the other hand, the cloth was sold directly to the consumer, and the effects of the increase would be minimized, for as the judge said, it was up to the buyer to decide if the price was fair or not. In yet a third example, almost a century later, the judge settled a dispute between the makers of silver thread and a type of luxury cloth over a price increase in the thread by bringing in a blue-ribbon panel of merchant witnesses who determined collectively what the fair price should be.[45] In all three cases, the request for a price increase had come as the guilds were faced with rising costs in commodities that were not price-controlled, emphasizing the inherent weaknesses in the Ottoman price-control scheme. The underlying principle in the judges' rulings seems to have been to maintain the status quo, as change invariably would bring injustice.

The same attitude also governed the courts' decisions in disputes that arose between the guilds and the merchants. It was, perhaps, inevitable that the two groups would come into conflict in Ottoman Syria, as they did in Europe, given that they held as producers on the one hand and marketers on the other economic philosophies that were diametrically opposed. While the merchants were relatively unhindered in their pursuit of profits, the guilds exercised a tight control over their membership in regards to profits, prices, and quality. But as in Europe, merchants realizing that innovation and profits were hindered by the guild structure sought to circumvent the guilds' authority, with varying degrees of success.

Of all the guilds in the city of Aleppo, those of the various dyers of cloth and thread were most closely linked to the merchants' interests. Aleppo's international trade rested in large part on raw silk and cotton, thread, and textiles. This included more than just the broadcloths imported from Europe and the raw silk brought in from Iran. Various kinds of locally produced cotton textiles from Aleppo and the smaller provincial centers of Diyarbakır and Kilis were exported to Europe in the seventeenth century, and Aleppo's luxury textiles, especially its cotton and silk mixture known as *alājā*, were exported throughout the Empire.[46]

The dyers' trade was essential to the many merchants dealing in textiles, and that dependence created conflict between the two groups over the course of the seventeenth and eighteenth centuries. It was also a matter of grave concern for the city's tax collectors. Under the Ottoman *kanun*, a principal source of urban revenue was generated through the operation of state-controlled dye houses *(miri boyahane)* where all dyeing of cloth and thread was to take place. The centralization of the operation, in theory, allowed for the maintenance of standards, but it also provided a convenient means to tax cloth production in the city.[47]

Despite these attempts by the government to preserve order in the textile crafts, an underlying tension in the marketplace remained, created by the merchants' desire to circumvent the dyers' guilds and deal directly with individual workers. This circumvention would provide them with a means of exercising control over the quality of the work and at the same time of reaching a more competitive price for the work to be done. In this ongoing dispute, the Ottoman government and legal system walked a careful line between the principles of maintaining revenues and of preserving justice in the marketplace. Unfortunately, the two seem to have been largely incompatible, given the often contradictory rulings the two goals evoked.

In this battle, personal considerations often influenced which side the officials chose to support. In 1684, Ali the tax collector *(muḥaṣṣil)* of Aleppo sided with the merchants. Writing to the central government, he complained that in the past, the merchants who brought *khām* to the city were free to choose the dyer of their choice. Later on, in contradiction of past practice, the *shaykh* of the guild had started taking the cloth from the merchants himself to be divided up equally among the dyers. This innovation (notice again the dread of *bidʿa*) had resulted in an increase in the prices charged for dyeing, and the merchants in response were no longer bringing their cloth to Aleppo to be dyed. This, in turn, adversely affected the revenues of the tax collector and the government dye house. The response from Istanbul was ambiguous, restating simply the principle of *kanun* that all cloth was to be dyed in the government dye house, leaving the question of whether the guild was legal or not in the first place to the *shari^c^a* to determine.[48]

The conflict between the merchants and the dyers' guild was apparently never fully resolved. In 1693, there was a complaint to the central government from representatives of the dyers' guild to the effect that "important people" *(zi'l-kadret kimesneler)* had entered into their trade, and, contrary to custom, the cloth to be dyed was no longer being divided up among all the guild members. Custom, it would seem, was a double-edged sword, to be evoked either to support the guilds or to undermine them. In this particular case, the Porte supported the guild's version of what custom was. The cloth was ordered divided up among the dyers according to guild rules.[49] Similarly, in 1702, the *shaykh* of the dyers complained that various creditors and other members of the *a^c^yān* were financing the operations of individual dyers, telling them that they did not have to follow their *shaykh* any longer. As seen in the previous chapter, the guild members were increasingly indebted to members of the military and civilian upper classes, and those individuals were beginning to call in their markers. Here again, the ruling supported the integrity of the guild.[50]

Alternatively, in 1707, a delegation of dyers complained before the court that certain merchants of *khām* were handing over their cloth to individual dyers, disregarding the guild's practice of sharing the work among the entire membership. The dyers, who had been chosen by the merchants, responded that this seeming discrimination had come about at the request of the merchants themselves, who had wanted particular dyers to do the work for them. When the merchants confirmed their story, the judge ruled that the merchants had the right to choose freely to whom they would distribute their merchandise.[51]

This principle was even more firmly elaborated almost a half century later, when the dyers' guild sought to stop certain dyers from independently dealing with merchants who brought cloth from Diyarbakır, Mardin, and Urfa to be dyed in Aleppo. In that case, the judge, supported by *fatwās*, agreed with the independents that they could not be forced into guild membership. Furthermore, he made the seemingly groundbreaking decision that any attempts by the guild to collect dues from the independents were illegal, constituting bribery *(rashwa)*. Any contribution owed by the independent dyers to the general *avariz* and *tekalif* levied on the dyers of the city as a whole was, thereby, the responsibility of the *malikaneci* of the dyers to collect, and not of the guild *shaykh*.[52] This example obviously undermines the contemporary scholarly interpretation, which held that the guilds were an instrument of Ottoman fiscal administration. The principle of an "open shop" had reared its head in Aleppo.

But lest we come to the conclusion that the courts were antiguild in the middle of the eighteenth century, we have only to look at a ruling roughly contemporary to the one just discussed, from 1754. In that case, a group of merchants who were bringing cloth from Konya to be dyed and sold in Aleppo appealed to the judge concerning what they considered to be the monopolistic practices of the dyers of rose-colored cloth. They claimed the monopoly had resulted in a rise in the cost of dyeing their cloth. The guild members responded that all the membership had voluntarily entered into their labor agreement and that all increases in the cost of their labor were the result in a rise in the price of gallnuts, essential to their operations, on the open market. Here, the judge ruled that since all the dyers had agreed to the formation of the guild (significantly for our understanding of Ottoman guilds, the term *sharika*, "partnership," is explicitly applied to the arrangement), then the merchants had either to deal with the guild on its terms or, alternatively, to find other dyers to do the work.[53]

What had happened between the middle of the seventeenth century, when the integrity of the guilds was almost invariably upheld against all challenges by the courts, and the middle of the eighteenth, when for all extents and purposes guild practices were permitted only when they enjoyed the voluntary approbation of those practicing a certain craft? In the absence of any clearly articulated economic philosophy, it is difficult to say with certainty. There is the purely economic explanation, which would say that once the government had hit upon *malikanecis* to collect taxes from practitioners of a certain craft, it no longer needed the services of the guilds, whose principal function under that interpretation was tax collecting, after all. This explanation would follow in the tradition that sees the guild system in the Ottoman Empire as having been imposed from above. While this explanation clearly has its merits, it neglects, or at least underplays, the role of the courts in interpreting guild practices. While it might be argued that the courts were but an arm of the state, it is clear that especially in the eighteenth century, when the central government was less able to assert its interpretation of Muslim law, the local courts often acted on their own to implement their version of God's law.

It is difficult to know whether the guilds' unraveling, which we can date to the eighteenth century, was a product of a reassertion of a Muslim business ethic by the courts or a result of an economic deterioration the government was ill-equipped to halt. But whatever the cause, the guilds were caught in an economic vise. The clearest indication of this in this period is the assertion by certain guilds, the block printers of cotton cloth and spinners of silk thread, for example, that their practices were not really traditional anyway. Such declarations were then followed by the membership's dissolution.[54] Interestingly, in the nineteenth century, when the bureaucratic arm of the government again reasserted itself, the erosion of guild authority was halted and the guilds, at least in Istanbul, enjoyed more far-reaching control over their membership than they had in eighteenth-century Aleppo.[55] This suggests that state interests may have coincided with the guilds while the local courts, when free to act on their own, were able to emphasize somewhat different ideals of the Muslim marketplace. These included the responsibility of individuals for contract implementation and the corresponding absence of the idea of corporate capital, as well as an abhorence of compulsion in determining how the individual would make his or her living. Perhaps it was also only coincidental that these same principles benefited the local elites from which the judges would have come.

The guilds' status had clearly changed. In most cases, however, the guilds were able to resist merchant attempts to bypass them, at least until 1750, if not beyond.[56] Nonetheless, there were already indications that the merchants were able to circumvent the guilds in at least some instances by hiring workers directly, as in the cases of the dyers discussed above. This was an apparent parallel to the "putting out" system *(verlagssystem)* employed by merchant capitalists in Europe.[57]

As in Europe, the Syrian merchants, faced with guild resistance, found that it was easier to move their operation to the countryside. In the countryside, or more correctly in the villages in the immediate vicinity of the city, peasants were hired to spin and twill cotton and silk thread in their villages, and their output was then marketed by the merchants themselves.[58] The process seems to have accelerated by the middle of the eighteenth century, as cotton thread became one of Syria's major exports. Besides peasants, women, as another marginalized part of the labor force, were hired in Aleppo by the merchants to circumvent the guilds as well.[59]

Although the "putting out" system was employed in eighteenth-century Aleppo, one has to be careful not to compare too closely the situation there with conditions in sixteenth- and seventeenth-century Europe. In the first place, the European merchants were able transfer new techniques of manufacture to villages, thereby circumventing the urban guilds. This, in turn, gave rise to new woolen and flax cottage industries. In Syria, the kinds of work performed in this way were extremely simple and did not lead to the creation of new industry, nor were there any attempts by the merchants to introduce new techniques among the peasant workers. Furthermore, given the conditions of rural instability created by the nomadic incursions mentioned in chapter 4, it is doubtful that any major industrialization of the countryside, following the models that developed in either Britain or Germany, could have occurred, even had the merchants been inclined to promote it.

Within Aleppo itself, economic conditions in the second half of the eighteenth century apparently grew worse, generating a greater willingness on the part of craftsmen to enter into direct wage relationships with individual merchants. Al-Ghazzī reports a major depression in the city's textile industry in 1758.[60] Such setbacks seem to have helped break down a few guilds and to have given rise to a limited use of the "putting out" system in the city as well.[61] To make matters worse, the practice of selling *malikane*s for various craft guilds intensified, bringing hardships to the craft industries. The selling of these positions gave outsiders new and wider controls over the guilds' output and was a direct affront to the guild *shaykh*s' authority. This development was often met by work stoppages. In 1772, for example, the cloth makers of the city went on strike for 129 days, during which time the holder of the *mukata'a* was unable to collect a *ghurūsh* in revenue.[62]

An example of the types of conditions the cloth makers were striking against is provided by the complaint brought by Mugerdiç w. Bagras against the agent of Mehmed Ağa, kapıcı başı. Mugerdiç was a cloth glosser *(ṣaqqāl)* who had worked in a shop, owned jointly with his wife, Qādisīya bnt. Naṣūr. But it seems that Mehmed Ağa obtained the *mukata'a* of the glossers' guild and used that authority to close the shop, forcing Mugerdiç to work in a different workshop. Mugerdiç complained that when he had worked independently, he had earned 8 *ghurūsh* a week, but under the new system he was only paid 2 and 1/2 *ghurūsh* a week, of which he had to pay the workshop owner one. He stated that this was the way he had worked for eight years, but he now wanted to open up the old shop and work independently. Furthermore, he wanted a settlement of 2,112 *ghurūsh* to compensate for the wages he had lost over the past eight years. The judge ruled that Mugerdiç had, in fact, been wronged and that he could go back to his old workshop, but as no one had forced Mugerdiç to work as a cloth glosser, he could not rightfully claim damages for the lost income.[63]

In addition to attempts to undermine their authority by merchants and others, the various guilds were also faced increasingly with direct competition from European imports. In the case of the dyers this challenge came in the early eighteenth century when the French began to import into the Ottoman Empire a lighter broadcloth, dyed in various vibrant colors that were new to the Levant trade.[64] As one source of revenue for the dyers' guild had been the dyeing of imported European broadcloth to meet local tastes, their livelihood was adversely affected by the innovation.

In response to the challenge, the dyers developed their own brighter dyes and temporarily kept their competitive edge with the importers. Typically, they were not supported in their efforts by the Ottoman government tax collectors, who claimed that the new colors were innovations and not covered by previous regulations. That being the case, they slapped new taxes on them. The increase was protested by the dyers, who petitioned Istanbul asking that seven new colors—among them light blue, lemon yellow, tan, and gold—be declared their *emek* ("livelihood'), free of taxation, as three other colors—red, crimson, and light yellow—had previously been declared to be. Their request was turned down by the government, and the new higher tax rate remained in effect.[65] Despite these governmentally imposed hardships, however, the dyers seem to have adapted to the new conditions created by European competition. By the second half of the century, the European factors were sending home samples of the colors developed by the Aleppo dyers in order to compete more effectively with the local dyeing industry. Perhaps a further indication of the resiliency of both the local textile guilds and the dyers lies in the fact that throughout the eighteenth century, two of the major items imported by the Europeans into Syria were indigo and cochineal, which would hardly have found a market had the European textiles totally supplanted local production.[66]

Having looked at a few individual policy issues, we are left with the question of whether the economy of Ottoman Aleppo was Islamic. This question should be answered with a qualified yes. The traditional wisdom of the Islamic states of the Middle East held that the caravan trade was to be supported, even at the expense of local production. This was a policy clearly followed by the Ottomans. While it might be argued that such a policy was not in itself derived from the *sharīʿa*, neither did it run counter to it. The low taxes placed on commerce, compared to a much higher rate imposed on agriculture and to some extent on crafts production, clearly found precedents in the tenets of Muslim law, derived as they were from the historical tradition of a society that had lived primarily off trade.

Furthermore, it can be argued that the Ottoman state policy toward the guilds was also conditioned by more than a mundane interest in the preservation of tax revenues. This higher motivation, as it were, lay in the concern of the state for the maintenance of justice in the marketplace. This, in itself, was colored by what might be termed as a Muslim code of business ethics. This unwritten code included the sanctity of personal property, the importance of contract, and the tenuous idea that business profits should be neither exploitative nor exorbitant.

On the other hand, the court registers of Aleppo demonstrate that the guilds enjoyed a great deal of autonomy, derived partly from their distance from the capital and partly from the interpretation of the courts, which upheld them as contracts entered into willingly by individuals. While some scholars have suggested that the guilds were an arm of state control, such a characterization seems to be very far from the actual conditions in Aleppo during the Ottoman centuries. There is little doubt, however, that given the traditions of Iranian statecraft, a universal control of the economy to provide for the smooth turning of the circle of justice was in fact among the goals of the Ottoman bureaucracy. But it must be recognized that it was not only the Ottomans' inability to impose firm central control that hampered the pursuit of this goal, as the independence granted to the judiciary at times also played a part.

Finally, we see more clearly the role of policies implemented by the Ottomans, out of their understanding of what was the best fiscal policy for themselves, in speeding up the incorporation of the Middle East into a European world economy. There is little doubt that the process would have gone ahead anyway, with or without Ottoman official action, but some of the more severe dislocations seemingly might have been avoided. Most important, the penalties imposed on the local crafts production in order to compensate for lost transit-tax revenues seems crucial. The Ottoman concern to preserve low import duties on imports while placing an increasing burden on local producers, in both the agricultural and crafts sectors, seems with hindsight to have been a perfect formula for eliminating the competitiveness of local industry.

Yet the Ottomans did not embark on these potentially destructive policies because they had to. There were no European gunboats in their harbors forcing these favorable concessions. Rather, their policies seemed at the time they were implemented by the Ottoman officialdom to be eminently sound and, in the case of the guilds, just.

NOTES

1. Robert Olson, "The Esnaf and the Patrona Halil Rebellion of 1730: A Realignment in Ottoman Politics?" *JESHO* 17:329–44.
2. Inalcik, "The Ottoman Economic Mind" in *Studies in the Economic History of the Middle East*. ed. M. A. Cook (London, 1970) pp. 207–18. Ann Lambton, "Justice in the Medieval Theory of Kingship," *Studia Islamica* 17:91–119.
3. Uriel Heyd, *Studies in Old Ottoman Criminal Law* (Oxford, 1973).
4. I. Metin Kunt, *The Sultan's Servants: The Transformation of Ottoman Provincial Government* (New York, 1983).
5. Russell 1:330.
6. Volney 2:160.
7. SP 105/116:442, 21 June 1722.
8. Gibb and Bowen, pp. 19–38.
9. Naima 4:293–94; English translation, Thomas, pp. 144–45.
10. MM 2960:4, 4 Müharrem 1118/18 April 1706.
11. MM 7326:43, 1 Cemaziyelevvel 1070/14 Jan. 1660; MM 2964:129, 28 Safer 1127/4 Feb. 1715.
12. MM 3595:26, 27 Şevval 1113/27 March 1702.
13. MM 2964:129, 28 Safer 1127/5 March 1715; MM 9924:220, 18 Şaban 1143/16 Feb. 1731.
14. de Vries.
15. Bernard Lewis, "Some Reflections on the Decline of the Ottoman Empire," *Studia Islamica* 9:111–27.
16. Davis, *Aleppo and Devonshire Square, passim.*
17. Individual studies of this process in different parts of the empire include Cohen, *Palestine in the 18th Century* (Jerusalem, 1973); Afaf Lutfi al-Sayyid Marsot, *Egypt in the Reign of Muhammad Ali* (Cambridge, 1984); Gilles Veinstein, "Ayan de la région d'Izmir

et commerce du Levant (Deuxieme moitié du XVIIIe siècle)," *Études Balkaniques* 12:71–83, Inalcik, "The Emergence of Big Farms, Çiftliks: State, Landlords, and Tenants," *Contributions à l'histoire économique et sociale de l'Empire ottoman,* eds. Jean-Louis Bacqué-Grammont and Paul Dumont. vol. 3. (Paris, 1983), pp. 105–26.

18. AS 1:34; Aleppo 27:105; Aleppo 52:3.

19. SP 110/32:82, 1 Aug. 1754.

20. SP 105/112:332, 18 Nov. 1659; SP 110/25:38, 21 Aug. 1725; SP 110/29:34, 25 Sept. 1749.

21. SP 110/30:234, 29 June 1756.

22. Davis, "English Imports from the Middle East," in *Studies of the Economic History of the Middle East,* Ed. M.A. Cook (London, 1970), p. 197.

23. Davis, *Aleppo and Devonshire Square,* p. 139.

24. SP 110/25:54, 22 Sept. 1725; SP 110/32:73, 23 June 1754; SP 110/32:100, 25 Oct. 1754; SP 110/32:194, 31 May 1755.

25. AS 2:124.

26. Aleppo 45:32.

27. Davis, "English Imports from the Middle East"; Chaudhuri, *The Trading World of Asia,* pp. 294–95.

28. MM 3774:238–240, 16 Zilhicce 1075/30 June 1665; MM 9850:77–78, 8 Şevval 1083/27 Jan. 1673.

29. Sahillioğlu, "Taghayyur ṭurūq, p. 7.

30. Aigen, p. 16.

31. MM 9855:148, 7 Zilhicce 1091/29 Dec. 1680.

32. MM 2742:103, 16 Ramazan 1076/22 March 1666.

33. MM 9855:148, 7 Zilhicce 1091/29 Dec. 1680.

34. MM 2777:96, 18 Şaban 1124/20 Sept. 1712.

35. Among others, Gibb and Bowen; Inalcik, *The Ottoman Empire: The Classical Age;* Rafeq, "Maẓāhir min al-tanẓīm al-ḥirafī fī bilād al-Shām fī al-ʿahd al-Uthmāni, *Dirāsat Taʾrīkhīya* 4:30–62"; Galal el-Nahal, *The Judicial Administration of Ottoman Egypt in the 17th Century* (Minneapolis, 1979); Gabriel Baer, "The Administrative, Economic and Social Functions of Turkish Guilds," *IJMES* 1:1–23, "Monopolies and Restrictive Practices of Turkish Guilds," *JESHO* 13:145–65, and "Ottoman Guilds: A Reassessment," in *Social and Economic History of Turkey (1071–1920);* ed. Osman Okyar and Halil Inalcik (Ankara, 1980); Haim Gerber, "Guilds in Seventeenth Century Anatolian Bursa," *Asian and African Studies* 11:59–86.

36. Huri Islamoğlu and Çağlar Keyder, "The Ottoman Social Formation," in *The Asiatic Mode of Production: Science and Politics,* ed. Anne Bailey and Josep Llobera (London, 1981), p. 303.

37. Aleppo 3:715.

38. Aleppo 80:48; MM 3595:82, 5 Zilhicce 1113/3 May 1702.

39. Aleppo 28:518.

40. Aleppo 55:187.

41. Mübahat Kütükoğlu, *Osmanlılarda Narh Müessesi ve 1640 Tarihli Narh Defteri* (Istanbul, 1983).

42. Aleppo 94:47.

43. Aleppo 3:715.

44. Aleppo 3:918; Aleppo 25:22.

45. Aleppo 105:159.

46. SP 110/11:113, 20 Feb. 1660; SP 110/15:9, 15 March 1686; SP 110/19:3, 28 March 1695.

47. MM 2931:41, 8 Rebiyülevvel 1094/7 March 1683; MM 3462:252–53, 24 Şaban 1108/ 18 March 1697.

48. MM 2931:124, 26 Rebiyülahır 1095/12 April 1684.

49. AS 1:90.

50. MM 3598:82, 5 Zilhicce 1113/3 May 1702.

51. Aleppo 3:69.

52. Aleppo 80:143. Although the dyers had no recourse in this particular case, a few years later they were able to get a court order banning a particular individual from working as a dyer in the city. In that case, they claimed that the person named was incompetent to practice the trade and had given false testimony about guild practices. When they produced witnesses from outside the guild who supported their charges, the judge issued an injunction, barring the man from the trade. Aleppo 85:103.

53. Aleppo 85:72.

54. Aleppo 45:151, 184; Aleppo 80:78.

55. Baer, "Monopolies and Restrictive Practices of Turkish Guilds."

56. Despite the existence of individual dyers who did not want to be bound by guild rules, there were frequent delegations of dyers who swore in court that they wished to follow the practice of the guilds and would abide by their legislation. Aleppo 78:190; Aleppo 85:72, 262.

57. Kriedte, *passim*.

58. Aleppo 53:99.

59. Russell 1:161.

60. al-Ghazzī, 3:300.

61. For an example of this practice among workers of silver thread, see Aleppo 105: 2, 4.

62. Aleppo 105:68.

63. Aleppo 85:127; for abuses of the *malikaneci* against the guild of the makers of *aṭlāṣ* cloth, see Aleppo 79:154.

64. Davis, *Aleppo and Devonshire Square*, pp. 96–107.

65. MM 2960:144–45, 24 Zilkade 1117/10 March 1706; MM 2960:349–50, 20 Ramazan 1118/26 Dec. 1706; MM 2960:387–88, 4 Zilhicce 1118/7 Feb. 1707.

66. Henry Grenville, *Observations sur l'état actuel de l'Empire Ottoman* (Ann Arbor, 1965), p. 163; Davis, *Aleppo and Devonshire Square*, pp. 122–23.

Conclusion

Işte geldik, gidiyoruz. Şen olasın Halep şehri.
(So we have come and now we are parting. Be of good cheer, City of Aleppo.)—Turkish Folk Saying

---

The choice of 1750 as the cutoff point for this study was not completely random, but neither can we say that 1750 was a true watershed year in the history of Aleppo. As in trying to date any social or economic trend, there is no universally accepted time to which we can point as having marked the definitive end of the caravan trade. Steensgaard's masterful study links it with the fall of Hormuz in 1622. This dating is clearly problematic. While his analysis seems correct in its determination of the underlying strengths of the European trading companies, which would eventually enable them to best the traditional trade of Asia, his dating of that trade's demise seems premature, given the fact that the silk trade of Iran with the West continued to be carried by caravan well into the eighteenth century. By 1750, that was no longer the case. Yet the caravans remained important in regional commerce, within the Ottoman demi-world, playing the traditional routes connecting Syria with Iraq, Anatolia, and the Hijaz. In fact, the absolute triumph of the West over the traditional trade of the Levant only came in the nineteenth century, with the advent of the steamship and the railroad. And so 1750, like 1622, is not definitive, as it witnessed no transformation of the institutions of the caravan trade, of the trade itself, or of how commerce was conducted in Aleppo.

Still, 1750 seems a good disembarkation point. Besides being the year that the Levant Company factors gave as the last in which caravans arrived in Aleppo from Iran, something not borne out by the Aleppo court records,[1] economic and social conditions in Aleppo differed in 1750 from those in 1600. The middle of the eighteenth century found Aleppo, like Syria and the Ottoman Empire as a whole, at a major turning point in its collective history. The social, economic, and political institutions that the peoples of the region had inherited no longer seemed capable of staunching the political disintegration of empire and *umma* or of competing successfully with a steady Western economic encroachment upon the trade of the Levant. Neither had any new institutions yet developed that were capable of revitalizing the region's formerly premier commercial position in the East-West trade.

But this perception is a gift of historical hindsight. Today we can point to the eighteenth century as the period in which the Ottoman Empire lost conclusively any competitive edge it might have previously enjoyed over the West. At the time, however, there seems to have been little of the painful soul-searching, coupled with an acknowledgement of political and economic inferiority vis-à-vis the West, that colored the ideology of the nineteenth-century Ottoman political and intellectual elite. Instead of the radical approaches of the Tanzimat period (1839–76), what was advanced as the solution to the problems of the age was a return to the halcyon days of Sultan Süleyman the Lawgiver and a reestablishment of the center's control over the periphery.

But financially and militarily, hence politically, this was no longer possible. Needless to say, the difficulties faced by the House of Osman in Istanbul were not viewed with the same degree of trepidation by everyone within the realm. The growing weakness of the center provided new opportunities for economic enrichment, both for the Europeans and for those Ottoman subjects who could use the empire's decrepitude for their own advantage. In the case of the latter, we have seen how the need for cash in Istanbul opened up new avenues for capital investment in the form of tax farms. Investors who might have previously put their money in trade or moneylending could find more profitable rates of return in a new government-sponsored sphere of investment.

In this pattern, the Ottoman Empire was not really so different from eighteenth-century France, which also suffered from a top-heavy and archaic bureaucracy.[2] Additionally, the apparent relaxation of the interpretation of what constituted legitimate endowments led many of Aleppo's wealthy, in this period, to channel their investments into semilegal family *waqf*s.

These new opportunities coincided with a narrowing of the horizons of what had been traditionally a leading source of wealth for Aleppo's Muslims: commerce. Even before its demise, the profitable Iranian silk trade had been largely the specialized venue of the Armenians, whether subjects of the sultan or of the shah. Added to this, the mid–eighteenth century saw the virtual capture of the Syria-Egypt trade by Syria's Christians and an increasing level of European economic penetration into the Red Sea and the Persian Gulf. In the early decades of the eighteenth century, indigo and Indian cloth, as well as Yemeni coffee, had arrived in Aleppo by caravan from Basra or Jeddah. After 1750, almost all Indian goods, and even oftentimes Yemeni coffee, arrived in the city via Iskenderun and the sea, brought in on ships flying the flags of western European nations.

Syrian Muslims might have used commerce as a vehicle to create wealth, but once they had joined the ranks of the wealthy, they invariably diversified their holdings. As such, the narrowing of commercial opportunities was not necessarily a matter of concern, as it coincided with an opening up of opportunities in tax farming and the commercial transformation of Syria's agriculture production to export crops for Europe, with its promise of ready wealth. Rather, the contraction of the commercial role Muslim Aleppines could play necessarily fell the heaviest on those who might have aspirations to follow in Sindbad's footsteps and become *fakhr al-tujjār*s in their own right: young Muslims with ambition, if not wealth.

This contrasts with the widening opportunities that were becoming available to the city's Christians at roughly the same time. The Syrian Christians, like the Armenians before them, were a minority in a predominantly Muslim world. This limited their options for both obtaining wealth and investing it. Despite their legally sanctioned position of inferiority, however, changes in the trading patterns of the Levant had pushed both communities to the forefront, and both were quick to capitalize on their opportunities.

While the Muslim elite of Aleppo may have had new opportunities that served to preclude the formation of a merchant class to promote their economic interests in a changing world, their poorer coreligionists were finding that their advancement opportunities had contracted, witness the impoverishment of the peasantry and the tensions in the guilds. While this did not create an economic class identity in their case either, it did lead to conflict. The economic pressures on Aleppo's Muslim population, when compared to the Christians' newfound prosperity, sowed the seeds of fear in the minds of many Syrian Muslims that the Christians were going to outpace them economically and perhaps even politically. It does not seem all that strange, therefore, that Aleppo, which in the seventeenth and eighteenth centuries had been labeled the most tolerant of all Ottoman cities, was host, in 1850, to the first of many acts of violence directed by Muslims against Christians in nineteenth-century Syria.

Wallerstein has posed the question as to the timing and the process by which the Ottoman Empire was brought into the "modern world economic system," leaving the incorporation itself as a historical fact. Aleppo's case helps to elucidate that there was not, in fact, one process. Different parts of the empire had greatly differing experiences. However, none emerged into Wallerstein's slightly elevated category of "semiperipheral" (as in the case of Russia, for example) as opposed to "peripheral," the apparent fate of the Levant in its entirety.

With the Qazdoghli amirs in the eighteenth century, Egypt was already governed by a semiindependent, centralizing political leadership. This trend was merely accelerated by Mehmed Ali in the nineteenth century, who succeeded in transforming the Egyptian export economy, linking it inextricably with that of industrializing western Europe. In southern Iraq, on the other hand, no real local political leadership emerged, and the incorporation of the region occurred under the direction of the British and their Indian surrogates.

Northern Syria, and especially Aleppo, seems to have fallen somewhere in between these two examples. Unlike Egypt, the period of disintegration for the Ottoman state did not engender a local dynasty capable of taking control of the region's economy. Instead, Aleppo was governed by an uneasy balancing act between various factions, headed by the *ashrāf* and the janissaries, each of whom tried to jockey their way to power through the obtainment of wealth and its accompanying political influence. The result was political confusion and often outright anarchy, which descended into violent faction fights. In northern Syria, after the demise of the Canpulatoğlus, there was no political leadership to help or hinder the region's incorporation into the world system. But there were individuals, Christian merchants and Muslim *malikaneci*s alike, who personally profited from its happening and so moved to take advantage of the situation, speeding the process along.

Mercantilism had triumphed over the Ottoman Empire's version of an Islamic economy, or to use Wallerstein's terminology, Syria had become a peripheral region, supplying colonial products to capitalist Europe. But this process differed from what was happening in many other parts of the world, in that it had required no force of arms on the parts of the Europeans. Rather, they had encountered local elements who, for differing reasons, aided the process.

Nonetheless, there were obviously various internal factors that aided the incorporation along as well. The weakness of the central government meant that it could not effectively oppose the European economic penetration, even if it had so wanted. This allowed the Europeans to extract concessions from the Porte that gave their merchants and products advantages over the local ones. An important example of this trend were the concessions the Europeans were able to obtain for their Christian protégés as *beratlı*s.

In the end, however, we return to two important local conditions that seemingly abetted the Western designs more than anything else. The first was strictly economic. The traditional patterns of investment for Aleppo's wealthy demonstrate no real inclination to invest primarily in trade. The disinclination could only have been strengthened in the eighteenth century by new, extremely profitable investment opportunities and by the growing role played by Europeans even in internal Ottoman trade, including, for example, the sea routes to Egypt. We have seen that in some cases the Europeans actually discriminated against Muslim merchants in favor of Christian ones. But even where they did not, the status of *beratlı* held by some of the more prominent Christian merchants, as well as their knowledge of Western languages and willingness to deal with the Franks, gave them an advantage few Muslims could equal.

Simply put, then, the question in the minds of most wealthy Muslims was probably, "Why not leave the trade to the infidels?" This abdication would have catastrophic results, but at the time, the brunt of the choice's effects fell on those elements of the Muslim population, peasants and guildsmen, who were least able to give political voice to their distress or to form a united course of action. A modern Marxist sense of class identity was, after all, still a long way off.

A second factor lay in a belief in the basic moral rectitude of an Islamic economic policy as it had been interpreted over the preceding centuries. Despite the setbacks the Ottomans were facing, nothing had caused Muslims by that time to ask serious questions, as they would in the twentieth century, about their understanding of the nature of an Islamic state. In 1750, as in 1250, most Muslims were content to let the Muslim courts decide what was Islamic and what was not. The courts, in turn, promoted a commercial ideology that, while it favored trade, was hardly mercantilist. On the contrary, the tenets of this economic approach as the courts interpreted it were almost diametrically opposed to the creation of conditions similar to those found in the regions of Europe that were just beginning to see a development of protoindustry.

The law's interpretation could change. We have evidence of this in the allowal of interest under the legal guise of terming it profit rather than usury and in the seemingly antiguild rulings of eighteenth-century Aleppo. But even in these cases, the underlying ideology of justice in the marketplace, including the idea of fair pricing, the sanctity of contract, and the right for labor to receive a just wage, makes us wonder whether conditions for a capitalist protoindustry such as arose in Europe could ever have appeared in Aleppo without a total collapse of the Ottoman system of government, with its courts and bureaucrats.

NOTES

1. Aleppo 80:130, 20 Nov. 1752, speaks of a shipment of Iranian silk from Tabriz.
2. de Vries, pp. 63–4, 200–02.

Glossary

The following terms have had different meanings in various Muslim states over the centuries. The glosses are meant simply to serve as a guide to their meanings as they were used in Ottoman Aleppo during the period from the sixteenth through the eighteenth century. The terms have been identified as to their language of origin: (A) Arabic, (T) Ottoman Turkish, (F) Frankish (i.e., one of the European languages). In a case where a term was originally from Arabic, but had a specialized meaning in the Ottoman period, its Turkish form is given (e.g., *mukata'a* rather than *muqāṭaʿ*.) In some cases, both the Arabic and the Ottoman Turkish forms have been given, as the two were often radically different.

ağa (T)	chief, head; especially in the janissary corps
ahidname (T)	treaty agreement, especially the *imtiyazat* or capitulatory agreements between the Ottomans and the European powers
amāna (A)	security; safekeeping
arpalık (T)	livelihood; the tax revenues assigned to members of the *askeri* class
ashrāf (A)	plural, singular *sharīf;* descendants of the family of the Prophet Muhammad
askeri (T)	the tax-exempt Ottoman military, bureaucratic, and religious ruling establishment
avania (T)	an illegal impost; a bribe; Arabic, *rashwa*
avarız (T)	name given to all sorts of extraordinary taxes collected in times of fiscal deficits for the central treasury
aʿyān (A)	collective used to designate the locally important families in an Ottoman provincial city
b./bnt. (A)	abbreviations for *ibn* and *bint* ("son of" and "daughter of," respectively); used in Muslim names
bayt al-māl (A)	office of the state treasury authorized to take charge of estates of persons who had died without leaving any known heirs
bazarbaşı (T)	the administrator of a market; also the officer in charge of provisioning the governor's residence

bedestan (T)	(A) *bāzīstān;* covered central market area where valuable goods were stored and sold
berat (T)	(1) an official government patent of office; (2) the exemption from taxation and prosecution by Muslim courts granted to the Europeans resident in the empire and their local non-Muslim employees
beratlı (T)	a person holding a *berat*
Çelebi (T)	an honorific added to a man's name; it usually connotes civilian status
dallāl (T)	commercial broker
dār al-ghanam (A)	government office responsible for taxing livestock
Dār al-Islām (A)	the House of Islam; the Muslim nations as opposed to the *Dār al-Ḥarb* ("the House of War") or those lands under a non-Muslim sovereign.
dār al-wakāla (A)	government station where large, bulky agricultural products were weighed and taxed
defter (T)	register book
devşirme (T)	the child tax, levied on the Christian populations of Anatolia and the Balkans to provide recruits for the Ottoman military
dhimmī (A)	non-Muslim subjects of a Muslim state
dizdar (T)	officer in charge of a citadel's garrison
dragoman (F)	translator; derived from the Arabic *turjumān*
emin-i gümrük (T)	official charged with the collection of customs receipts
fatwā (A)	a religious ruling, not necessarily binding but admissible evidence of precedence in a Muslim court; issued by a *muftī* or by the *Şeyhülislam,* the highest religious authority in the Ottoman state
ḥājj (A)	pilgrimage to Mecca; in someone's name, a honorific indicating that he or she has made the pilgrimage; feminine from *ḥājja;* in Turkish names *hac*
hane (T)	house; taxable household
ḥawāja (A)	honorific attached to non-Muslims' names; corruption of the Persian *khʷaja*
ḥawāla (A)	(T) *poliça;* letter of credit
ḥisba (A)	market regulations; enforced by the *muḥtasib*
ḥujja (A)	document attesting to a decision taken by a Muslim judge
imtiyazat (T)	capitulatory agreements; commercial treaties between the Ottomans and various European powers, granting extraterritoriality to European merchants living in the Ottoman Empire
jizya (A)	poll tax placed on non-Muslims; Turkish spelling, *cizye*
kafāla (A)	guaranty; sponsorship; surety; *kafīl* quarantor
kanun (T)	law issued by imperial fiat by the Ottoman sultan
kanun-name (T)	collection of laws, not a part of the *sharīʿa*

kethüda (T)	representative of a guild, neighborhood, etc. to the government; steward
khān (A)	structure designed as a residence and trading facility for traveling merchants
laqab (A)	personal name indicating origin or occupation, e.g., the Damascene, or the Baker
mahr (A)	bridal dower
malikane (T)	tax farm granted to the holder for life; held by a *malikaneci*
millet (T)	officially recognized non-Muslim religious community
mizan-ı harir (T)	government scales where raw silk was weighed and taxed
muḍāraba (A)	commercial agreement where an investor entrusted capital to an agent who traded with it, after which the accrued profit was divided between them according to a prearranged formula; *commenda*
muftī (A)	see *fatwā*
muḥaṣṣil (T)	tax collector
muḥtasib (A)	see *ḥisba*
mukata'a (T)	tax farm; held by a *mukata'acı*
mukhallafāt (A)	(T) *tereke;* an estate of a deceased person
mulk (A)	privately held property
mutawallī (A)	executor of a *waqf*
naqīb al-ashrāf (A)	officially designated leader of the *ashrāf* faction
Paşa (T)	Ottoman title applied in the early centuries only to those officials holding the rank of general or provincial governor; in Ottoman Aleppo, the colloquial form *basha* was by the eighteenth century being applied with much less discrimination
Porte (F)	the Ottoman government in Istanbul; a shortened form of the Sublime Porte, an English translation of the Ottoman *bab-i ali* ("high gate"); in contemporary Arabic accounts from Aleppo, Ottoman officials were often referred to as *rijāl al-bāb* ("men of the Gate")
qāḍī (A)	judge who administered the *sharīʿa* and *kanun*
qassām al-ʿaskarī (A)	official charged with the disposition of the estates of the *askeri* members
qaysārīya (A)	building designed to be a residence of merchants, or a workplace for craftsmen
raʿāyā (A)	(T) *reayet;* tax-paying elements of the Ottoman population, as opposed to the *askeri*
saray (T)	palace; governor's residence
sayyid (A)	honorific applied to a member of the *ashrāf,* or a *sharīf;* see *ashraf*
shāhbandar	(Arabic form of a Persian term) the officially designated head of the merchant community
sharīʿa (A)	body of Muslim law, variously interpreted

shaykh (A)	leader; chief of a guild, tribe, quarter, or a religious order
simsār (A)	commercial broker
sūq (A)	(T) *çarşı;* market, in Aleppo usually covered
taife (T)	group; sect; guild
tekalif (T)	extraordinary tax, supposedly only imposed in times of emergency for the state
timar (T)	fief, the revenue of which was granted to the holder in return for military service
ʿulamā (A)	body of Muslim religious officials and scholars
ümera (T)	Ottoman bureaucratic elite
w. (A)	abbreviation for *walad* ("son of"), used in records only for non-Muslim males; interestingly, the form *bnt.* was used for both Muslim and non-Muslim women alike
waqf (A)	pious endowment
yave cizye (T)	head tax placed on nonresident *dhimmī*s
zāwīya (A)	(T) *tekke;* residence established for a Muslim Sufi religious order *(ṭarīqa)*

Selected Bibliography

ARCHIVAL SOURCES

Damascus. National Archives.
(1) Sharīᶜa Court Records. Aleppo.
(2) Awāmir al-Sulṭānīya. Aleppo.

Istanbul. Başbakanlık Arşivi.
(3) Cevdet. Maliye.
(4) Maliyeden Müdevver.
(5) Mühimme Defterleri.

London. Public Records Office.
(6) Foreign Office Documents.
(7) State Papers. Series 105 and 110.
(8) Calendar of State Papers. Venice.

CONTEMPORARY ACCOUNTS

Aigen, Wolffgang. *Sieben Jahre in Aleppo, 1656–1663*. Ed. Andreas Tietze. Vienna, 1980.

Ali Efendi. *Fetava-yı Ali Efendi*. Cairo, 1283/1866–67.

Arvieux, Laurant, chevalier d'. *Memoires du Chevalier d'Arvieux*. 6 vols. Leipzig, 1756.

ibn Ayās, Muḥammad Aḥmad. *Badā'iᶜ al-zuhūr fī waqā'iᶜ al-duhūr*. 5 vols. Istanbul, 1932.

Barker, John. *Syria and Egypt under the last Five Sultans of Turkey*. 2 vols. Ed. Edward Barker. London, 1876.

Berchet, Guglielmo. *Relazioni dei consoli veneti nella Siria*. Turin, 1866.

Carré, the Abbé. *The Travels of the Abbé Carré in India and the Near East, 1672 to 1674*, 3 vols. The Hakluyt Society. 2nd ser., nos. 95–97, 1947–48.

Carruthers, Douglas, ed. *The Desert Road to India: Being the Journals of Four Travellers by the Great Desert Caravan Route between Aleppo and Basra, 1745–1751*. London, 1929.

Evliya Çelebi. *Evliya Çelebi Seyahatnamesi*. 10 vols. Istanbul, 1896–1938.

Green, P. A. *A Journey from Aleppo to Damascus*. London, 1736.

Greenville, Henry. *Observations sur l'état actuel de l'Empire Ottoman*. Ann Arbor, 1965.

Ismail, Adel. *Documents diplomatiques et consulaires relatifs à l'histoire du Liban et des pays du Proche Orient du XVIIe siècle à nos jours*. 15 vols. Beirut, 1975–.

Maundrell, Henry. *Journey from Aleppo to Jerusalem at Easter 1697*. London, 1832.

McCulloch, J. R., ed. *Early English Tracts on Commerce*. Cambridge, 1954.

al-Muḥibbi, Muḥammad al-Amīn. *Khulāsat al-athār fī aʿyān al-qarn al-ḥādī ʿashar*. Cairo, 1869.

al-Murādī, Muḥammad. *Silk al-durar fī aʿyān al-qarn al-thānī ʿashar*. Cairo, 1291–1301 A.H.

Naima, Mustafa. *Tarih-i Naima*. 6 vols. Istanbul, 1864–66.

Pococke, Richard. *Description of the East and Some Other Countries*. In *Voyages and Travels in All Parts of the World*, vol. 10. Coll. John Pinkerton. London, 1811.

Polonyalı Simeon. *Polonyalı Simeon'un Seyahatnamesi, 1608–1619*. Istanbul, 1964.

Purchas His Pilgrims. Ed. Samuel Purchas. 20 vols. The Hakluyt Society.

Qarāʾlī, Būluṣ. *Ahamm ḥawādith Ḥalab*. Cairo, n.p.d.

Rabbath, Antoine. *Documents inédits pour servir à l'histoire du Christianisme en Orient*. 2 vols. Paris, 1905, 1911.

Rauwolf, Leonhart. *Aigentliche Beschreibung der Raiss inn die Morgenländer*. Graz, 1971.

Russell, Alexander. *The Natural History of Aleppo*. London, 1794.

Sanderson, John. *The Travels of John Sanderson in the Levant, 1584–1609*. London, 1931.

Tavernier, Jean-Baptiste. *Les six voyages en Turquie*. Paris, 1679.

Teixeira, Pedro. *The Travels of Pedro Teixeira*. London, 1902.

Thevenot, Jean de. *Voyages du Monsieur de Thevenot en Europe, Asie, et Afrique*. Paris, 1689.

ibn Ṭulūn, Muḥammad. *Aʿlām al-warā bi-man wuliya nāʾiban min al-Atrāk bi-Dimasq al-Shām al-kubrā*. Damascus, 1964.

al-ʿUrdī, Abūʾl-Wafā. *Maʿādin al-dhahab fīʾl-aʿyān al-musharrafa bi-him Ḥalab*. MS. British Library, London. Or.3618.

Volney, Constantine. *Travels through Syria and Egypt in the Years 1783, 1784, and 1785*. 2 vols. London, 1787.

SECONDARY SOURCES

Abdel-Nour, Antoine. *Introduction à l'histoire urbaine de la Syrie Ottomane (XVIe–XVIIIe siècle)*. Beirut, 1982.

Abu-Husayn, Abdul-Rahim. *Provincial Leaderships in Syria, 1575–1650*. Beirut, 1985.

Akdağ, Mustafa. *Türk Halkının Dirlik ve Düzenlik Kavgası*. Ankara, 1979.

——. *Türkiye'nin İktisadi ve İçtimai Tarihi*. Ankara, 1979.

Allen, Calvin H., Jr. "The Indian Merchant Community of Masqat." *BSOAS* 44:39–53.

Ambrose, Gwylim. "English Traders at Aleppo, 1658–1756." *Economic History Review* 3:246–67.

ʿAnūtī, Usāmā. *al-Ḥaraka al-adābīya fī bilād al-Shām khilāl al-qarn al-thāmin ʿashar*. Beirut, 1970.

Ashtor, Eliyahu. "The Economic Decline of the Middle East during the Late Middle Ages: An Outline." *Asian and African Studies* 15:253–86.

——. *Levant Trade in the Late Middle Ages*. Princeton, 1983.

al-ʿAzzāwī, ʿAbbās. *ʿAshāʾir al-ʿIrāq*. Baghdad, 1935–56.

Baer, Gabriel. "The Administrative, Economic, and Social Functions of Turkish Guilds." *IJMES* 1:28–50.

——. "Monopolies and Restrictive Practices of Turkish Guilds." *JESHO* 13:145–65.

——. "Ottoman Guilds: A Reassessment." In *Social and Economic History of Turkey (1071–1920)*. Ed. Osman Okyar and Halil Inalcik. Ankara, 1980.

Bağış, Ali. *Osmanlı Ticaretinde Gayri Müslimler*. Ankara, 1983.

Bakhit, Muhammad Adnan. "Aleppo and the Ottoman Military in the 16th Century." *al-Abḥāth* 27:27–38.

——. *The Ottoman Province of Damascus in the Sixteenth Century*. Beirut, 1982.

Barbir, Karl. "From Pasha to Efendi: The Assimilation of Ottomans into Damascene Society, 1516–1783." *International Journal of Turkish Studies* 1:68–83.

——. *Ottoman Rule in Damascus, 1708–1758*. Princeton, 1980.

Barkan, Ömer Lütfi. "Edirne askeri kassamına ait tereke defterleri, 1549–1659." *Belgeler* 3:1–479.

——. "Essai sur les donées statistiques de registres de recensement dans l'Empire Ottoman aux XVe et XVIe siècles." *JESHO* 1:9–36.

Betts, Robert. *Christians in the Arab East*. Atlanta, 1978.

Bodman, Herbert. *Political Factions in Aleppo, 1760–1826*. Chapel Hill, 1963.

Bosscha Erdbrink, G. R. *At the Threshold of Felicity: Ottoman-Dutch Relations during the Embassy of Cornelius Calkoen at the Sublime Porte, 1726–1744*. Ankara, 1975.

Boxer, C. B. *The Portuguese Sea-Borne Empire, 1415–1825*. London, 1969.

Braudel, Fernand. *Civilization and Capitalism, 15th–18th Century*. 3 vols. New York, 1982, 1984.

——. *The Mediterranean and the Mediterranean World of Philip II*. New York, 1975.

Çagatay, Neşet. "Osmanlı İmparatorluğunda riba-faiz konusu, para vakıfları ve bankçılık." *Vakıflar Dergisi* 9:39–56.

Charles-Roux, François. *Les échelles de Syrie et de Palestine au XVIIIe siècle*. Paris, 1928.

Chaudhuri, K. N. *The English East India Company: The Study of an Early Joint-Stock Company*. London, 1964.

——. *Trade and Civilisation in the Indian Ocean: An Economic History from the Rise of Islam to 1750*. Cambridge, 1985.

——. *The Trading World of Asia and the East India Company, 1660–1760*. Cambridge, 1978.

Çızakça, Murad. "A Short History of the Bursa Silk Industry." *JESHO* 23:142–52.

Cohen, Amnon. "Local Trade, International Trade, and Government Involvement in Jerusalem during the Early Ottoman Period." *Asian and African Studies* 7:5–12.

——. *Palestine in the 18th Century*. Jerusalem, 1973.

——, and Bernard Lewis. *Population and Revenue in the Towns of Palestine in the Sixteenth Century*. Princeton, 1978.

Cook, M. A. *Studies in the Economic History of the Middle East*. London, 1970.

Curtin, Philip. *Cross-Cultural Trade in World History*. Cambridge, 1984.

Dalsar, Fahri. *Türk Sanayi ve Ticaret Tarihinde Bursa'da İpekçilik*. Istanbul, 1960.

David, Jean-Claude. *Le waqf d'Ibšir Paša à Alep*. Damascus, 1982.

Davis, Ralph. *Aleppo and Devonshire Squire*. London, 1967.

——. "English Imports from the Middle East, 1580–1780." In *Studies in the Economic History of the Middle East*. Ed. M. A. Cook. London, 1970, pp. 193–206.

Dengler, Ian. "Turkish Women in the Ottoman Empire: The Classical Age." In *Women in the Muslim World*. Ed. Lois Beck and Nikki Keddie. Cambridge, 1978.

Düzdağ, Ertuğrul. *Şeyhülislam Ebussuûd Efendi Fetvaları Işiğında 16. Asır Türk Hayati*. Istanbul, 1983.

Encyclopedia of Islam, 2nd ed. (Leiden: 1960–)

Faroghi, Suraiya. "Notes on the Production of Cotton and Cotton Cloth in 16th and 17th Century Anatolia." *Journal of European Economic History* 8:405–17.

——. "Rural Society in Anatolia and the Balkans during the Sixteenth Century, II." *Turcica* 11:103–53.

——. "Textile Production in Rumeli and the Arab Provinces: Geographical Distribution and Internal Trade (1560–1650)." *Journal of Ottoman Studies* 1:61–83.

——. *Towns and Townsmen in Ottoman Anatolia: Trade, Crafts and Food Production in an Urban Setting, 1520–1650*. Cambridge, 1984.

Fawaz, Leila. *Merchants and Migrants in Nineteenth Century Beirut*. Cambridge, 1983.

Ferrier, R. W. "The Armenians and the East India Company in Persia in the 17th and Early 18th century." *Economic History Review*, 2nd series, 26:38–62.

Floor, W. M. "The Merchants *(tujjar)* of Qajar Iran." *Zeitschrift der Deutschen Morgenländischen Gesellschaft* 126:101–35.

Frazee, Charles. *Catholics and Sultans: The Church and the Ottoman Empire*. London, 1983.

Gaube, Heinz, and Eugen Wirth. *Aleppo: Historische und geographische Beiträge zur baulichen Gestaltung, zur sozialen Organisation und zur wirtschaftlichen Dynamik einer vorderasiatischen Fernhandelsmetropole*. Wiesbaden, 1984.

Gerber, Haim. "Guilds in Seventeenth Century Anatolian Bursa." *Asian and African Studies* 11:59–86.

——. "The Monetary System of the Ottoman Empire." *Turcica* 15:311–48.

——. "The Muslim Law of Partnership in Ottoman Court Records." *Studia Islamica* 53:109–19.

——. "The Population of Syria and Palestine in the Nineteenth Century." *Asian and African Studies* 13:58–80.

al-Ghazzī, Kāmil. *Nahr al-dhahab fī tāʾrīkh Ḥalab*. 3 vols. Aleppo, 1923–26.

Gibb, Hamilton, and Bowen, Harold. *Islamic Society and the West*. London, 1950.

Gregorian, Vartan. "Minorities in Isfahan: The Armenian Community of Isfahan 1587–1722." *Iranian Studies* 7:652–80.

Griswold, William. *The Great Anatolian Rebellion 1000–1020/1591–1611*. Berlin, 1983.

de Groot, A. H. *The Ottoman Empire and the Dutch Republic: A History of the Earliest Diplomatic Relations, 1610–1630*. Leiden, 1978.

Hachico, Mohammad Ali. "English Travel Books about the Near East in the 18th Century." *Die Welt des Islam* 9:1–206.

Haddad, Robert. *Syrian Christians in a Muslim Society*. Princeton, 1970.

Hattox, Ralph. *Coffee and Coffeehouses: The Origins of a Social Beverage in the Medieval Near East*. Seattle, 1985.

Heyd, Uriel. *Studies in Old Ottoman Criminal Law*. Oxford, 1973.

Heyd, Willem. *Histoire du commerce du Levant au Moyen-Age*. Leipzig, 1886.

Hoskins, H. L. "The Overland Route to India in the Eighteenth Century." *History* 9:302–18.

Hourani, Albert. "The Changing Face of the Fertile Crescent in the XVIIIth Century." *Studia Islamica* 8:89–122.

——. *The Emergence of the Modern Middle East*. Los Angeles, 1981.

——. *Europe and the Middle East*. Los Angeles, 1980.

——. "Ottoman Reform and the Politics of Notables." In *Beginnings of a Modernization in the Middle East*. Ed. W. Polk and R. Chambers. Chicago, 1968.

Hurewitz, J. C., ed. *Diplomacy in the Near and Middle East: A Documentary Record, 1535–1919*. New York, 1972.

Inalcik, Halil. "Adaletnameler." *Belgeler* 2:49–145.

——. "Bursa and the Commerce of the Levant." *JESHO* 3:131–42.

——. "Bursa I. XV asır sanayi ve ticaret tarihine dair vesikalar." *Belletin* 24:45–110.

——. "Capital Formation in the Ottoman Empire." *JESHO* 29:97–140.

——. "The Emergence of Big Farms, Çiftliks: State, Landlords, and Tenants." Eds. Jean-Louis Bacqué-Grammont and Paul Dumont. In *Contributions à l'histoire économique et sociale de l'Empire ottoman*, vol. 3 (Paris, 1983) pp. 105–26.

——. "The Hub of the City: The Bedestan of Istanbul." *International Journal of Turkish Studies* 1:1–17.

——. "Introduction to Ottoman Metrology." *Turcica* 15:311–48.

——. "Military and Fiscal Transformation in the Ottoman Empire." *Archivum Ottomanicum* 6:283–337.
——. "15. asır Türkiye iktisadi ve içtimai tarihi kaynaklar." *İktisat Fakültesi Mecmuası* 15:51–75.
——. "Osmanlı idare, sosyal ve ekonomik tarihiyle ilgili belgeleri: Bursa kadı sicillerinden seçmeler." *Belgeler* 10:1–91.
——. "The Ottoman Economic Mind and Aspects of the Ottoman Economy." In *Studies in the Economic Histories of the Middle East.* Ed. M. A. Cook. London, 1970, pp. 207–18.
——. *The Ottoman Empire: The Classical Age, 1300–1600.* London, 1973.
Ingram, Edward. "From Trade to Empire in the Near East—I: The End of the Spectre of the Overland Trade." *Middle Eastern Studies* 14:3–21.
Islamoğlu, Huri, and Çağlar Keyder. "The Ottoman Social Formation." In *The Asiatic Mode of Production: Science and Politics.* Eds. Anne Bailey and Josep Llobera. London, 1981.
Israel, Jonathan. *European Jewry in the Age of Mercantilism, 1550–1750.* Oxford, 1985.
Issawi, Charles. "Comment on Professor Barkan's Estimate of the Population of the Ottoman Empire, 1520–1530." *JESHO* 1:329–31.
Itzkowitz, Norman. "Eighteenth Century Ottoman Realities." *Studia Islamica* 16:73–94.
Jennings, Ronald. "Loans and Credit in Early 17th Century Ottoman Judicial Records." *JESHO* 16:168–216.
——. "Urban Population in Anatolia in the Sixteenth Century: A Study of Kayseri, Karaman, Amasya, Trabzon, and Erzurum." *IJMES* 7:21–57.
——. "Women in Early Seventeenth Century Ottoman Judicial Records: The Sharia Court of Anatolian Kayseri." *JESHO* 18:53–114.
Joseph, John. *Muslim-Christian Relations and Inter-Christian Rivalries in the Middle East.* Albany, 1983.
Kampman, A. A. "XVII. ve XVIII. yüzyıllarda Osmanlı İmparatorluğunda Hollandalılar." *Belletin* 23:513–23.
Kevonian, Keram. "Marchands Arméniens au XVIIe siècle." *Cahiers du Monde Russe et Sovietique* 16:199–244.
Khalidi, Tarif, ed. *Land Tenure and Social Transformation in the Middle East.* Beirut, 1984.
Kreiser, Klaus. "Bedestan-Bauten in Osmanischen Reich. Ein vorlaufiger Überblick auf Grund der Schriftquellen." *Istanbul Mitteillungen* 29:367–400.
Kriedte, Peter. *Peasants, Landlords and Merchant Capitalists: Europe and the World Economy, 1500–1800.* Cambridge, 1983.
Kritzeck, James. *Anthology of Islamic Literature.* New York, 1966.
Kunt, I. Metin. "Derviş Mehmed Paşa, Vezir and Entrepreneur: A Study in Ottoman Political Theory and Practice." *Turcica* 9:197–214.
——. *The Sultan's Servants: The Transformation of Ottoman Provincial Government, 1550–1650.* New York, 1983.

Kurdakul, Necdet. *Osmanlı Devleti'nde Ticaret Antlaşmaları ve Kapitülasyonlar*. Istanbul, 1981.

Kütükoğlu, Mübahat. *Osmanlı-İngiliz İktisadi Münasebetleri, 1580–1838*. Ankara, 1974.

——. *Osmanlılarda Narh Müessesi ve 1640 Tarihli Narh Defteri*. Istanbul, 1983.

Lambton, Ann. "Justice in the Medieval Theory of Kingship." *Studia Islamica* 17:91–119.

Lapidus, Ira. *Muslim Cities in the Late Middle Ages*. New York, 1984.

Lewis, Bernard. "Some Reflections on the Decline of the Ottoman Empire," *Studia Islamica* 9:111–17.

Lewis, Warren. *Levantine Adventurer: The Travels and Missions of the Chevallier d'Arvieux, 1653–1697*. New York, 1962.

Longrigg, Stephen. *Four Centuries of Modern Iraq*. Oxford, 1925.

Mandaville, Jon E. "Usurious Piety: The Cash-Waqf Controversy in the Middle East." *IJMES* 10:289–308.

Mantran, Robert. *Istanbul dans le seconde moitié du XVIIe siècle*. Paris, 1962.

Marcus, Abraham. "Men, Women, and Property: Dealers in Real Estate in 18th Century Aleppo." *JESHO* 26:138–63.

——. "People and Property in Eighteenth Century Aleppo." Unpublished Ph.D. thesis, Columbia University, 1979.

——. "Privacy in Eighteenth-Century Aleppo: The Limits of Cultural Ideals." *IJMES* 18:165–84.

Marsot, Afaf Lutfi al-Sayyid. *Egypt in the Reign of Muhammad Ali*. Cambridge, 1984.

Masson, P. *Histoire du commerce français dans le Levant au XVIIe siècle*. Paris, 1896.

——. *Histoire du commerce français dans le Levant au XVIIIe siècle*. Paris, 1911.

Masters, Bruce. "Patterns of Migration to Ottoman Aleppo in the 17th and 18th Centuries." *International Journal of Turkish Studies*. 4, no. 1.

McGowan, Bruce. *Economic Life in Ottoman Europe: Taxation, Trade, and the Struggle for Land, 1600–1800*. London, 1981.

Meilink-Roelofsz, M. A. *Asian Trade and European Influence in the Indonesian Archipelago between 1500 and about 1630*. The Hague, 1964.

Meriwether, Margaret. "The Notable Families of Aleppo, 1770–1830: Networks and Social Structure." Unpublished Ph.D. thesis, University of Pennsylvania, 1981.

Mishkimin, Harry. *The Economy of Later Renaissance Europe, 1460–1600*. London, 1977.

Naff, Thomas, and Owen, Roger, eds. *Studies in Eighteenth Century Islamic History*. Carbondale, 1977.

el-Nahal, Galal. *The Judicial Administration of Ottoman Egypt in the Seventeenth Century*. Minneapolis, 1979.

Olson, Robert. "The Esnaf and the Patrona Halil Rebellion of 1730: A Realignment in Ottoman Politics?" *JESHO* 17:329–44.

Orhonlu, Çengiz. *Osmanlı İmparatorluğunda Aşiretleri İskan Teşebbüsü*. Istanbul, 1963.

Owen, Roger. *The Middle East in the World Economy, 1800–1914*. New York, 1981.

Özbaran, Salih. "Osmanlı İmparatorluğu ve Hindistan yolu." *Tarih Dergisi* 31:66–146.

Philipp, Thomas. "Jews and Christians: Their Changing Position in Politics and Economy in Eighteenth Century Egypt and Syria." In *Egypt and Palestine: A Millenium of Association (868–1948)*. Ed. Amnon Cohen and Gabriel Baer. New York, 1964.

——. *The Syrians in Egypt*. Berliner Islamstudien 3. Stuttgart, 1985.

Prakash, Om. *The Dutch East India Company and the Economy of Bengal*. Princeton, 1986.

Rafeq, Abdul-Karim. *al-ᶜArab wa-al-ᶜUthmānīyūn*. Dasmascus, 1974.

——. "The Impact of Europe on a Traditional Economy: The Case of Damascus, 1840–1870." In Économie et Sociétés dans l'Empire Ottoman. Ed. Jean-Louis Bacque-Grammont and Paul Dumont. Paris, 1983.

——. "The Law Court Registers of Damascus." In *Les Arabes par leurs archives: XVIe–XXe siècles*. Ed. J. Berque and D. Chevallier. Paris, 1976.

——. "The Local Forces in Syria in the Seventeenth and Eighteenth Century." In *War, Technology, and Society in the Middle East*. Ed. V. J. Parry and M. E. Yapp. London, 1975.

——. "Maẓāhir min al-tanzīm al-ḥirafī fī bilād al-Shām fī al-ᶜahd al-ᶜUthmānī." *Dirāsāt Tāʾrīkhīya* 4:30–62.

——. *The Province of Damascus*. Beirut, 1966.

——. "Qāfilat al-ḥājj al-Shāmī wa-ahammiyatuha fī al-dawla al-ᶜuthmānīya." *Dirasāt Tāʾrīkhīya* 6:193–216.

——. "Economic Relations between Damascus and the Dependent Countryside, 1743–71." In *The Islamic Middle East, 700–1900: Studies in Economic and Social History*. Ed. A. L. Udovitch. Princeton, 1981, pp. 653–85.

——. "The Revolt of ᶜAlī Pāshā Jānbulād (1605–1607) in the Contemporary Arabic Sources and Its Significance." In *VIII. Türk Tarih Kongresi: Kongreye Sunulan Bildiriler*. Ankara, 1983.

Raymond, André. *Artisans et commerçants au Caire au XVIIIe siècle*. 2 vols. Damascus, 1973–74.

——. *Grandes villes arabes à l'époque ottomane* (Paris: 1985).

——. "The Ottoman Conquest and the Development of the Great Arab Towns." *International Journal of Turkish Studies* 1:84–101.

——. "The Population of Aleppo in the Sixteenth and Seventeenth Centuries According to Ottoman Census Documents." *IJMES* 16:447–60.

Refik, Ahmet. *Anadolu'da Türk Aşiretleri (966–1200)*. Istanbul, 1930.

Richards, D. S., ed. *Islam and the Trade of Asia*. London, 1970.

Riedlmayer, András. "Ottoman-Safavid Relations and the Anatolian Trade Routes: 1603–1618." *Turkish Studies Association Bulletin* 5:7–10.

Rogers, J. M. *Islamic Art and Design, 1500–1700*. London, 1983.

van Rooy, Silvio. "Armenian Merchant Habits as Mirrored in the 17th–18th Century Amsterdam Documents." *Revue des Études Arméniennes* 3:347–57.

Sahillioğlu, Halil. "Bir tüccar kervanı." *Belgelerle Türk Tarihi Dergisi* 2:63–70.

——. "Bursa kadı sicillerinde iç ve diş ödemeler aracı olarak 'Kitabü'l-Kadi' ve süfteceler." In *Türkiye İktisat Tarihi Semineri (8–10 Haziran)*. Ed. Osman Okyar. Ankara, 1975.

——. "Taghayyur turūq al-tijāra wa'l-tanaffus bayna mina'ay Ṭarablūs al-Shām wa'l-Iskandarūn fī al-qarn al-sābiᶜ ᶜashar." In *Mu'tammar al-duwwalī li-tā'rīkh bilād al-Shām*. Damascus, 1980.

Salibi, Kamal. "The Sayfas and the Eyalet of Tripoli." *Arabica* 20:63–70.

Sanjian, Avedis. *The Armenian Communities in Syria under Ottoman Domination*. Cambridge, 1965.

Sauvaget, Jean. *Alep: Essai sur le développement d'une grande ville syrienne des origines au milieu du XIXᵉ siècle*. Paris, 1941.

Sella, Domenico. "Crisis and Transformation in Venetian Trade." In *Crisis and Change in the Venetian Economy in the Sixteenth and Seventeenth Centuries*. Ed. Brian Pullan. London, 1968.

Shmuelevitz, Aryeh. *The Jews of the Ottoman Empire in the Late Fifteenth and the Sixteenth Centuries*. Leiden, 1984.

Steensgaard, Niels. *The Asian Trade Revolution of the Seventeenth Century: The East India Companies and the Decline of the Caravan Trade*. Chicago, 1973.

———. "Consuls and Nations in the Levant from 1570 to 1650." *Scandinavian Economic History Review* 15:13–55.

al-Ṭabbākh, Mahammad Rāghib. *Aᶜlām al-nubalā bi-tā'rīkh Halab al-shahbā*. 7 vols. Aleppo, 1923–26.

Thieck, Jean-Pierre. "Décentralisation ottomane et affirmation urbaine à Alep à la fin du XVIIIᵉ siècle." In *Mouvements communautaires et espaces urbains au Machreq*. Ed. Guy Leonard. Beirut, 1985.

Thomas, Lewis. *A Study of Naima*. New York, 1972.

Turan, S. "Venedik'te Türk ticaret merkezi." *Belletin* 32:247–83.

Turner, Brian. *Marx and the End of Orientalism*. London, 1978.

Udovitch, Abraham, ed. *The Islamic Middle East, 700–1900: Studies in Economic and Social History*. Princeton, 1981.

———. *Partnership and Profit in Medieval Islam*. Princeton, 1970.

Veinstein, Gilles. "Ayan de la région d'Izmir et commerce du Levant (Deuxième moitié du XVIIIᵉ siècle)." *Études Balkaniques* 12:71–83.

Voll, John. "Old ᶜUlama Families and Ottoman Influence in Eighteenth Century Damascus." *American Journal of Arabic Studies* 3:48–59.

de Vries, Jan. *The Economy of Europe in an Age of Crisis, 1600–1750*. Cambridge, 1976.

Wake, C. H. H. "The Changing Pattern of Europe's Pepper and Spice Imports, ca. 1400–1700." *Journal of European Economic History* 8:361–403.

Wallerstein, Immanuel. *The Modern World System*. 2 vols. New York, 1974, 1980.

Wirth, Eugen. "Aleppo in 19. Jahrhundert: Ein Beispiel für Stabilität und Dynamik spätosmanischer Wirtschaft." Corrected reprint of article with the same title published in *Osmanistische Studien Zur Wirtschafts und Sozialgeschichte*. Ed. Hans Georg Majer. Wiesbaden, 1986.

Wood, Alfred C. *A History of the Levant Company*. London, 1935.

Index

Abaza Hasan Paşa, 22
Abbas, shah of Iran, 23, 24, 83
Abide Hanım, daughter of Kara Mustafa Paşa, 124, 125
Abū Rīsha, 116, 117, 118
ʿĀ'ida, Jirjīs, 98, 99, 175
ʿĀ'ida, Shukrī, 98
Akdağ, Mustafa, 14
Aleppo: geopolitical situation, 8, 11, 13, 14; European trade with, 10, 22, 24, 205, 206; hinterlands, 13, 14, 53, 139, 156, 205, 206; cultural life, 14, 34*n*.15, 49, 60, 133, 134; European consuls in, 14, 15; political leadership, 32, 45, 47, 48, 120, 196, 219; population, 38, 39, 41; migration to, 40, 42, 46, 84, 85, 86, 92, 93, 157; quarters, 42, 111
Alexandria, 17
Amık Gölü, 42, 119
Amır al-ʿArab, 116, 117
Anatolia, 13, 14, 28, 53
ʿAnāza beduin, 118, 120
Ankara: 87; wool trade, 28, 53, 90
Antioch: 8, 31, 197; see of, 92, 95
Arabistan defterdarı, 12
Arīḥāwīzādah, Niʿmat Allah, 64, 65, 174
Armenians: 173; in Iran trade, 23, 24, 63, 64, 82, 87; in Anatolian trade, 53, 63; trade with Europe, 60, 83, 84, 88, 141; growth of Aleppo community, 84, 85, 86, 93; cultural life, 84, 141; service workers, 125; government service, 140, 141
d'Arvieux, chevalier, 38, 40, 41, 57
Ashrāf: 45, 46, 48, 136; involvement in trade, 47
Askeri (Ottoman military/bureaucracy): 45, 57, 141, 142; moneylenders, 158, 166; investment patterns, 165, 166, 169, 172
Aʿyān, 48, 196, 207
ʿAẓm family, 32, 120

Baghdad, 13, 64, 88, 152, 153
Bānqūsā, 42, 111, 121, 127
Barkan, Ömer Lütfi, 39
Barter trade, 25, 31, 148, 149
Basra, 13, 31, 34*n*.11, 88, 153
"Battalation," 67
Bedestan, 123, 127, 128
Beduin: 111, 199, 200; raiding caravans, 29, 112, 114, 116, 118; migration to Aleppo, 42; monopoly over caravans, 111; raids on peasants, 117, 118
Beirut, 13, 17
Berat, 96, 97, 98, 99, 108*n*.81
Braudel, Fernand, 14, 153
Broadcloth, 25, 26, 30, 31, 62, 148, 151
Brokers and agents, 47, 129, 130, 131

Canpulatoğlu, Ali, 16, 19, 20, 21, 22
Canpulatoğlu, Hüseyin, 19, 20
Capitulatory agreements, 67, 76, 77, 78, 88, 96
Caravans: routes, 8, 9, 11, 13, 111, 112; challenges to, 22, 23, 29, 31, 118, 186, 193, 194, 195; transportation costs, 29, 113, 114, 121; Baghdad caravan, 32, 112, 118; size, 111, 112; Anatolian, 112; organization, 114, 115; Aleppo-Iskenderun caravan, 120, 121. *See also* Hajj caravans
Caravansaries (khāns): along caravan routes, 115, 116; urban, 122, 123, 124, 125; financing, 123, 124, 125; administration, 125
Celali revolts, 18, 19
Central Asians, in Aleppo, 80, 81
Christians: 175; population in Aleppo, 39,

Christians (*Continued*)
42, 107*n*.61; migration to Aleppo, 40, 84, 85, 86, 92, 93; sects in Aleppo, 42, 91, 93; Syrian Christians in trade, 62, 63, 64, 96, 97, 98, 99, 100, 101, 102, 103, 104, 130; legal status in Islam, 77, 93; inheritance laws, 178
Coastal shipping, 100, 101, 102, 103
Coffee, 29, 54, 55, 79, 132, 133, 134
Coffee shops, 132, 133, 134, 135
Coins: imported, 22, 25, 31, 148, 149, 150, 151, 152; counterfeiting, 149, 150; Ottoman, 150, 151
Commercial contracts: 50, 51, 52, 61, 135; partnership agreements, 50, 52, 208. *See also Muḍāraba*
Cotton, 10, 22, 32, 104, 195, 196
Courts, Islamic: 50, 61, 125; European involvement with, 65, 66, 67, 68, 154; caravan trade, 115; commerce, 61, 134, 135, 136, 151, 152; women, 179, 180; guilds, 201, 202, 204, 205, 208, 209
Curtin, Philip, 72, 104
Customs office: 121, 136, 137; regulations, 56, 137, 138, 139, 149, 194, 195; officials, 137, 138, 139, 140, 141, 142

Damascus: 12, 14, 15, 38, 46; geopolitical situation, 9, 10, 27; rivalry with Aleppo, 10, 13, 19, 22, 32
Dīb, Yūsuf, 98, 99, 175
Diyarbakır, 13, 41, 85, 93, 113, 198, 206, 207
Dowry *(mahr)*, 178, 179
Dragomans, 96, 97, 98, 99, 108*nn*.77, 80-81

East India Company, 23, 26, 27, 30, 31, 87, 88, 148, 194
Ebusuûd Efendi, 134
Economic theory, Islamic: 2, 75, 76, 97, 110, 199; trade, 136, 137, 187, 188, 189, 191, 198; guilds, 200, 203, 204, 212, 213; Iranian tradition, 188, 189, 192, 195, 200, 212
Egypt: 12, 196, 219; trade with Syria, 62, 64, 100, 101, 102, 103, 104, 139
England: consul in Aleppo, 15, 78, 97, 142; ambassador at Porte, 16, 17, 67, 152, 153; trade with Aleppo, 22, 27, 30, 31, 36*n*.64, 148; silk industry, 25, 26; local commercial agents, 86, 96, 97, 99
Euphrates, 8, 13, 29, 31, 117, 191
Erzurum, 63, 85, 87, 88, 194

Fakhr al-tujjār, 48, 49, 61, 97
France: consul in Aleppo, 15, 78; trade with Aleppo, 22, 27, 30, 31, 36*n*.64, 148; trade with Syria, 27, 30, 32; missionary activity, 94, 95, 96, 100; commercial agents, 96, 97, 99, 103

Gaziantep, 41, 130
al-Ghazzālī, Jānbirdī, 12, 21
Greek Orthodox *(Rum milleti)*: 42, 91, 92, 93, 94, 173; migration to Aleppo, 93; uniate church, 94
Guilds (craft corporations): 47, 70*n*.41, 128; pressures on guilds, 46, 47, 206, 207, 208, 209; retailers' guilds, 54, 55; craft guilds, 54, 55, 56, 57, 130; service guilds, 120, 121, 122; indebtedness, 159, 207; women in guilds, 176; organization, 54, 55, 56, 201, 202, 203, 204

Hajj caravans: 112, 114; economic role, 10, 29, 54, 55; beduin attacks against, 29, 114, 115, 118, 120
Hama, 9, 93, 118, 120
Heyd, Uriel, 189
Homs, 9, 93, 118, 120
Hüsrev Paşa, 18

Idlib, 8, 139, 156
India trade, 13, 29, 62, 63, 64, 82, 147, 153
Indians, in Aleppo, 81, 82
Indigo, 22, 29, 62, 64, 79, 212
Inheritance laws, 165, 178, 180
Iran: Ottoman wars with, 13, 20, 23, 30, 74; silk production, 24, 30, 31, 194, 195; trade with Ottoman Empire, 27, 30, 31, 62, 63, 74, 80, 193, 194, 195, 197
Ireland, 31
Iskenderun, 16, 17, 18, 102, 120, 141
Issawi, Charles, 39
Istanbul: 13, 27, 28, 38, 119, 198; Syria's trade with, 102, 151, 152, 197, 198

Italian merchants. *See* Venice
Izmir, 17, 27, 28, 32, 38, 87, 88, 194, 196

Jabal Samʿān, 118, 119, 135, 136
Janissaries: Damascus, 13, 19, 46; in Aleppo, 46, 48; rivalry with *ashrāf,* 46, 47; involved in trade, 47, 130
Jennings, Ronald, 158, 159, 160
Jews: 174; population in Aleppo, 42, 89; in trade, 53, 60, 64, 89, 90; legal status in Islam, 77; Sephardi community, 60, 89; foreign protection, 89, 90; government service, 140, 141, 142
Jizya: 39, 40, 81, 84, 85, 86, 106*n*.28; *yave cizye,* 85, 86
Judayda, 93, 127, 159
Julfa: 82, 83, 84, 141; New Julfa, 83, 87

Kanun, 189, 195, 206
Kanun-name, 56, 137, 139
Karagözoğlu, Sanos and Bedik, 140, 141
Khān al-wazīr, 124, 125
Kilis, 19, 22, 42, 121, 139, 206
Kurds: 119; military force, 19, 20; migration to Aleppo, 19, 42, 46, 111; brigandage, 22, 28, 121; competition with Arab villagers, 118

Landownership, 157, 169, 171, 172
Lebanon, 10, 21, 22, 27, 119, 193
Letters of credit, 132, 146, 151, 152, 153
Levant Company: 15; factors, 15, 26, 78, 79; competition with East India Company, 23, 26, 30, 31, 87, 148; organization, 26, 78, 87, 148; strengths, 26, 148; trade levels, 27, 28, 30, 31; operations in interior, 87, 88; relations with Syrian Christians, 99, 101, 102, 104; changeover to Syrian silk, 191, 194, 196, 197

Malikane, 60, 130, 207, 208
Mamluks, 9, 12, 13, 82
Mandaville, Jon, 161
Maʿnīs, 19, 21, 192, 193
Mardin, 41, 85, 93, 207
Marj Dābiq, battle of, 12
Markets *(sūqs):* construction, 18; organization, 54, 127, 128, 132; taxation of, 56, 127, 129, 203, 204, 205; porters, 122; size, 126; guards, 132
Maronites, 42, 92, 173
Marseilles: 90; trade with the Levant, 26, 27
Mawālī beduin, 116, 117, 118, 120
Mercantilism: 2, 37, 110, 146, 148, 149, 150, 192, 193, 198, 199
Merchants (Aleppo): social origins, 48, 64, 65, 68, 174; status, 49, 60, 61; organization, 56, 60
Millets, 93, 94
Money changers *(ṣarrāfūn),* 161
Moneylending: European involvement, 67, 68, 153, 154, 172; patterns, 158, 159, 160, 170; guarantors, 157, 163; interest, 160, 161, 162, 163; defaults, 163, 164. *See also Waqf,* cash
Mosaic theory, 43, 44, 55
Mosul, 11, 13, 113, 115
Muḍāraba, 50, 51, 52, 53, 62, 63
Muftī, 58, 134
Muḥtasib, 203, 204, 205
Mukhallafāt. See Qassām al-ʿaskarī
Mūsā w. Isḥāq al-Khākhām, 139, 140, 141

Naqīb al-ashrāf, 136
Nasuh Paşa, 20
Netherlands: 23, 83; trade with Aleppo, 22, 27; trade with the Levant, 25, 27, 148; local commercial agents, 97, 99; consul in Aleppo, 78, 141
North Africans, in Aleppo, 131, 132

Ottoman Empire: policies toward trade, 16, 17, 22, 23, 102, 118, 119, 120, 123, 197, 198, 200, 203, 204, 212, 213; relations with Europeans, 16, 17, 67, 75, 76, 77, 78; trade with Europe, 27, 186; society, 43, 44, 45; leadership, 186, 189, 190

Peasants: 200, 209; rural flight, 39, 40, 41, 117, 118, 157, 200; indebtedness, 154, 156, 157, 158, 161, 162, 170, 196
Peddlers, 53, 54
Piracy, 16, 101, 102
Portugese, 13, 23, 73, 74, 75
Price control *(ḥisba),* 55, 57, 203, 204, 205
"Putting out" system, 209, 210, 211

Qānsūh al-Ghāwrī, 11, 12
Qassām al-ʿaskarī, 135, 136, 159, 165
Qassām al-baladī, 135
Qaysārīya, 123, 124

Raqqa, 119, 120
Raymond, André, 39, 41
Real-estate, 165, 166, 167, 168, 170, 180, 181
Russell, Alexander, 39, 49, 62, 63, 78, 79, 123, 126, 127, 133

Safi, shah of Iran, 23, 24, 83
Şah vekili, 86
Sasun, 85, 87, 106*n*.40
Sayfā family, 15, 16, 19, 119
Selim, Sultan, 12
shāhbandar, 57, 58, 59, 136, 158
Sherley, Robert, 23
Sidon, 27, 104
Silk: Syrian, 10, 31, 32, 64, 196, 197; Iranian, 11, 23, 24, 30, 32, 62, 63, 148, 193, 194, 195, 197; silk trade in Aleppo, 15, 22, 24, 62, 63, 104, 196, 197, 198; Lebanese, 27, 31, 32, 196, 197, 198; Anatolian, 28, 197, 198; industry in Aleppo, 198, 199, 200, 202
Soap, 53, 62, 64, 139, 200, 201
Steensgaard, Niels, 3, 29, 53, 142
Suryanis (Jacobite/Syrian Orthodox Church): 42, 173, 205; migration to Aleppo, 93; uniate movement among, 94, 107*n*.74
Syria: rural conditions in, 40, 41, 117, 118, 119, 120, 157, 172; beginnings of commercial agriculture, 195, 196

Ṭahazādah family, 136, 167, 170, 174
Taife, 43, 44, 45, 55, 60
Tax farming, 130, 131, 137, 171, 172, 195, 202
Taxation: detriment to trade, 28, 198, 199; on trade, 56, 77, 101, 121, 138, 139, 140, 194, 195, 206; market, 56, 59, 60; assessment, 56
Textile industry: 93, 176, 197, 198, 203, 204, 205, 206; dyers, 203, 205, 206, 207, 211; pressures on, 197, 198, 209, 210, 211, 212, 215*nn*.52, 56
Trabzon, 17
Trading diasporas: 72, 79, 80, 90, 104
Tripoli: 12, 14, 27, 93, 102, 104, 199, 200; Aleppo's port, 11, 15, 16
Türkmen: 42, 111; role in caravans, 11, 112, 120; forced resettlement in Syria, 119, 120
Turks, in Aleppo, 14, 42, 46

ʿUlamā, 45, 48, 60, 64, 95, 167, 170
Uniate movement, 94, 95, 96, 98
al-ʿUrdī, Shaykh Abū al-Wafā, 158, 159
Urfa, 41, 207
Urmia, battle of, 20
Usury: 52, 153, 160, 161; permissible usury, 161, 162, 163. *See also* Moneylending

Van, 20, 63, 85
Venice: trade with Aleppo, 10, 16, 22; consuls in Aleppo, 14, 15, 34*n*.16, 78; decline of trade, 24, 25, 26; Muslim traders in, 73, 74; Levantine trade, 75, 148

Wallerstein, Immanuel, 3, 7*n*.2, 14, 219
Waqf: commercial, 17, 18, 123, 125; promotion of trade, 18, 124; beneficiaries, 124, 172, 173; cash waqf, 160, 161, 162, 163; as investment, 172, 173; non-Muslim, 173, 174
Women: waqf administrators, 124, 125, 179; taxfarmers, 130, 179; craft workers, 130, 176, 209, 210; wealth, 168, 180, 181; status in Islamic society, 175, 176; marriage patterns, 177; money-lending, 180